Eirik Vold: Hugo Chávez The Bolivarian Revolution from Up Close

Original title in Norwegian: *Hugo Chávez Revansjen*

First published in English 2016 by Irene Publishing

Translation from Norwegian by Paul Russell Garrett
With generous financial support from NORLA
www.norla.no

ISBN 978-91-88061-16-4

Irene Publishing
Sparsnäs 1010, 66891 Ed, Sweden
irene.publishing@gmail.com
www.irenepublishing.com

Copyright by Eirik Vold and Irene Publishing ©

Cover photo by Jorge Silva ©

Layout by Jørgen Johansen

Hugo Chávez The Bolivarian Revolution from Up Close

'Our revolution is peaceful, but armed'

Hugo Chávez

Contents

'WELCOME TO VENEZUELA'	10
FROM COUP TO COUP: THE MAKING OF A LEGEND	25
THE OIL	81
THE VOICE OF THE BARRIORS	98
A POLITICAL SURVIVOR: The World's First Presidential Referendum	130
SOCIALISM FOR THE TWENTY-FIRST CENTURY	158
THE BOLIVARIAN CRUSADE IN LATIN AMERICA	164
DISTRIBUTING THE OIL BOOM	177
TAKING ON BIG OIL	198
A PHONE CALL FROM CHÁVEZ	233
WHO WAS HUGO CHÁVEZ?	320
Endnotes	368

Caracas, Venezuela, 2008:
The first thing I registered was the sound of the baseball bat striking my skull.

A sharp, dry crack. Then the taste of blood in the back of my mouth, along with the feeling of having skipped a few seconds. Suddenly I found myself on the ground trying to get my bearings. I tried standing, but every time I attempted to get up, I heard another crack and everything went black again. As the sounds of the bat striking me and the kicks to my head and torso faded into the distance, they were gradually replaced by terror and pain – and a numbing resignation. By the time I saw the silhouette of the pistol in the faint light, I had long since been incapable of standing. There was no point in resisting. The moment seemed to go on forever as I watched the pistol being lowered towards me. Right up until I heard the crack. Luckily for me it wasn't a shot but the butt of the gun striking my skull. The only thing I sensed as I tried to shield my head was the cool, red earth beneath me and the beggarly shanties with lopsided corrugated metal roofing. And the blows that struck me over and over again.

I was in the *barrios*. One of the suburban slums on the outskirts of the Venezuelan capital of Caracas.

I didn't recognise which one I had ended up in. The steep earthen slopes and the improvised shanties differed from some of the other *barrios* with their paved streets and brick dwellings, suggesting I was in one of the most deprived areas of the city. For decades, the people here had waged a daily battle to keep hunger at bay. On some weekends, the raw violence that ravaged these slums, mostly drug-related, saw Caracas surpassing war-torn Iraq in the number of murders, according to some of the gloomiest estimations. And during every rainy season – when the amount of water pouring down surpassed the absorption capacity of the porous earth – deadly landslides swept entire families away.

Over the past fifty years, Latin American governments from across the political spectrum have at various points attempted to bulldoze entire *barrios* to the ground. Sometimes to prevent catastrophes like the one which occurred outside Caracas in 1999, when thirty thousand people were killed in the continent's worst ever landslide. But often for purely aesthetic reasons, such as to give the impression of order and prosperity ahead of international summits and sporting events. Nevertheless, the inhabitants of these slums returned time after time. In Caracas, it is estimated that half of the five to six million inhabitants live in the barrios. Public services and infrastructure barely exists here. The precipitous earthen paths meandering upwards amongst the homes of the poor are impassable for police vehicles. The people who live here are used to being left to their own devices.

I had no idea how I had ended up here of all places. In this manifestation of terror itself, in the violent suburban hell of Venezuela. But even as I struggled to stay conscious, one thing remained clear to me: I knew exactly why I had travelled to Venezuela and I did not regret coming for one second.

Since 2002, I had spent the bulk of my time living in Venezuela. I did return to Norway for a year, but in the summer of 2007 I decided to return with one end in mind: to interview the president, Hugo Chávez. I had been curious about this man ever since my first visit to Venezuela, a man who over the years had become the most loved and loathed president in the world. For every year that passed, I was drawn deeper and deeper into the political maelstrom that began when a young Lieutenant Colonel Hugo Rafael Chávez Frías came to power in 1998. Several fundamental questions crystallised for me during that time: Who was Hugo Chávez really? What drove him and where would it lead him? Clearly the president wanted to break US dominance over Latin America and create an alternative to the prevalence of global capitalism. But was it possible? Would Chávez become the first world leader to lead society to the far left without lapsing into a totalitarian regime, and at the same time avoid succumbing to military coups and civil wars, like the majority of Latin America's leftist leaders had done before him?

The answers to some of these questions were revealed to me over the years as I observed Venezuelan society at close quarters. I had been witness to the Bolivarian Revolution, as Chávez dubbed it, both in triumph and on the verge of collapse. I had observed Chávez' seemingly countless controversial reforms from several perspectives: at street level, through the official statistics and from the reactions they provoked in my acquaintances – including zealous Chávez supporters, fanatical opponents and confirmed sceptics. I had familiarised myself with their reality through my personal experiences. Both good and bad: in the poverty-stricken slums where I lived for some time, as well as at the conservative elite university where I studied. I wanted to speak to Chávez face to face, hear his side of the story. However my timing was not the best. Chávez was at the forefront of the international political scene. Even readers of the liberal-minded American news weekly, *Time Magazine*, selected him as Person of the Year, a fact that should have been enough for an unknown Norwegian freelance journalist to abandon any hopes of interviewing him. I was on the verge of throwing in the towel when I received a message from the president's office that I was number 1000 in the queue. One thousand. Still, I continued to wait. One year later – after nine hundred and ninety-nine other foreign journalists, a Colombian bombing raid that brought the region to the brink of war, and my own personal blunders had delayed my path to the interview – I was finally offered a seat on the presidential plane for a trip to Ecuador.

A few months later, I was attacked on the streets. Twelve hours after the attack I found myself recovering in a military hospital in Caracas. My head and face were stitched up but the doctors remained uncertain as to whether I had recovered from all the blows and whether I had any potentially fatal internal wounds. I was to be kept under observation for seven days. Shortly after the doctor left me, two guards arrived, sent by the authorities to keep me under twenty-four-hour watch until the matter was resolved. When I was discharged from hospital, I was given an alias and instructed to find a new place to live. There was a genuine fear that the attack was linked to my meeting with Chávez, and worst yet, that corrupt police officials had been involved. There was a real danger of reprisals against me if I decided to report the incident. With bodyguards observing me twenty-four hours a day, severely restricted freedom of movement and the sense of being subject to some unknown threat, it was not the best time to be starting the arduous task of writing a book. But I had no choice. The material I was sitting on had to get out.

'WELCOME TO VENEZUELA'

13 April 2002, Oslo, it must have been around one o'clock when I found myself completely absorbed by a sensational front-page story during my coffee break at the care home where I worked.

'Venezuelan Leader Orders Troops on Demonstrators: People's Protest Topples President,' the headline read.[1] According to the article, President Hugo Chávez had attempted to suppress a popular uprising using military force, but had resigned when the military turned against him – in protest at the crackdown. Following that, Pedro Carmona, the president of Fedecámaras – the Venezuelan Federation of Chambers of Commerce – formed a transitional government with broad support 'from the country's democratic forces, from the right and the left, from business and trade unions.' The newspaper article, based on a *Washington Post* story, described Chávez as a 'Latin American military dictator.' In a fact box he was given the titles 'coup leader and populist.' Pedro Carmona was introduced as a 'diplomatic troubleshooter,' a leader with vast experience and one who always 'surrounds himself with competent people.'

Until then there had been little coverage of Hugo Chávez or Venezuela in the Norwegian press. Still this country, most famous for having the worst football team in South America and holding the record for most international beauty pageant winners, had already caught my attention. The manner in which Chávez was portrayed, both in the time before he became president in 1998 and afterwards, left me first and foremost with a feeling of uncertainty. At the beginning of his presidency, I wasn't even sure whether he belonged to the right or to the left.

After a few years in power, however, the media began to paint a clearer image of him. There was no doubting that he was a controversial leader. A politician who used populist rhetoric, had authoritarian tendencies, was elected on airy election promises of ending injustice and corruption. He was popular among poor Venezuelans but had a strained relationship with the media, business and the USA. I once asked a Chilean friend, a refugee from General Pinochet's right-wing dictatorship, what she thought of the

Venezuelan president. She was sceptical. 'We Chileans don't like presidents in uniform.' I understood what she was getting at. The few times I had seen Chávez on Norwegian television, I was really struck by his military uniform. His bellowing voice and harsh words against the opposition also left a chilling impression. It was only a few decades since the majority of Latin America was ruled by brutal military dictators. Of course they had been extreme right-wing governments with close ties to the United States, but if the events of the twentieth century have taught us nothing else, it is that the left is certainly not free from authoritarian rulers with brutal methods. Perhaps Chávez was the latest in a long line. And as I understood it, he had recently secured even more presidential powers for himself with a constitutional amendment in 1999.

Even so, it was impossible to judge the situation without observing it in the light of Latin America's poverty problem.

Ever since the colonial period, the region's indigenous peoples, as well as African slaves and their descendants, have been treated as second-class citizens in Latin America. For most of that time, they have suffered from the world's greatest disparity in living conditions, with few political, social or economic rights. On a continent usually governed by anonymous presidents from the rich elite, the fact that Chávez considered himself a revolutionary and 'a man of the poor' undoubtedly made him intriguing. But by 13 April 2002, it had all come to an end. Both for Hugo Chávez and the hope of him signalling a turning point in Latin America's history of suppression. As I read in another newspaper later that day: 'Chávez is the only leader in Latin America who ventured a move to the left in defiance of the prevailing liberal economic model.' The *Washington Post* story was of a president who came to power with the support of the poor, but failed due to a misguided economic policy and by brutally gagging the opposition, thereby confirming what most people already suspected. These kind of projects always end badly. I could almost hear Margaret Thatcher in the background with her famous postulate: *There is no alternative*, there is no alternative to economic liberalism. The Iron Lady may have been right.

Reading about the dramatic rise and fall of Hugo Chávez during my coffee break at work, the world around me seemed to disappear. Still, I was left with the feeling that the full story had not been told in the *Washington Post* double-page spread reprinted in the Norwegian paper. Later that day I came across a bulletin from the Norwegian News Agency (NTB). It told an entirely different story. Vegard Bye, the Latin America expert at the Norwegian Institute of International Affairs, called the takeover a 'coup d'état.' 'It is an ominous sign that the military and the oligarchy are taking over. If they remain in power, they threaten democracy in all of Latin America,' he wrote. I didn't know what to believe – the *Washington Post/Aftenposten* article, which embraced the regime change as a victory for democracy, or Bye and his sombre warning. As I was reading about Chávez' down-fall, across the Atlantic, enormous demonstrations were taking place in an effort to have the president released and reinstated, while a number of soldiers refusing to follow orders and sided with the protesters instead. But that news had not yet reached Norway by the evening of 13 April. On 14 April Chávez was again in the presidential chair – a spectacular return to power. Clutching the newspaper in my hand and still unaware of the popular uprising, I had reached a decision. No matter what the future held for the South American country, I had to travel there in order to find out what had happened for myself.

Four months later I was on a plane to Venezuela.
During my stopover in Paris, I got first-hand experience of how Chávez was not everyone's cup of tea. I got to chatting with a friendly, middle-aged Venezuelan woman who was doing her best to ensure I would enjoy my stay in her country. In her best English, she told me of spectacular beaches, shopping centres and fashionable areas that I just *had to* visit. The woman had recently vacationed in Europe. 'I needed a break from the dictator,' she said. 'Chávez has turned Venezuela into a dictatorship.' Then she made an earnest appeal to me: 'Make the most of your opportunity to get to know my beautiful country. Because it is likely that Chávez is soon going

to ban foreigners from the country. He hates gringos.'* I had begun my journey just in time.

And there I was. At Simón Bolívar International Airport in Caracas, one summer's day in 2002.

The air was heavy and humid, and I felt rather small waiting for *el señor* Vicente, the driver from the language school I had signed up to. He was supposed to meet me at the airport and drive me to the city. The dust had hardly settled after the April clashes and many embassies had warned their citizens against travelling to Venezuela for fear of new outbreaks of violence. If that wasn't enough, all of the horror stories about the airport I had come across in the days before my trip were still fresh in my mind. Caracas was meant to be one of the most violent capitals in the world. The airport was practically crawling with criminals passing themselves off as taxi drivers who would rob their customers and leave them naked in the slums, stripped of their bags, money and documents. Just before I departed from Norway, I read that eleven people had been decapitated in a clash between rival gangs in a prison outside Caracas. Fortunately I found Vicente. My worries quickly disappeared when he greeted me with a broad smile, gave me a firm pat on the shoulder and with a heavy accent said, 'Welcome to Venezuela.'

If it were true that Chávez hated foreigners and was going to close the borders soon, I soon found many reasons to be pleased that I had got my foot in the door before it was slammed shut. Jovial and outgoing Venezuelans made it easy for me to feel welcome. The Caracas climate was hot but pleasant. Everywhere I went in the city, there were tall trees bearing tonnes of mangos – and I had arrived at peak season. Colonialism's sweetest fruit, both figuratively and literally, had come to Latin America from the Philippines in the 1500s, brought by the Portuguese. Green, yellow and red, they crashed to the ground in huge quantities, faster than anyone could

---

* In some countries *gringo* is used as a derogatory term for people from the USA. In Venezuela, gringo is commonly used to refer to any white foreigner, without it having any derogatory connotation.

ever eat them. I did my best to keep up. Strolling between the skyscrapers and the mango trees, it was impossible not to notice the beautiful women, scantily clad as the climate dictated, wearing high heels and lots of make-up. The nightlife was electric; I usually ended up at a trendy nightclub or an impromptu street party in the slums. And only a couple of hours outside the city centre, nestled between the eastern extension of the Andes and dense jungle, were some of the most paradisiacal beaches on the Caribbean coastline.

Like most Europeans who travel to Venezuela – though there appeared to be fewer and fewer of us – my first port of call was the urban middle-class environment.

Here, support for Chávez was limited, something which my host family testified to. *Señora* Mireya was a kind lady who passed the time by cleaning the house, at least a couple of times a day, and by looking after her grandchild while her daughter focussed on her career in dentistry. Her husband was the hard-working *señor* Héctor. He held a middle-management position at a private sector company with troubled finances. Their four-storey house was relatively new and was well situated under the cooling shade of tall mango trees in the fashionable district of El Marqués in east Caracas. The family struggled to make ends meet. The simple fact was that the lifestyle that Venezuela's upper middle class ascribed to during the oil boom in the seventies came at a high price. In those days, shopping-mad Venezuelans would board a flight to Miami on a Friday, their pockets lined with Venezuelan currency buoyed by high oil prices, and return on a Sunday with their suitcases packed with products most Latin Americans could only dream of. This had such a strong impression on the local population in Miami that they gave the Venezuelans a rather long and telling nickname: *'ta barato dame dos* – roughly translated as 'so cheap, I'll take two.' The economic downturn of the eighties and nineties severely reduced the buying power of the middle class, but the status seeking continued. Vintage Scotch, fancy cars, eating out at restaurants every week and holidays abroad, or one of the Venezuelan islands in the Caribbean at least, preferably one that could only be reached by plane. Many middle-class families just about managed to keep up the facade by taking out large loans.

Mireya and Héctor, like many other hard-working middle class families, feared that Chávez would now take whatever they had left.

I learnt my first Spanish curse from Héctor when the president appeared on the living room TV one evening. The mere sight of Chávez was enough to make this otherwise sober-minded, Catholic family man lose his temper. *Hijo de puta, maldito dictador comunista!* 'Son of a whore, bloody communist dictator!' This was a typical example of what I heard in the living room on Sundays when Chávez aired his weekly programme, *Aló Presidente.*

There was a similar tendency at the language school, though the president was usually referred to as el loco, the madman. The head of the school was quick to inform us that 'any romantic notions of the president fighting for justice for the poor and such,' were delusional. On the school's TV in the reception room, every news programmed showed images of demonstrators shouting, *Chávez dictador.*

One day, I was invited to a party at a penthouse flat near Plaza Altamira.

This part of Caracas was the stronghold for Chávez's fiercest opposition. Here, the allegations about him ran rampant and were extremely crass. Some claimed that the president was in league with Osama bin Laden. Others compared him to Hitler. The opposition was going to be executed soon, according to the worst predictions. If Hugo Chávez, behind the facade of mango trees, a vibrant nightlife and beautiful women, was in the process of establishing a tropical Gulag*, I wanted to know about it, if for no other reason than to escape in time. I was often tempted to ask

---

* The Gulag was a system of slave labour and concentration camps in the Soviet Union.

people whether it was true that the president was so ruthless. But I noticed early on that most Venezuelans considered it bad etiquette to delve too deeply into other people's political views. Familiarity with the Venezuelan temperament and a good intuition were needed to know when and where it was appropriate to broach the subject. Bringing up Chávez at the wrong place, the wrong time or in the wrong way, could easily create a bad vibe or provoke a heated argument.

That evening however, my biggest priority was having fun. So I decided to set aside my curiosity and forget about politics. It went surprisingly well. At the front door I was pleasantly surprised when a smiling and unusually friendly – even by Venezuelan standards – middle-aged man named Antonio offered me a *roncito*, a small rum. Among the Venezuelan upper class, no matter the quality, rum has long been considered a low-status drink, a drink considered far too Venezuelan and far too cheap to be served to guests. Apparently that was not the case with Antonio, who turned out to be the host of the party. There was something about the atmosphere, in combination with the rum, which must have allowed me to relax more than I normally would at a party like that, surrounded by smartly dressed men and women from the capital's upper echelons. Perhaps a little too relaxed, as at the end of the evening, I found myself sitting on the kitchen floor in the Lotus position, holding a spoon, with the contents of the fridge spread out before me. Much to my surprise, I was invited back to Antonio's a few weeks later. Anyone who responded like that had to be a good man, I thought, and I thumped Antonio approvingly on the back when he introduced me as his *alto pana*, 'good mate' to the other guests. And good mates is exactly what we would become.

Antonio was a tall man, white, with dark hair that was just beginning to show signs of grey.

As a medium-sized business owner, he belonged to the privileged segment of Venezuelan society. His company sold lighting products and it had done rather well supplying other businesses in the commercial and service industry. Antonio was born and raised in the fashionable east of Caracas to wealthy parents. He studied at an international university and spoke fluent English. Like most people in his position, Antonio was an *anti-Chavista* through and through.

'I was suspicious of Chávez from the start. I value democracy and civil society. Why should we have a lieutenant colonel as president,' he asked.

Antonio was also alarmed by Chávez' obvious admiration for Castro. Ever since he came to power, Chávez was on a first-name basis with his Cuban colleague. He praised Cuba's health and education system and *Fidel's* unwavering determination to stand up to the USA. Antonio heard Chávez' statement about Cuba being 'a sea of happiness' and couldn't help contrasting it with the lack of freedom he had witnessed when visiting Cuba some years earlier.

Neither did he care for Chávez' aggressive tone. The *cadena nacional* he unwittingly heard on the car radio on his way home from work one night gave him a genuine feeling of being unwanted by the government of his own country.

At least a couple of times a month, Chávez took advantage of a law which entitled the government to address the population through *cadenas*, broadcasts produced by the state channel, but which all radio and TV stations with a public service broadcasting license were compelled to transmit. It was an old law, but no president had ever delivered as many *cadenas* as Chávez. He would talk for hours about everything from the government's latest initiative to his childhood experiences and baseball, the national sport, before denouncing the former rulers in opposition and the economic elite. 'Traitors, stateless oligarchs,' Chávez would rail against the opposition to viewers who had likely only switched on the TV to watch their favourite soap opera.

It was around nine o'clock in the evening when Antonio was driving home from work one evening, exhausted, stuck in traffic, and looking forward to the well-deserved whiskey he was going to pour himself when he got home. That was the moment Chávez – recently elected president – interrupted the radio transmission and launched into a tirade against 'whiskey drinking oligarchs.' Antonio did not care much for that. *'Coño,* I thought. Should a hard-working businessman like myself, someone who toils his life away creating jobs for this country, feel bad about having a whiskey after a long day's work? Is this what we want for our country, for people who struggle to make a decent living to get hung out to dry by the president?'

For Antonio, the answer was no. Chávez did not get a second chance from him.

You could safely say that it was not very *fashionable* – a word often said with a feigned English accent by many Venezuelans – to be a *Chavista*.* The media usually divided the population into sociedad civil and those it sometimes called *las hordas*, 'civil society' and 'the hordes.' The latter were those who supported Chávez. The papers were ruthless in their description of *los Chavistas*: 'Hordes of gangsters and women leading dark lives.'[2] 'Swarms of marihuana smokers.'[3] 'Adventurers, opportunists, parasites and criminals.'[4] 'Chávez and his beasts. Brown, black and white monkeys, animals with no dignity,' they were once labelled in the major newspapers, *El Nacional* and *El Universal*.[5]

'Monkey' might have been interpreted humorously, if it were not one of the most common racist insults the Venezuelan upper and middle class use for poor people with dark skin. Referring to Chávez supporters in this way was also prevalent on television and radio, without ever leading to any form of reprimand. The segment of the population who were the object of these malicious terms had no means of responding to this abuse by the media. When the newspaper El Nuevo País printed a picture of Venezuela's most popular soap star, the gorgeous blonde actress, Roxana Díaz, a furore arose. In the picture, she was holding a sign that read: 'I'd rather be a prostitute than a *Chavista*.' It was certainly not unthinkable for a Venezuelan actress, whose career was dependent

---

* A supporter of Hugo Chávez.

on positive press coverage, to prefer almost anything to a political stance that placed her in the same stall as 'hordes, beasts and monkeys with no dignity'. But not prostitution. It turned out that the image had been manipulated. Roxana Díaz had never held such a sign and sued the newspaper. All the same, the photo became a big hit.

On top of being accused of being uneducated and unintelligent and having bad genes, the people's support of Chávez was often attributed to envy. They were lazy and unsuccessful, with no desire or ability to achieve prosperity, and through the president, they saw an opportunity to take revenge on the clever and the successful. Several of the students at my university subscribed to this idea. For an opposition claiming that the president only had the support of a small minority, it was difficult to deny the size of the pro-Chávez marches. No thanks to the private TV channels, who rarely broadcast images revealing the true size of the processions, but Chávez and his hundreds of thousands of red-clad supporters often forced their way into middle-class homes through his despised *cadenas*. The solution for the commercial media and the opposition was to explain away the large street processions in support of Chávez as being due to coercion, intoxication, or simply a matter of uneducated riffraff dressed up in red, bussed in from villages on the promise of free food and alcohol. After a massive pro-Chávez demonstration in October 2002, *El Nacional* launched its most infamous description of the crowds that filled the streets: 'The same riffraff as always, transformed into eternal bus passengers for a piece of bread and a bottle of rum.'[6]

My new friend Antonio did not come across as an obsessive political fanatic. During our conversations, he often drew upon his knowledge of music, arts, girls, whiskey and hidden beach gems, which unfortunately he rarely had time to visit due to commitments at work. Obviously, I had nothing against learning more about them. And then there was his business. Antonio often invited me to lunch and allowed me to see his business from the inside, explaining the problems politics created for him and introducing me to the co-owners and employees. During our many conversations, I was given a first-hand insight into what it was like to be a successful businessman in Chávez's Venezuela. Most fascinating though, was his account of the maelstrom that struck the country on 11 April of that year and how Antonio found himself at the centre of the events: the battle for Miraflores, the presidential palace, where conflicting ideologies, classes and economic interests came to blows, with fatal consequences for an as yet undetermined number of victims.

I was about a month into my stay in Venezuela when I strolled out of Capitolio Metro Station in the centre of Caracas, bound for Plaza Bolívar and the presidential palace.

Faced with the highly confrontational political atmosphere in the country, the chaos of the big city and the vastly conflicting accounts of the events, it was with mixed emotions and some confusion that I approached the area where the dramatic scenes had unfolded on 11 April. My host mother, Mireya, had advised me in the strongest possible terms against taking this route. According to her, there were very few *Chavista* remaining – people had by and large come to their senses and joined the opposition – but the few who were left kept to the city centre. 'Many of them are violent,' she said, 'particularly if they see a foreigner and think you're American. They often carry knives and if you're lucky, you'll only get robbed.'

Only one block from Miraflores on Avenida Urdaneta, which passed right in front of the presidential palace, I found myself on Puente Llaguno Bridge. Austere in structure, straight and no more than twenty metres across, the bridge had a single lane in each direction with a narrow pavement on each side. Since its construction in the fifties, the bridge had never been anything more than an anonymous building block in the Venezuelan capital's infrastructure. Puente Llaguno's primary function was to take several hundred thousand workers making their daily commute from the west of the city to their workplaces in the city centre or further east, elevating them above the heavily trafficked Avenida Baralt. This ensured one less infernal traffic jam during peak time, which could last from five in the morning until eight in the evening. For pedestrians, it spared them the task of crossing Avenida Baralt, hazardous at any time of day, as well as escaping the sharp stench of urine that filled the narrow passages that had to be taken if the bridge had not been there.

Puente Llaguno was only a stone's throw from the presidential palace, the parliament and a number of government ministries, as well as Plaza Bolívar and the childhood home of the eponymous liberation hero, Simón Bolívar. But stepping onto the bridge and gazing at the streets below, there was little to indicate that you were in the country's political power centre and surrounded by the country's most important cultural monuments.

The sight of street vendors, traffic jams and filthy streets, if nothing else, provided a clue as to why Venezuela's financial sector had long since abandoned the area and established a new and fashionable business district amongst luxurious shopping centres and residential areas in the east of the city.

I was mostly engrossed by the vultures landing on a nearby roof, when I happened to stroll across Puente Llaguno one autumn day in 2002. The sight of the enormous carrion birds gliding between Caracas' skyscrapers had a sombre and futuristic feel to it. I accepted it as a bad omen when I almost walked straight into a large cross that had been erected on the pavement in the middle of the bridge. It was a frugal wooden structure, painted white wood and adorned with a few wreaths.

'Those who die for life, cannot be called dead.' The words were etched into the wood next to the date, 11 April 2002.

Continuing across the bridge, I spotted some large, black circles on the brick wall of the building on the corner. A cluster of bullet holes. Painted next to them in large letters, *Peña es de la CIA*. Obviously someone believed that the mayor of Greater Caracas, Alfredo Peña, was working for the US intelligence services. It seems I had stumbled upon a central point of the battles that surrounded the removal and reinstatement of Hugo Chávez several months earlier.

Much of what took place in the military barracks, on the streets and inside the presidential palace over the course of the forty-eight hours in which Chávez was imprisoned, seemed to have been taken directly out of a Hollywood action film.

The whole world had witnessed Chávez's spectacular return, arriving on the roof of the presidential palace by helicopter in front of thousands of supporters, after a military rescue operation had been launched on a coastal island during the night of 13 April. But the cause of the violent conflict and the exact course of events was still unclear to me. A thick veil of conflicting accounts, sensational rumours and conspiracy theories surrounded the events. And in contrast to Hollywood's usual ability to convincingly portray the noble and nefarious motives of the main characters early on in their movies, six months after Chávez' triumphant return, it was still unclear who the good guys and bad guys were in this story. The battle to define the heroes and villains of those April days raged on. In the media, in the streets, and not least, in the courts.

Not long after I arrived in the country, Venezuela's Supreme Court declared that the military had acted 'full of good intentions' when Chávez disappeared and Pedro Carmona became the new head of state.

The day the high court ruling was announced, unaware of what had taken place, I ended up in the middle of a group of furious *Chavistas* who were protesting the judgement. They believed that the court had legally established the oligarchy's right to launch a military coup against any elected government that places the interests of the people above the privileges of the elite. Some of them threatened to burn down the high court building. The police arrived and the situation quickly escalated into a violent confrontation. The embassies of several European countries that advised their citizens against travelling to Venezuela, evidently did so for a reason. They assessed the situation as such: the power struggle between the

Chávez government and Venezuela's former rulers was far from over. Worst case scenario, it could escalate into a military confrontation. Fear and curiosity pulled me in every direction as the street battle raged on around me. But finally, tear gas and what sounded like gunshots made me race towards the nearest metro station.

In the meantime – I only discovered this when I got home – Chávez appeared on TV and ordered his supporters to end the protests and go home to their families. This declaration may have prevented the battle outside the Supreme Court from turning into a bloodbath. It was my first encounter with the passion that consumed Venezuelan politics under Chávez. Various components of the state apparatus continued to face off on either side of the front line dividing Venezuelan society. The clashes outside the Supreme Court building gave few answers to my questions about Chávez and the April events. But the rush of adrenaline from being at the centre of events that day gave me a taste for more. I wanted to stay in Venezuela and dig deeper.

FROM COUP TO COUP: THE MAKING OF A LEGEND

El Comandante – The Revolutionary

On the evening of 3 February 1992, a young paratrooper puts on his uniform.

The lieutenant colonel tells his wife that he has to leave, that he might not come home. He opens the door to the bedroom where his son and two daughters are sleeping, presses the crucifix to his chest and offers up a silent prayer for God to protect them, before shutting the door and setting course for the Venezuelan capital. His objective: to lead a military operation against the government of President Carlos Andrés Pérez.

During the night, armed commandoes take control of the strategic cities of Maracay, Valencia and Maracaibo. In Caracas, the rebels manage to surround the military airbase and the presidential residence in the east of the city. While a tank crashes through the gates of the presidential palace, the lieutenant colonel entrenches himself on a hill a few hundred metres away in order to direct the attacks on the capital – as well as to coordinate the operations across the entire country.

The following morning, the rugged mestizo features* and red beret of the previously unknown 37-year-old Hugo Chávez appear on Venezuelan television for the first time.

Several cities awake to the sound of gunfire. Rumours of a coup abound in the country. Maracaibo and Maracay are still under the control of the rebels. In Valencia, students and workers have joined the rebellion. But something has gone wrong in Caracas. The communications equipment fails, one of the tanks has no ammunition. The rebel forces still manage to secure the area around the presidential palace but they encounter heavier resistance than expected. President Pérez has escaped. Apparently he was warned by the security services. With pro-government forces streaming towards the capital, Pérez appears on TV announcing that he has just spoken

---

* Mestizo is the term for a Latin American of mixed ethnic origin. Chavez had distinctive African and indigenous features.

to President George Bush to assure him that the uprising will be defeated. Shortly afterwards, it is all over. Chávez, entrenched in a military museum with a group of soldiers, has negotiated the terms of their surrender. They are arrested and transported to a location where they are met by microphones and cameras from the country's biggest broadcasters.

With cameras flashing all around him, he speaks to the reporters in a deep and serious tone: '*Compañeros*, unfortunately, the objectives we set were not achieved in the capital city, *por ahora* [for now]. This means that we have failed to seize power here in Caracas.' The *compañeros* Chávez refers to are his co-conspirators, still holding their positions in the cities they conquered during the night: 'You have all done a good job. But we must avoid more bloodshed. It is time to reflect. New occasions will arise, and the country must definitively get on a path towards a better future.'

Chávez, not particularly accustomed to the media at this time, blinks and looks around. The cameras do not catch the surname embroidered on his uniform. But it does not matter. The lieutenant colonel introduces himself: 'So listen to me, listen to *el comandante* Chávez when he sends you this message. It is time to put down your weapons; the objectives we set on a national level are now impossible to achieve. I thank you for your loyalty, your courage and your sacrifice. Before the country and before you, I accept full responsibility for this Bolivarian military action.'

A government official grabs the microphone. He thanks the press for coming on such short notice and for their part in getting the rebels in the rest of the country to surrender. Chávez is led away, taken to the headquarters of the intelligence services and later sentenced to seven years in prison by a military court. Shortly afterwards, the government of neighbouring Colombia presents a declaration signed by the leaders of sixteen Latin American countries, condemning what they call *la insurrección*, one of the many Spanish terms for rebellion. Venezuela's media, political parties and business organisations offer the institutions and political establishment their full support.

The Pérez regime appeared to have weathered the storm. The leaders of *los insurrectos*, the insurgents, were imprisoned, cross-party support had been offered by the national assembly, the president had the support of the Bush administration, and with that the entire international community. But something had happened. Chávez' military campaign in 1992 was not a popular uprising but a secret operation by a few select military personnel. However, the thirty seconds in which Chávez was given to speak to the nation were imprinted on the collective consciousness of Venezuelans. In the neglected rural communities and in the impoverished suburban slums, the coup commander had started something that was nothing short of a revival. The words *por ahora*, 'this time,' were a battle cry for all those who would have liked to see Chávez and his Bolivarian movement succeed in their attempted coup. There were a lot of them.

Chávez had regular visitors in prison. Of the numerous journalists who travelled to Yare Prison to interview him, many became fascinated by the young Lieutenant Colonel. One of the journalists was so enthralled by him that she later married him, becoming Chávez' second wife. Another visitor, an anonymous *Caraqueño** wrote him a poem inspired by the Lord's Prayer.

Our Chávez, who art in prison,
hallowed be thy coup,
avenge thy people,
thy will be done,
in Venezuela as it is in the army.

Give us this day our trust,
that which has been stolen,
do not forgive our traitors,
as we shall not forgive those who have imprisoned you.

---

* A person from Caracas.

Lead us not into corruption,
but deliver us from Carlos Andrés Pérez.
Amen

It is not exactly clear who 'our traitors' refers to in the poem. Most assumed it meant that Chávez' secret movement had been infiltrated, a key reason for the failure of the coup. Whoever these infiltrators were, they saw no reason to come forward. Perhaps they knew they would not be welcomed as heroes.

The reasons for Chávez being regarded as a hero were many. One was a crime President Pérez had committed three years earlier in 1989. The president had just persuaded voters to side with him, primarily for lambasting the International Monetary Fund (IMF) and its neoliberal reforms, reforms the people viewed as the primary cause for the decline in living standards at the time. But Pérez had barely stepped foot in the presidential palace when he did an about-turn and sent his finance minister to Washington to sign a deal with the IMF. It was one of the most dramatic liberalisation packages in history. The deal included a comprehensive deregulation of prices, cuts to subsidies and reductions in the public sector. A country in which more and more people were struggling to fend off starvation, awoke on 27 February of that year to find that prices for transport and basic foodstuffs had more than doubled.

In Latin America, neoliberal shock policies entailing privatisation and public sector cuts were first introduced by brutal, yet market-friendly military dictators.* Most who had tried to force through similar policies – which largely made the rich richer and the poor poorer – knew these changes were incompatible with democracy. Yet behind closed doors, President Pérez reportedly

---

* Known as the Chicago boys - economists who implemented the first comprehensive neoliberal experiment in Augusto Pinochet's Chile. More military coups followed with subsequent neoliberal shock treatment.

boasted to his allies that he was the only elected president able to implement such a radical liberalisation package.

He was not prepared for the reaction that followed. In Caracas, the poor descended from the hillside slums in their tens of thousands. The riots later came to be known as *el Caracazo*. Soon the entire city centre, including the area around the presidential palace, was filled with hundreds of thousands of indignant Venezuelans. Cars and rubbish were set alight and there were clashes with the police. Shops were looted in places. Pérez sent in the army to quell the protests. It ended in a bloodbath. The government reported 276 deaths, all civilians. The remaining unreported victims were dumped in a mass grave known as *la peste*, 'the stench,' due to the bodies being left unburied for days after the event.

Immediately after the massacre, the government held a press conference to announce that everything was under control and to congratulate law enforcement officials for their efforts. In the midst of the press conference, the government spokesman broke down in tears, discarded the prepared statement and left the podium.

The final death toll was never established but some reports estimate that upwards of three thousand people were killed.[7]

In 1989, Chávez and his future co-conspirators of the 1992 coup attempt were mostly low-ranking officers in the military. Some of them were called on to quell the riots. They all refused. Many poor Venezuelans felt that in Chávez, they finally had someone who cared about them, an avenger willing to risk everything to hit back at the authorities who had humiliated, abused and oppressed them.

While Chávez was in Yare Prison a few miles outside of Caracas, scraps of information began to emerge about the soon-to-be legendary revolutionary. Letters and recordings were smuggled out by visitors, allowing Chávez to explain his views. The press were sceptical, but having the imprisoned Lieutenant Colonel on the front page sold papers. Slowly but surely, an image and a story began to emerge about the hero who had been born before the cameras after his failed coup attempt.

A Poor Boy from Sabaneta

Hugo Chávez wore his boyhood sandals thin on the dirt roads outside the small village of Sabaneta, in the heart of Venezuela's *llanos*, the open plains that cover vast swathes of the interior. His parents were teachers. For long periods, they worked in a village several kilometres away and left the two oldest children, Hugo and Adán, with their grandmother, Rosa Inéz. The house was beggarly, with an earthen floor and a roof made from palm leaves, not dissimilar to the other houses in a village that at the time had only three roads.

During the 1960s little Huguito, as his grandmother called him, was often seen on the roadside with a rucksack full of Grandma's homemade papaya sweets, *arañas*, which he sold to contribute to the strained family finances. As a boy, he had an avid interest in small game hunting. Even after he became president it was said that the distinctive smell of grilled capybara, the largest rodent in the world and a favourite amongst *llaneros*, the people of the Venezuelan plains, would often give Chávez away when he arrived at a meeting.

Long afternoons on the country roads were spent dreaming of being a baseball star. He wanted to play in *las grandes ligas*, the major leagues, playing American professional baseball, preferably pitching for the San Francisco Giants.

Chávez did well in school. When he was in the final year of secondary school, Hugo's father, Hugo de los Reyes Chávez, wanted to take him to Mérida to see if he could get a place at the city's university. However, Huguito had heard that there, in the Andes Mountains near the Colombian border, they played football, not baseball. The road to San Francisco does not lead through Mérida, he thought. Nobody in the Chávez family was known for giving in, especially not his father, a tall, strong, dark-skinned man with an air of authority about him. But from an early age young Hugo displayed a fierce determination. He was not going to a football town and that was that. His recourse was the military. The military had good baseball teams and US talent scouts often scoured them on the hunt for promising players – he would also have the opportunity to study at a military academy. That way his dream of *las grandes ligas* and his parents' hopes of him continuing his education were both kept alive.

But thoughts of playing baseball were soon thrust to the background in favour of a new passion. During his time in the military, Chávez began to take an interest in Venezuelan and Latin American history. Simón Bolívar in particular. Chávez established a secret movement in order to carry out a revolution based on the thinking of Latin America's liberation general. The movement was founded in 1982 with the name *Movimiento Bolivariano Revolucionario*, The Bolivarian Revolutionary Movement. The goal was to bring about a revolution and overthrow the ruling regime.

Simón Bolívar, often referred to as *El Libertador*, the liberator, led the Latin American Wars of Independence at the beginning of the 1800s. He freed the north of South America from Spanish colonial rule in an area that today roughly includes Bolivia, Peru, Ecuador, Colombia, Panama and Venezuela. In these countries, there is a Plaza Bolívar centrally placed in almost every city, village and urban area. The independence war that began with only a few hundred horsemen is considered one of the greatest achievements in military history. Venezuelans are extremely proud that Bolívar was born in Caracas, and the fact that Chávez referred to him resonated with the people. But what relevance did this historical figure have now, more than one hundred and fifty years after the colonial rulers were defeated?

From the tapes smuggled out of Yare Prison, it emerged that Chávez intended to revive both Bolívar the *thinker* and Bolívar the *politician*. Bolívar was born into a rich, aristocratic family in Caracas but on his travels he was inspired by the revolutions in the USA and Europe, the French Revolution in particular, as well as the enlightenment philosophy that formed the basis for those upheavals. In South America, he put the battle cries of the French revolution *'liberté, egalité and fraternité'* into practice, for example by ending slavery and abolishing feudal privileges in the lands he conquered from the Spaniards. This provided Bolívar with vital support from slaves, peasants and labourers. It also presented him with a powerful enemy: the oligarchy. The oligarchy were the rich land and slave owners and those at the highest levels of the mercantile community – the powerful elite that had developed under colonial rule. In 1830, a pale and emaciated Simón Bolívar died in the city of Santa Marta in what is now Colombia, having failed in his bid to unite the freed territories into a greater republic. Some remain convinced that regret over this failure was the cause of the liberation general's deteriorating health and death. In reality however, it was the oligarchy who crushed him and his project.

In 1982, Chávez and his co-conspirators swore an oath underneath a tree outside Maracay:

'I swear by the God of my fathers, by my honour and my country, that I will not allow my hands to grow idle or my soul to rest until I have broken the chains which the powerful use to suppress my people.' The words were drawn from a pledge Bolívar made in 1805 before going to war to liberate Latin America from Spanish colonial rule. Chávez and his companions merely replaced the word 'Spanish' with 'powerful', i.e. the oligarchy. Chávez believed that the same oligarchy who had defeated Bolívar's project continued to maintain real power in Venezuelan society at the end of the twentieth century. He accused politicians of serving this small, but incredibly rich group of elites and of keeping the rest of the population in poverty. Only by breaking the oligarchy's monopoly on power could the poor have any hope of a better life. Chávez promised to do that through *la revolución bolivariana*, the Bolivarian Revolution. The armed revolutionary bid of 1992 had failed but the oath remained.

During his years in prison, Chávez was persuaded to make a fresh attempt at gaining power. This time through peaceful means.

Beauty and the Beast

In 1994, Chávez was pardoned by President Rafael Caldera after two years in prison and released to rousing celebrations. He had barely stepped through the prison gates when he began his campaign for the presidential election, four years down the road.

Leading politicians who maintained a good relationship with the owners of Venezuela's TV stations had a direct route to the country's twenty-five million citizens. It was simply a matter of showing up at the RCTV or Venevisión studios in Caracas and obliging journalists and the country's expansive cable and antenna network took care of the rest. Chávez did not have such alliances, making the path considerably longer. It was true that the young Lieutenant Colonel had become a media sensation, but he knew he could never compete with his opponents for positive press coverage. Instead Chávez concentrated his efforts on going from village to village, door to door, face to face. This also enabled him to become familiar with the living conditions throughout the country, a familiarity his rivals could not achieve by passing from office to make-up room to TV studio. Determined as he was to win the election, he regarded his journey both as an election campaign and as preparation for the challenge he would face as president: to fulfil the millions of expectations he was faced with in villages and suburban slums where poor Venezuelans crowded around him, embraced him, shouted, cried and prayed that he would help them. Chávez travelled around in an old red car he received as a gift, staying with friends, allies, or anyone else who offered him a bed or a sofa to rest on.

During his time in prison, Chávez was visited by representatives of several small left-wing parties who had expressed an interest in the rebellious Lieutenant Colonel. He welcomed everyone. But Chávez wanted his own party. Shortly after his release, he founded the *Movimiento Quinta República* (MVR), The Movement of the Fifth Republic. The powerfully symbolic name played on two things. First, Chávez wished to implement such fundamental changes to Venezuelan society that it would have to be considered a new republic. Second, the name marked a continuity from the secret movement he had founded in the military, *Movimiento Bolivariano Revolucionario* (MBR) which when abbreviated sounds identical to MVR since the letters *b* and *v* have identical pronunciations in Spanish. Chávez wanted to make it clear that he was still leading a revolutionary movement, even though he now sought to win power through the despised party-political system. This was difficult to swallow for the Americans. When Chávez went to the US embassy in Caracas to apply for a US visa, the ambassador made sure his application was refused. On the surface, Chávez took it in good humour. On a popular TV programme he joked that he did not need a visa because he already had one, then pulled a Visa card out of his wallet and laughed. However, within his close circle, the decision was taken very seriously. The USA had approved visas for some of Latin America's most brutal dictators. When Chávez had his rejected, it was an indication that Washington viewed him as an enemy.

In its first parliamentary election in 1996, MVR captured a massive twenty-one per cent of the votes. It was the same figure obtained by the former ruling social democratic party *Acción Democrática* (AD), the undisputed giant of Venezuelan politics for forty years based on their party machinery, number of activists, electoral experience and financial backers. Many saw this election as a trial run for the 1998 presidential race. Concern amongst the elite grew significantly that year. AD and the other former governing social Christian party, COPEI, continued to fall in the polls. Ahead of the presidential election, the private sector decided to allocate its financial resources in support of the charismatic businessman, Henrique Salas Römer, and former Miss Universe, Irene Sáez. Both ran independently from the traditional ruling parties during this election.

Römer had his power base in Valencia, a city in Carabobo State, home to the most traditional segment of the Venezuelan upper class and known as the country's conservative stronghold. He had ruled as state governor there since the early nineties. Römer had founded an organisation that brought together the country's state governors, with him and his son taking turns as its president. He was educated at an exclusive private school outside of New Jersey and later studied at Yale, the famous Ivy League university. With his assured and distinguished manner of speaking and an appearance as European as his German surname, Römer was typical of Venezuela's leading politicians. The name of his party was *Proyecto Venezuela*, Project Venezuela, and his rhetoric painted a picture of an apolitical pragmatist. His supporters hoped that Römer's success as a businessman would rub off on the entire nation in the form of increased investments, resulting in higher levels of employment and greater prosperity.

Irene Sáez, the blonde beauty queen, had received a lot of attention for her hard work as mayor in the Caracas district of Chacao, Venezuela's wealthiest municipality. Steel and glass structures, luxurious shopping centres and trendy nightclubs were characteristic of Chacao, which had also taken over as Venezuela's leading business district. At a time when the majority of the country's population lived in surroundings with steadily increasing poverty, chaos, crime and visible decline, the municipality served as an effective shop window for Sáez. With no stated ideology, she appealed to all those who were impressed by the clean streets, low crime and police officers who wore uniforms and hats styled after the London Metropolitan Police. For a long time Sáez was best placed to battle Chávez. This continued right up until COPEI announced their support of her candidacy in the hopes of securing even more votes for her. But gaining the support of one of the established ruling parties had the exact opposite effect. As a result, Sáez ended up withdrawing just prior to the election in an attempt to help Römer's cause.

It was not enough.

The poor boy from Sabaneta had proposed to the Venezuelan people.

On 6 December 1998, Hugo Chávez received a resounding 'yes' through the ballot boxes.

With 56.5 per cent of the votes, the margin of victory was among the largest in the country's history. Venezuela's political and economic elite reacted with nervous anticipation. In the slums around the centre of Caracas, the victory was celebrated for many nights with the chanting of slogans, fireworks and huge quantities of beer and spirits.

Chávez' Little Blue Book

'I swear, upon this dying constitution ... '

Lieutenant Colonel Chávez had been president for only a few seconds when on 2 February 1999, he shocked everyone with his improvised version of the traditional oath that Venezuelan presidents make during their inauguration ceremony at the national assembly. He swore upon a 'dying constitution,' signalling that he was going to implement a new constitution, as he had proposed during the election campaign. Televised images of the ceremony showed parliamentarians' serious but shocked faces, with some even laughing as Chávez spoke the unexpected words. 'What does Chávez want with a new constitution? He'll be forgotten by the next election anyway,' one journalist wrote.[8] But Chávez was very serious. 'Until we reconstruct the architecture of the political system, one which has lost both legitimacy and ethical substance with its worm-eaten and decadent power structures, it will be impossible to implement a coherent national plan for social, economic, political and cultural development,' he said in one of his first speeches as president.

Six months after his inauguration, Chávez had won two new elections: a referendum to initiate the process of making a new constitution, and shortly afterwards, a vote to form a constitutional assembly – receiving over seventy per cent support in both. All that remained was the task of writing the new constitution and having it approved through yet another referendum.

In December 1999 the bill was ready, unsurprisingly entitled *Constitución Bolivariana*, the Bolivarian Constitution. Venezuela's official name was to be changed from *República de Venezuela*, the Republic of Venezuela, to *República Bolivariana de Venezuela*, The Bolivarian Republic of Venezuela. The first article established that the constitution was based on 'Símon Bolívar's doctrine of liberty, equality, justice and international peace.' Furthermore the country's form of government would be redefined as a 'democratic and social constitutional state.' The parliamentary system was changed from a bicameral to a unicameral system. Apart from that, the other original institutions – the judicial system, parliament and government – remained formally unchanged for the most part, but were to be complemented by new forms of 'participatory democracy.' The indigenous population had their languages recognised and there was a greater emphasis on human rights. There were separate articles giving special protection to women, children and minorities whilst all forms of discrimination based on gender, skin colour or sexual orientation were explicitly prohibited. These kinds of discrimination have been ingrained in social structures across the continent ever since colonial times. No Latin American constitution had ever been so uncompromisingly explicit on these points as the proposed Bolivarian constitution.

The bill also allowed for more government intervention in the economy. The country's natural resources, including the enormous oil reserves, were irrevocably 'public property' and should be used to raise the quality of life of the people of Venezuela. Food, health, education and housing were defined as constitutional rights for the people, and the constitution made the state legally responsible for fulfilling these obligations. 'Know your rights and know what you are voting for,' Chávez pleaded, making sure that a vast number of copies of the constitutional proposal were made available. He promised that once the Bolivarian constitution was in place, the oligarchy would no longer be able to trample all over the people.

This was the first time in Venezuelan history that a constitution was subject to the will of the people via a referendum. But even before the vote, it started to create problems for the president. 'Chávez has made it clear that he will accept nothing less than a complete and permanent overhaul of the Venezuelan state structure,' the *New York Times* correspondent in Caracas, Larry Rohter, wrote.[9] The headline left no doubt as to Chávez' intentions: 'Thirst for more power drives President as Venezuelans go to the polls.' The opposition's congressional representative, Alberto Franceschi chimed in: 'He wants absolute power, a banana republic where his supporters go to the constitutional assembly to propose a tropical monarchy with Chávez as emperor.' In an open letter to the people, Chávez' predecessor, the former president Rafael Caldera, declared that his conscience prevented him from participating in a vote which was meant to 'destroy, not strengthen the constitutional state.' Politicians, analysts, and businessmen – everyone who was interviewed for the *New York Times* article – rejected the proposed constitutional changes. Apart from one, a bellboy working at the Caracas hotel of the dispatched journalist. He believed that the old 1961 constitution 'was not [created] to give people the opportunity to express their will, but to allow a gang of corrupt politicians to line their pockets and remain in power.' Therefore he believed it was a good idea to replace it with a new constitution.

In the weeks before the vote, Chávez was interviewed by the three main TV stations. The editorial teams were all well prepared. Surveys showing a clear majority against the proposal were prepared ahead of Chávez' arrival at each studio. Video reports broadcast during those same programmes confirmed the view that the entire population was against the president. Even in the poorer districts of the capital where support for Chávez was strongest, there were only negative comments, people shaking their heads at the proposal. The host from the RCTV network began his interview with Chávez as follows: 'You fight with the church, you fight with the business community, you fight with the political parties, you fight with the trade unions. This fight has cost millions of dollars, and everywhere in the world, they are talking about how you pick fights with the most respected segments of society.' The interviews on the other major channels, Globovisión and Venevisión, followed a similar pattern. The hosts concluded that plans to provide constitutionally guaranteed rights to free healthcare and free education, and to ban privatisation in the oil industry, were 'pathetic,' and that Chávez was bringing about the 'total destruction' of the Venezuelan economy. The RCTV host concluded with an unambiguous warning: 'If this government becomes radical, you're through.'

Nonetheless the referendum on 12 December 1999 resulted in seventy-one per cent support for the Bolivarian constitution. The bellboy from the *New York Times* article, it seems, was not alone in rejecting the advice of Venezuela's politicians, journalists and former presidents.

Chávez' constitutional initiative had provoked a tremendous response from the Venezuelan people.

After the referendum, suddenly little blue books began to appear everywhere. Chávez always carried a copy in his breast pocket and pulled it out every time he appeared in public. Constitutional fever still raged years later. One of the things that had the greatest impact on me when I first arrived in Venezuela was observing poor Venezuelans purchasing street vendors selling miniature editions of the constitution alongside newspapers, plastic watches and fruits and vegetables, and observing poor Venezuelans as they purchased it.

Mechanics, domestic workers and bus drivers followed Chávez' example and made sure to always carry a copy of the little blue book that was no bigger than a pack of cards. I saw them studying, memorising and discussing the individual laws. Observing political discussions on the bus, at snack bars and in many other situations, the constitution was like a road map that Chávez supporters pulled out with stirring pride. They could use it to trump all arguments of the more eloquent opposition supporters from the middle and upper class. 'Here is the constitution. Chávez has opened our eyes. We are no longer ignorant and gullible people for you to trample on. We have rights now, and we have learnt to demand them,' was a typical declaration after hearing the mini constitution slammed onto the table. Chávez supporters believed that the words contained within the thin blue plastic binding were the key to a better life.

But not everyone was so enthused. The overwhelming majority who voted in favour of the new constitution did not lessen my friend Antonio's scepticism. Like most other Venezuelan business owners, he was concerned about the consequences it could have for private property rights and for private enterprise in the country.

In 1999, following a powerful landslide which hit the coast of Vargas State just north of Caracas – occurring at almost the exact time as the referendum – there was a wave of illegal squatting which would prove to demonstrate the political explosiveness of the new constitution. As many as thirty thousand people were killed when debris flows caused by torrential rain swept their houses out to sea, and many more lost their homes. The event was described as the worst natural disaster in South America in over a century, though it could hardly be considered entirely natural.

Chávez railed against the previous rulers and argued that their policies of serving the oligarchy, the property speculators and the rich, had virtually forced the poor up the perilous hillsides outside the city where the landslide had occurred. Encouraged by their newly elected president, people from Vargas arrived in Caracas in their thousands to demand a roof over their head. With the constitution in hand, they occupied vacant buildings – and sometimes buildings which turned out not to be vacant - demanding a home. Previously the authorities would have cracked down on this kind of activity. But with Chávez in Miraflores, the police allowed many of the squatters to remain, providing the buildings had been vacant for some time and the owners displayed no intention of using them. For years to come, the urban landscape of Caracas was filled by banners that marked the occupied buildings.

When the first squatters arrived in the capital in 1999, Antonio was one of many who believed that most of them had never lived in Vargas and were simply exploiting the new constitution in order to get a free home. According to him, Chávez was abusing the Vargas tragedy to legitimise the expropriation of private property, a situation made possible by the new constitution.

Antonio referred to it as *viveza*, a local term for a type of cunning that borders on the edge of social acceptability, something which Venezuelans subject each other to on a regular basis. It can be a question of being resourceful as a pure survival technique, telling a white lie, opportunistically switching allies, or outright fraud, and can occur in the streets, in families and in love affairs, business transactions or politics. Every local knows that *viveza* is not a new phenomenon to Venezuelan politics. Nevertheless Antonio believed that the constitution acted as an incentive, encouraging people's *viveza* by legally establishing the right to get something from the state without working for it, and that Chávez himself was committing political *viveza* by using poverty as an excuse to expropriate assets that belonged to others.

Most Venezuelans were sick of neoliberal economic policies and the old political elite and wanted a fairer distribution of assets. But tampering with private property rights was a taboo deeply engrained in Venezuelans, even among supporters of Hugo Chávez.

However the occupations of 1999 were just a sample of what was to come, displaying how Chávez and the movements of poor farmers, workers and political activists which shot up under his wings, were taking increasingly more daring steps to take back power from the Venezuelan economic elite.

Oil: The Ticking Time Bomb

In 2001, Chávez appeared on state television holding a large horn.

One by one, he called out the executives of the state-owned oil company PDVSA (pronounced *'Pedevesa'*, *Petróleos de Venezuela SA*) by first and last name, blew the horn and said: 'Thank you for your hard work, you're fired.'

Chávez had already handed the PDVSA management one surprise via the media when shortly after his inauguration he informed them that their fleet of aeroplanes had been sold to finance schools and health clinics for the poor. 'What use do we have of aeroplanes, oil and riches when millions of our poor brothers are starving,' Chávez had said, before accusing the PDVSA leadership of being a strain on the country's finances, managing the oil at their own discretion without consideration for the 'true owners, the Venezuelan people.'

These jilted oil bosses were probably the first people ever to be fired by a president on live television. However, the PDVSA management controlled what was undoubtedly the government's most important source of income. Oil was responsible for between eighty and ninety per cent of Venezuela's export revenues and around half of the government budget.* It was a considerable instrument of power that they would later use to exact their revenge on the president.

'Oil is a ticking time bomb for Chávez,' the Miami based newspaper *El Nuevo Heraldo* wrote on 24 March 2002, after speaking to Venezuelan oil industry insiders. An unnamed PDVSA executive said that the company was going to respond to the Chávez offensive 'with force,' while a former head of Shell's Venezuelan operations believed the conflict with PDVSA would 'explode into something much bigger.'

---

* The exact figure could fluctuate from one month to the next with the price of oil, but the annual average had been between eighty and ninety per cent for some time.

Within two weeks, the Venezuelan opposition, the national workers federation, *Confederación de Trabajadores de Venezuela* (CTV) and Fedecámaras stood before a group of supporters and presented their unanimous ultimatum to the Chávez government: Reinstate the PDVSA leadership or attempt to govern Venezuela with no oil money.

In 2001, Chávez had enacted a series of laws that dramatically altered the power dynamics of the Venezuelan economy. A land act was adopted which formed the basis for the redistribution of farmland, and new regulations in the banking and financial sectors were introduced. Internationally, it was the new oil law that received the most attention. With sixty-eight articles in a small book the size of the constitution, and almost as thick, the new oil law was a significant break from oil politics of the past. The sums of money foreign oil companies were extracting from Venezuela were enormous, not to mention difficult to keep track of. Chávez suspected that a decreasing amount of the assets was remaining in Venezuela. The new statute required them to contribute more in tax. In some cases, the royalties increased from one dollar per barrel of oil to fifty per cent of its market value, with the tax on profits rising from thirty per cent to fifty per cent. In addition, a loophole in the 1975 oil law was closed, one which had allowed foreign companies to be majority owners of certain Venezuelan oil fields. With the new law, PDVSA had to own at least fifty-one per cent in the so-called joint ventures with foreign companies. This resulted in increased operational control of the business and an increased share of the juicy oil profits for the state.

If Chávez intended to go through with this law, foreign companies stood to lose huge sums of money.

At the time, the USA was the world's largest importer of oil. When Chávez came to power, the US imported around fifteen per cent of their oil from Venezuela. As the only major supplier far removed from the unstable Middle East, Venezuela had even more importance for US energy security than the figure indicated. For this reason, Chávez caused significant unease in Washington. When the topic of oil came up in the US Congress, CIA director George Tenet expressed his concerns, stating that 'Venezuela is obviously important because of the oil' but it was ruled by Chávez, 'who probably does not have the best interests of the United States at heart.'[10] If Chávez was able to implement even a few of his proposals, then worst-case scenario, it could lead to an energy crisis for the USA. Best case, it would only lead to a substantial reduction in profits for American oil companies and more expensive petrol for the country's motorists. Oil companies and motorists were two interest groups US politicians could not afford to let down.

An acquaintance of mine who worked for PDVSA shared her thoughts on Tenet's statement with me over a beer: 'When it's the CIA and not the US Department of Energy or the press slating your oil policy, then you have a big problem.' She had a certain degree of sympathy towards Chávez and the prospect of him rooting out corruption in the oil industry to ensure that a little more of the assets were diverted to the public purse and to the poor. But she believed that attempting to seize control of America's most stable source of oil and using it to fund a revolution that was contrary to American interests was 'madness' and 'playing with fire.'

Hugo Chávez' struggle with the USA is now one of the most talked-about aspects of his time in power. But it was not always like that. The relationship got off on the wrong foot when Chávez was denied a US entry visa before the Venezuelan presidential election campaign in 1998. But as a newly elected president, he received an invitation to the White House. Venezuelan diplomats still remember how Bill Clinton greeted him at the door wearing jeans and neglected to offer his Venezuelan counterpart the standard presidential reception. But Chávez had mostly positive things to say about the cigar-smoking man from Arkansas. 'It was a relationship characterised by mutual respect,' he often recalled the brief period when their presidencies overlapped. He once described their relationship during a TV appearance: 'We talked on the phone. "How are you, Mr Clinton?" "I'm good, thank you, and how about you Mr Chávez?" And then we would discuss important issues, sometimes we agreed and sometimes we did not agree. But we were always respectful.'

When George W Bush became US president, the presidential relationship quickly soured. Chávez' meeting with the US ambassador in Caracas, Donna Hrinak, was a defining moment.

After the terrorist attack on the twin towers on 11 September 2001, Chávez was quick to condemn the terrorists. On the state-owned TV channel, he expressed his condolences for the bereaved and asked for a minute's silence for those who were killed. But Chávez shocked the entire world when he became the only head of state in the Western Hemisphere who vehemently condemned the subsequent invasion of Afghanistan. 'Let's find the terrorists, but not like this,' he said during a live televised address, holding up pictures of dead and wounded Afghan children, wrapped in bloodied white sheets, with distraught mothers at their sides. 'You say you made a mistake? Will you continue making mistakes?' The questions were directed at the screen, as though he was speaking directly to the US government. This was also how Washington perceived it. All the same, the Bush administration decided to give the Venezuelan president a chance to repent. US ambassador Hrinak was sent to the presidential palace to explain to Chávez that if he publicly retracted his statements, the entire matter would be considered an unfortunate misunderstanding. Chávez considered the suggestion imperialistic and humiliating, and later admitted to having lost his patience during their meeting. The US ambassador did not even get a chance to present Bush's demand, because as Chávez later described the encounter: 'I had to interrupt her. "You're speaking to the President of the Bolivarian Republic of Venezuela," I said, then kindly asked her to leave.' The Venezuelan media raged at the president's treatment of the USA, the country's most important ally. Soon after, Hrinak was recalled to Washington and a new man was sent to Caracas. Charles Shapiro. A man who had been stationed at the American embassy in Chile during the CIA-backed coup in 1973. What had been a cold conflict between Chávez and the White House was heating up. Would the episode between Chávez and Hrinak be a point of no return?

Towards the end of 2001, members of Fedecámaras and CTV, the AD-affiliated trade union, began making regular trips to the USA. They made sure that the visits were covered by the Venezuelan media. Their close contact with the Bush administration inspired Chávez' opponents with confidence. This relationship showed that the battle against the Venezuelan president was no longer an internal matter, but one that had international support from the world's biggest superpower.

From early April 2002, a number of front-page headlines in The Daily Journal, Venezuela's only English language newspaper, clearly indicated that the Bush administration had ended up in the middle of the conflict: 'USA cautions Chávez', 'USA denounces Chávez,' 'Bush warns Chávez.' Over the course of the year, fears had spread among *los Chavistas* of what Bush, the Pentagon and the CIA would do. Now it had reached all the way to Chávez' inner circles. Some began to waver. Was it really worth risking everything for a project that seemed to have gained many more powerful enemies than it had allies? Some had already made the decision to jump off the bandwagon.

In 2001, the outlook was bleak for Chávez. Pressure was increasing from all quarters – nationally and internationally. But instead of applying the brakes to his Bolivarian revolution, Chávez accelerated. With an uncooperative state apparatus and the private sector up in arms, the president decided to turn to the military. Plan Bolívar, approved by the national parliament the previous year, allowed the president to send soldiers to the slums and rural communities to construct bridges, repair roads and transport food and emergency aid to areas affected by floods and landslides. Bolivarian schools were built in poor areas, with the children receiving a glass of milk and a school meal every day. Chávez' men in green, and women in green, were gradually found in more and more positions within the civil administration. As were the Cuban advisors, brought to Caracas as a first part of the growing cooperation between Chávez and Castro. Amongst the economic elite and right-wing opposition, fears of communism were growing. They didn't equate Cuban conditions with zero illiteracy and the best education system in Latin America – a fact that Chávez liked to quote from the UN development statistics – but with the end of private property rights, seized assets and, if their worst fears came true, a life in exile. In the media, there was talk of communist indoctrination in the schools and even worse, that people would have their children taken from them, something a number of Venezuelans were convinced had occurred in Cuba.[*] *Con mis hijos no te metas*, 'Don't mess with my kids,' the newspaper headlines, TV programmes and protests banners declared. A community organisation was even inspired by the slogan.

'Are You Talking about a Coup?'

Towards the end of 2001, civil society, opposition parties, NGOs[†], business and the media united to form a broad coalition against the president.

Between July 2001 and the beginning of 2002, polling institute Datanálisis revealed a drop in Chávez' popularity from fifty-six per cent to from thirty-five percent. By early April, opposition politicians, journalists and experts were presenting figures as low as fifteen to twenty per cent. When political parties and key politicians from the Chávez alliance began to swap allegiances, the expression, *saltar la talanquera*, 'hopping the fence' became one of the most common expressions in Venezuelan politics. One such politician was the mayor of Greater Caracas and former communist, Alfredo

---

[*] The idea that Castro was stealing people's children was obviously pure fantasy, but this rumour was occasionally spread by the media in a number of influential Latin American countries.
[†] Non-governmental organisation – private, voluntary organisations.

Peña, who before the mayoral elections had been billed by Chávez and the revolution as their man in Caracas. 'Chávez, like so many other dictators, only supports freedom of speech when he is spoken well of,' Peña declared, a statement which landed him his first appearance on the front page of the long-established *El Nacional*.[11] Most leading papers, as well as radio and television stations, were now rampant with ex-*Chavistas*, all vying with each other to condemn the president.

At the same time, an impressive number of pop stars, actors, and other celebrities were appearing before the media, urging people, particularly young people, to join the opposition. One of the few positive things Antonio had to say about Chávez was that he 'forced many of us out of our complacency.' Protesting against the president became normal, even trendy among the urban middle-class youth. 'That hasn't happened in decades,' Antonio said.

'Power has gone to his head. He wants to turn Venezuela into the new Cuba.' This was the unanimous verdict of the chorus of opposition and media, who at that time almost exclusively referred to Chávez as 'the lieutenant colonel,' 'the dictator' or 'the madman.' Anything but 'president,' a word that became rare in the newsreaders' vocabulary. The opposition had taken to the streets, with their mass mobilisations steadily growing in size and frequency. Chávez supporters were a rare sight in the media.

The president's mental health also became the subject of scrutiny. Sometimes through humorous caricatures but often with deadly seriousness. It was certainly no joke when Venevisión asked its viewers to phone in their response to the question 'Do you think the president is crazy?' A psychologist they brought in for the show left the audience with no doubt that the president was mentally ill and had to step down. When the secretary general of AD, Rafael Marin, declared Chávez a 'psychopath,' the matter became an international story as well. His opinion of the president was quoted in a *Newsweek* article with the headline 'Is Hugo Chávez Insane?' In an *El Nacional* article where one of Venezuela's most renowned psychiatrists was interviewed, Chávez' madness was no longer a subject for discussion, but the actual premise of the interview: 'How does an *egomaniac** deal with losing control?' the journalist asked. The headline 'Losing power could teach Chávez a big lesson' also indicated that the swift demise of the president was now being taken for granted.[12] The question was how. There were fifteen formal complaints lodged against Chávez that were being considered by the Supreme Court. Among them was a demand for his removal from office due to mental incapacity.[13]

However the president showed no signs of caving in to the demands of so-called 'civil society,' so another player stepped forward. During a well-attended press conference at the luxurious Caracas Hilton on 7 February 2002, Rear Admiral Molina Tamayo urged Chávez to step down. He called the president 'anti-patriotic' and accused him of trying to 'weaken the operational capacity of the military' in order to 'establish an extreme left dictatorship.' In addition, Molina stated that 'at least ninety per cent of the armed forces' was dissatisfied with the government and warned the Chávez camp and the government of an 'impending risk of bloodshed' if the president didn't step down.

The media viewed Molina's press conference as definitive proof that Chávez had lost control of the military. On 10 April, a leading article in *El Nacional* warned of a conspiracy between Chávez and 'foreign agents' to dismantle the Venezuelan military and leave it under 'the command of the continental insurgency' which was supposedly led by Castro and Colombian left-wing guerrillas. 'The democratic officers will fall one by one, and then their families will be hunted down. They will be shown no mercy.' According to *El Nacional*, patriotic military commanders had to act quickly in order to avoid being eliminated by the president. 'Foreign agents have already assembled a list of the first to be "neutralised" in July.' No evidence was ever presented to support the claim of foreign agents and Chávez' secret plans for a murderous purge. But if the objective was to frighten more officers into siding with those demanding the

---

* A mental diagnosis of obsessive self-exaltation and egotism.

president's resignation, it seemed to be working. At a press conference on 10 April, Army General Nestor González González offered the clearest message to date: 'The military high command must tell the president, "You are the one responsible for all these problems – resign!" If the high command refuses to take responsibility, someone else will.' 'Are you talking about a coup?' one of the TV reporters asked. There was no reply.

To Miraflores

Antonio could already sense that something big was happening when he made his way onto a bridge to assess the size of the turnout near the starting point of the demonstration at Parque del Este. It was the morning of 11 April 2002. Below him and before him, he observed Autopista del Este, the motorway connecting the east of Caracas with the city centre. Four lanes and a massive central reservation, filled with opposition demonstrators as far as the eye could see. There was not room for a single person more. Even the side streets were packed. In the surrounding homes, enthusiastic housewives leaned out their windows and banged on pots and pans in support of those marching below.

Cacerolazos, with housewives making coordinated efforts to ensure that pots rang out in every district of the city, was a national protest activity for the growing movement against Chávez. Not even after seeing the enormous crowd did Antonio imagine that *La mega marcha* would end any differently than according to the official plans: 'A few kilometres of singing, chanting and waving flags. Happy people from all walks of life uniting in their opposition to Chávez.'

And then to Chuao, the headquarters of PDVSA. The demonstration was to protest Chávez replacing the leadership of the state-owned oil company. Outside the PDVSA headquarters, the scheduled destination of the demonstration, a stage awaited a list of speakers which included many of the former oil bosses Chávez had fired. There was good reason to expect that everything would be peaceful. The entire route for the procession was in the opposition's stronghold in the east of Caracas, passing mostly through opposition-led municipalities and far from the presidential palace and the surrounding slums which housed the majority of Chávez' supporters. The end point of the march was the only concern, as the PDVSA building in Chuao was just within the borders of a district run by a mayor loyal to Chávez. However he had approved an application by the organisers to end the march there and guaranteed their safety.

Outside the PDVSA building however, things took an unexpected turn. A number of opposition leaders began directing the crowds towards the presidential palace. 'On to Miraflores to cast out the tyrant,' they shouted. Nobody ever accepted responsibility for doing this, but video recordings show several opposition politicians and PDVSA executives shouting out the fateful marching orders from the stage. Suddenly the slogan, *ni un paso atrás*, 'not one step back,' was no longer a metaphor for sustained political opposition to Chávez. It now meant marching all the way to the presidential palace without stopping at the police cordons or the barricades. The objective was to force the president to resign. A man was also filmed with a megaphone, urging the crowd towards Miraflores. A middle-aged white man with slicked-back hair and a pressed shirt, he might have passed for a PDVSA executive or opposition politician, but in fact it was Rear Admiral Molina Tamayo, the same man who had recently demanded Chávez' resignation. It was an ominous sign for the president if active military personnel were directing the demonstration towards Miraflores. As they neared the city centre, the National Guard rained teargas down on the demonstrators, presenting Antonio with his first excuse to turn back. He knew that his life was in danger and that the situation had got of control. Only adrenaline kept him moving onward, not common sense. But when shots were heard a few blocks from Miraflores, he allowed himself to be convinced by a police officer who was shouting 'This is getting ugly, get out of here.' By the time Antonio managed to get to safety, complete panic prevailed in parts of the city centre. Many still refused to turn back. They didn't know what awaited them.

One of the many myths surrounding Hugo Chávez – in retrospect there is much to indicate that this one was fairly accurate – was that he only slept three or four hours a night. At 06.11 on Thursday, 11 April, as the sun began to climb the clear blue Caracas sky, he may not have had any sleep at all.

Those inside Miraflores that morning tell of panic-stricken meetings, messengers coming and going, and a president trying to maintain calm.[14]

The fact that CTV and Fedecámaras had announced a general strike only a few days previously was probably not enough in itself to deprive the former paratrooper of a good night's sleep. But how much did Chávez actually know about what was happening at the military bases? Away from Miraflores, Defence Minister José Vicente Rangel brushed aside rumours of a coup and spoke of absolute calm in the ranks. But could Chávez trust this to be realistic? The first grumblings to surface in the military were in fact over the president's appointment of Rangel as defence minister. He became the first civilian to take on that role in decades, making him a controversial choice. The silver-haired solicitor was better known for his interest in abstract sculptures than for handling a weapon. Worse yet, the books Rangel had written which revealed the human rights abuses the army and the police had committed against the former opposition, about corruption, and about the controversial loss of sovereignty in their close military collaborations with the Pentagon. Some of the officers he had named and shamed had been trying to get Rangel before a military court to answer for his publications when the newly-elected President Chávez appointed him Defence Minister. In one stroke, the officers had been placed under the command of their biggest critic.[15]

Still early in the afternoon on 11 April, Rangel sent word to the president that a general who refused to recognise the authority of the government had occupied the main base of the National

Guard in El Paraíso. The base was only two kilometres from Miraflores and situated near a massive interchange called 'The Octopus.' Built in the fifties and with its eight arms, The Octopus is an impressive result of military dictator Pérez Jiménez' passion for grand infrastructure. Whoever controlled this strategic junction could cut off the main arteries leading into the centre of Caracas. In addition to news of troop movements and of more officers declaring their opposition to the government, Chávez was informed that the demonstration was on its way to Miraflores, having left the PDVSA headquarters, the supposed destination of the march. Chávez ordered the National Guard to prevent the demonstration from entering the security radius around the presidential palace and the national assembly. Chávez supporters were gathered there, having arrived the previous day. In the event of any clash between the two groups of supporters, the president knew he stood to lose most.

TV images of the demonstrators getting closer and closer to Miraflores signalled that the president's orders were no longer being followed.

At almost the exact moment that shots were heard only blocks from the presidential palace, the private broadcasters had their programmes interrupted by the president. 'I have decided to address the entire nation through a *cadena nacional*.' He asked the marchers, now only a few blocks away from Miraflores, to pull back to avoid a confrontation with the thousands of government supporters gathered outside the presidential palace. 'Reconsider. Reassess. Do not allow yourselves to be manipulated by those who desire a confrontation which can only end in disaster,' Chávez said. The president spoke in a calm voice, but his eyes revealed a certain nervousness. The way he insistently repeated his message over and over again made it almost sound like he was pleading with them. 'Reconsider, reassess, do not allow yourselves to be manipulated,' he repeated.

Chávez was still on air when Antonio arrived home and switched on the telly. The private channels were broadcasting a split screen. On one side the president was urging for calm. On the other, there was a bloodbath. Horrific scenes showing people being carried off in a panic. Many bleeding from the head. Antonio was thankful that he had escaped the chaos but furious with Chávez for suggesting people go home. He interpreted his words as a gross trivialisation of the massacre of the people who had been his fellow demonstrators only minutes earlier. This TV appearance by Chávez, one that Antonio viewed as highly provocative, would be his last. For now.

The Battle of Llaguno Bridge

11 April 2002 around 4 p.m.

'We hear the discharge of firearms. Above us, there is a helicopter from DISIP [the Venezuelan security services.] There are several fires and *la Policía Metropolitana* [Caracas Metropolitan Police] are on location with armoured vehicles. There are supporters of Hugo Chávez here and the situation has become critical.'

The location was *Puente Llaguno*, a stone's throw from Miraflores. *Policía Metropolitana* was an eleven-thousand-strong, heavily armed police force under the control of Alfredo Peña, the mayor who had switched sides to join the opposition.* *La Policía Metropolitana* was advancing towards the presidential palace in armoured vehicles, but they were confronted by Chávez supporters on Llaguno Bridge. Globovisión reporter Del Valle Canelón was describing the situation to a news anchor at the studio as it unfolded. In the background, gunshots and sirens were heard. Amateur video recordings showed flames and smoke from what must have been the barricades set up by Chávez supporters, set alight to prevent the armoured vehicles from nearing the presidential palace. Llaguno Bridge and both approach roads were filled with Chávez supporters. Many of them had been there since the previous day and some had slept on the asphalt, in response to the MVR leaders' call for a *vigilia*, a kind of vigil to protect the presidential palace. Throughout the morning even more joined in. The biggest influx arrived when word spread that the opposition march was headed for Miraflores, with several leading figures of the movement behind Chávez warning that an attempted coup was already underway. The pleas from the improvised stage were defensive and showed signs of fear. The slogan, *no pasarán*, 'they shall not pass', was the same slogan shouted by supporters of the socialist government in Spain before they were crushed by General Franco's army in the 1930s. Some sang *el pueblo unido jamás será vencido*, 'the people united will never be defeated,' sung by Chilean socialists in 1973 – before they were drowned out by the explosions from General Augusto Pinochet's bombers during the military coup that year.

At 4 p.m. on 11 April 2002, the singing on Llaguno Bridge also came to an end.

Canelón described as the tightly-packed crowd fled to either side of the bridge when the first shots sounded: 'There are bullets everywhere. People are running for cover. People are crawling on the ground.' The armoured vehicles were slowly approaching the bridge when some of the Chávez supporters drew weapons. 'Those fleeing for cover are gone but there are now six people on the bridge firing; it appears that *Policía Metropolitana* are shooting at them [...] The civilians are firing short-barrelled handguns, 9mms, in a gun battle with *Policía Metropolitana*,' she said, clearly anxious. Her colleague at the studio asked her to be careful.

Close-ups showed lifeless limbs with trails of blood behind them. The bodies were carried from the bridge to an improvised field hospital, a tent outside the presidential palace. Three armoured vehicles from *Policía Metropolitana* approached the palace. The shooting from the bridge picked up again. The Chávez supporters emptied their magazines at the advancing police, took cover behind the corner buildings, reloaded and jumped up to fire again. The advancing vehicles were forced to stop about two blocks from the bridge. The battle appeared to have reached a stalemate.

In addition to the exchange of gunshots between Chávez supporters and *Policía Metropolitana*, snipers had taken positions in the high-rises near the presidential palace.

The first shots in the centre of Caracas occurred between three and four in the afternoon. Few realised where the shots were coming from. Victims collapsed, both amongst the Chávez supporters and the opposition ranks a few blocks away, but no one could see who had fired.

Bullet wounds to the head and neck indicated it had to be snipers. Only people trained to use long-barrelled rifles with telescopic sights from a secure and hidden position could achieve that kind of precision without being spotted. On Llaguno Bridge, a few people were seen pointing at a building with a large green sign on Avenida Baralt. It was a logical choice for the presumed mercenaries – Hotel Eden. In Venezuela, Catholic sexual (double) morality combined with a propensity for unfaithfulness and a housing shortage meant that most people lived with their parents until they were married, making hotels with hourly rates the only option for people who wanted to enjoy an hour and a half of uninterrupted time with a girlfriend, boyfriend, lover or prostitute. A rather vulgar and popular term for these places was *Mataderos*, slaughterhouses. Those who could not afford something a little more luxurious turned to Hotel Eden. For security reasons, all the buildings in the vicinity of Miraflores were kept under constant surveillance by the presidential honour guard but if there was one place where unfamiliar faces, dark sunglasses and baseball caps pulled low did not attract attention, it was the hourly-rate hotels.

Snipers are believed to have been responsible for many of the seventeen to twenty people who lost their lives that day. An independent commission led by two Catholic priests, one known to be sympathetic to Chávez and the other an open supporter of the opposition, discovered that eight of those killed were on or near Llaguno Bridge, while nine were killed near the opposition march, one of whom was a photojournalist unaffiliated with the protest. Of the Chávez supporters, some were killed by Policía Metropolitana and others by snipers. As far as the opposition fatalities, they determined that all were the result of sniper fire. The sharpshooters may have been agent provocateurs, used to spark a bloodbath and provide the necessary pretence to force Chávez from office.

These murders contributed to the confusion and chaos in Caracas. Several people – suspected snipers – were arrested. Some were apprehended by Chávez supporters, others by opposition protesters. The suspects were handed over to various branches of the police and military. A few were released immediately. Others were transferred to the courts, only to be released after a short period.

It is impossible to know the political allegiances of those who released the suspects and whether those arrested were actually snipers or merely people caught in the wrong place at the wrong time.

The identities of the snipers remains unknown.[16]

Blood, Lies and Videotape

Globovisión reporter Canelón's unique real-time eyewitness account of the clashes between the Chávez supporters and the armoured police units at Llaguno Bridge should have been the scoop of a lifetime. However Globovisión's management decided not to broadcast the footage. The recording only reached the public several years later when a whistle-blower at the station leaked the material to an investigative journalist working for the state-owned broadcaster.

Instead, on 11 April Globovisión broadcast an edited clip from Venevisión, another major commercial channel with a shared hostility for Chávez. The Venevisión footage painted an entirely different picture than that described by the Globovisión reporter.

When the battle broke out, a team of Venevisión reporters led by Luís Alfons Fernández had found a strategic location behind Llaguno Bridge. From there they were well out of firing range and had a good view of the bridge, but the angle from the location also meant that the police units were out of their camera range. While

Globovisión's on-the-scene reporter struggled to maintain her calm as she described the armoured units advancing towards the presidential palace, Venevisión's team of reporters kept the camera focussed on six armed Chávez supporters as they fired. From their secure position, they captured the faces and movements of each and every shooter, with the same deadly precision as the bullets fired from the far side of the bridge. For some of them – with equally deadly consequences.

At the Venevisión studio where Fernández' video images were edited and shared with the four major TV stations on the evening of 11 April, the Chávez supporters on Llaguno Bridge were assigned an entirely different role in the events of the day:

'See the man in the MVR* shirt. Watch closely as he pulls out a pistol and empties a magazine on defenceless, unarmed protesters on a peaceful mission. The man in the MVR shirt ducks down to reload, then fires on the peaceful demonstrators again and again.' The Venevisión reporter's voice was indignant and insistent. As he spoke, the camera panned to a man with a head wound being carried through the terrified crowds of people.

Appalled commentators on the various TV stations repeated the same message, only slightly varying the wording. A desperate Chávez had ordered his men to massacre the protestors. The ruthless gunmen, as they were referred to, had knowingly and intentionally fired on 'pregnant women and innocent children,' they explained.

The recording, however, had a fundamental weakness. While the faces and recoiling guns of the Chávez supporters were shown with merciless clarity, the angle it was filmed from did not allow viewers to see who or what they were shooting at. At a journalism conference a year after the event, a participant confronted the Venevisión reporter with the following point: 'You told the audience that the opposition was massacred, but there is no possible way you could know that since you could not see them from your position.'

---

* MVR (The Fifth Republic Party) The party founded by Chávez.

Fernández responded, 'I have never said [...] I have always made it clear that I did not have a clear view of Avenida Baralt.'[17] Venevisión and all the other major TV networks filled in this gap with images of bleeding opposition demonstrators mixed into the footage of Chávez supporters firing weapons in order to substantiate their repeated claims that the victims were shot by the Chavistas, but none of them had any video of opposition demonstrators within shooting range of Llaguno Bridge.

A series of amateur videos later emerged, taken at the same time but from different angles, including the commentary by Canelón, the Globovisión reporter. These images made it absolutely clear that no opposition demonstrators, pregnant women or innocent children were on Avenida Baralt when the Chávez supporters fired – only the armoured units of *Policía Metropolitana*, which went completely unmentioned in the broadcasts of 11 April.

The fact is that no opposition demonstrator was ever within firing range of Puente Llaguno, meaning that there was no way any of them could have been shot at by the Chávez supporters. However this revelation would only emerge later. The day following the events of 11 April, the only version of the killings to appear on the country's TV screens and newspaper columns was Fernandez'.

And it was these images that unleashed the events of the following hours.

Immediately after the footage was broadcast for the first time, with the Chávez government still standing their ground in Miraflores, Venevisión began showing still images of the gunmen and asking viewers to phone in with information about the identity and location of the 'ruthless murderers.' Armed police units soon swooped into their homes to arrest several of them. One was killed while being taken into custody.

With the images of bleeding victims rolling across the screens, a number of soldiers began appearing in the TV studios. Along with opposition politicians, they were invited to discuss the events. 'Chávez is a dictator. With the images we have now seen, can anyone deny that he is also a murderer and that he has blood on his hands?' a female presenter asked on Venevisión. 'Is it true what the leader of Fedecámaras and members of the armed forces are saying, that Chávez is a murderer?' the Globovisión news anchor asked.

Both received unambiguous replies from their respective guests in the studio. 'Chávez is a dictator, and now a murderer too,' Chávez is a psychotic killer,' Chávez is a criminal who has blood on his hands, he must be convicted,' Chávez is an agent for Castro and the Colombian narco-guerrillas,' Chávez is a tyrant who must be punished,' Chávez is responsible for all the killings, he is a power-crazed murderer.'

Asesino, assassin or murderer, seemed to be the word most used to describe the scenes by Venezuelan media that evening.

The generals had already decided to act. On the morning of 11 April, the media had already leaked rumours that Chávez had been arrested by the military high command. Chávez disproved this through one of his *cadenas*, but later that evening the rumour appeared to prove true. Around four o'clock in the afternoon, General Héctor Ramírez Pérez and a group of senior officers presented a conclusive video message to the military and the people of Venezuela:

'At this moment, as we count six dead in Caracas, we have decided to speak out against the regime and withdraw our recognition of the government of Hugo Rafael Chávez Frías.'

By the time night arrived the officers were appearing in even greater numbers, no longer calling for the president's resignation, but stating that he had already resigned.

'The armed forces have complete control of Caracas and the government has abandoned its functions,' Camacho Kairuz announced, a general from the National Guard, as well as deputy chief of defence. At Venevisión, one of the station's news veterans appeared on TV with what he claimed was a letter signed by Chávez.

The letter stated that he accepted responsibility for the murders, resigned as president and was seeking asylum in Cuba. The smiling Venevisión newscaster stated that it was all over.

The Fall of Miraflores

After his televised appeal urging the opposition demonstrators to turn back and to avoid confrontation, a pensive Chávez withdrew to the office of the presidential palace.

With reports of gunfire only a stone's throw from Miraflores, Chávez was unable to go outside to get an overview of the situation to assist him in making informed decisions. With rumours of an impending coup and officers making public statements encouraging the high command to overthrow him, it was impossible for Chávez to know who to trust in the military, either as a source of information or as an instrument to implement a possible emergency plan.

However the president was not completely unprepared. As an enthusiastic expert of the continent's history, he had long ago realised that challenging powerful business interests in Latin America was a risky exercise. The fact that Venezuela was the USA's third largest supplier of oil certainly did not make the matter any less dangerous. Chávez knew that there was far from unanimous support in the military for his Bolivarian project. Due to uncertainty about the loyalty of a number of generals, he had established a secret emergency radio network with his closest and most trusted allies in the military and the intelligence agencies. The time had arrived to set aside the usual lines of communication and initiate the secret radio network, setting into motion the necessary emergency measures against what the president perceived to be an attempted coup.

This did not go to plan either. Chávez' closest ally, a general by the name of Rosendo who was responsible for guarding the centre of Caracas against any potential military advance on the presidential palace, had disappeared. One of the few to answer Chávez' call on the secret network was the head of DISIP, the security police. He had only bad news to offer. That afternoon, yet another group of key military personnel had announced their support for the movement against the president. Even more were colluding in secret.

Chávez asked to be left alone in his office. He attempted to contact those he still considered allies. In the meantime, a group of around twenty people sat in a large waiting room outside. They were ministers, members of parliament, local politicians and some rank and file from the ruling alliance, as well as an Irish film crew who had come to Caracas to make a documentary about the president. While the politicians sat in front of the TV watching the images of the 'gunmen from Llaguno Bridge' on the private channels, the Irish journalists recorded everything that happened in the room outside the president's office. One of the few to speak to them was the former guerrilla, García Ponce: 'The media ... they were too strong for us ... we didn't even get a chance to form a media strategy.'

By that point, a state governor from the opposition had already sent an armed unit to shut down the state-owned television station. The activists trapped inside Miraflores had just given up on yet another attempt at getting out the message that many of those who had died that day were Chávez supporters. On TV, General Camacho Kairuz from the National Guard maintained that the military now had control of Venezuela. 'Every garrison in the country has joined the operation, with only a small pocket of resistance remaining around the presidential palace [...] Obviously we have no desire for a bloodbath. To those still outside the presidential palace: You are completely surrounded, there is no point in resisting. Withdraw so that we can avoid bloodshed.' The Irish documentary team panned the camera from face to face, stopping on the planning minister Jorge Giordani as General Camacho presented his ultimatum on TV. The elderly man raised his hand to his forehead, adjusted his glasses and stared at the floor. Many appeared to be in shock. Some were in tears. A young man in civilian clothes gripped the automatic rifle resting on his lap.

A little later that day, General Camacho arrived at Miraflores accompanied by two officers.

They had prepared a resignation letter for Chávez to sign.

Air Force General Fuenmayor explained that he had a squadron of F-16s ready to bomb the presidential palace if Chávez refused to sign the resignation letter. The president was given fifteen minutes to reach a decision.[18] In the book *Chávez Nuestro*, Defence Minister José Vicente Rangel described the discussion that ensued in the outer office of the presidential palace: 'I supported telling the coup leaders to go to hell and to offer armed resistance.' But since he was convinced they would all die, he attempted to persuade his son Pepe to try to leave the palace. To no avail. Defence Minister Rangel had spent several years in Chile and was married to a Chilean woman who had lived through Pinochet's military dictatorship. For him this was a reprise of 11 September 1973 in Chile. Even the finale, dying in a bombed out presidential palace just as President Salvador Allende had done, appeared destined to be repeated. When Rangel got through to his wife on his mobile, he left her a bleak message:

'It seems that all is lost. Pepe and I will remain here. You will be a widow and will lose your son.'[19]

'This is a victory for death,' Planning Minister Giordani stated dejectedly to the Irish journalists who continued filming. Most of the civilians had now been evacuated. Those remaining prepared themselves for a battle that could only have one outcome. The Environment Minister emerged from the president's office. With some difficulty, she explained that Chávez had negotiated his surrender to the military in order to stop them from bombing the presidential palace, which was now surrounded. 'But the president has not resigned. He has not abandoned the mandate that the people have given him. This is a coup. The president has not resigned.' She managed one final sentence before she was overwhelmed by tears: 'The world must know that this is a coup.' However nobody seemed to have any kind of plan for how the world, let alone the Venezuelan people, could be told. The armed raid on the state-owned TV station had cut off the government's only means of reaching the people to inform them of what had happened. Private media reports claimed that Chávez had resigned voluntarily and accepted responsibility for the murders in the centre of Caracas.

After the statement by the Minister of the Environment, Chávez emerged from his office in his olive-green uniform, military boots and distinctive red beret. Ten years older, but dressed exactly as he was the last time he was arrested in 1992. Those still in the waiting room flocked around him to say goodbye, but were asked to allow the president to get through quickly. Only five minutes remained before the deadline to bomb the palace expired. The strange mix of government ministers, secretaries, maintenance staff and bodyguards, who had all refused to leave the building despite the threat, sang the national anthem as the president left the building without saying a word.

Outside the palace, a young man ran after Chávez, seemingly causing no concern to the officers given the honour of bringing in the sought-after prisoner. With ill-disguised despair, the man attempted a final uplifting farewell: '*Presidente*, we will return,' he said. 'We are not defeated yet,' Chávez replied quietly, before being forced into the darkness of the waiting black sedan.[20]

'Good Morning Venezuela, We Have a New President.'

'Buenos días, tenemos nuevo presidente.'

A beaming Venevisión host wished Venezuela a good morning on 12 April, announcing that the country had a new president. The channel that had made history with its images of Llaguno Bridge also made the following appeal for the occasion. The message scrolled across the screen as the newsreader read:

'Today our children, our young people, the entire nation has seen the hope for a better life restored. At Venevisión we are proud of our contribution to the fatherland with which we have always walked hand in hand. We invite everyone to celebrate this day as the fatherland begins a new life. Venevisión: The feeling of believing in Venezuela!'

The previous afternoon, evening and night had been rife with conflicting rumours of the government's fall, of Chávez' resignation and of his possible escape to Cuba. All doubt was swept away when the president of Fedecámaras, Pedro Carmona, surrounded by military leaders, held a press conference at approximately five o'clock in the morning on 12 April.

He declared himself presidente de la republica.

'The military has confirmed they will be keeping Chávez under arrest ... We have decided to establish a transitional junta,' Carmona announced solemnly. According to the self-appointed leader of the junta, it was a 'democratic takeover' with a 'direct mandate from the people.'[21] The official inauguration of Carmona took place in Miraflores that same evening. The formal ceremony was broadcast by all the major TV stations, in the same room Chávez had held many of his speeches and press conferences. Dressed in a suit and tie, the slender, light-skinned figure of the ageing Carmona was a stark contrast to the robust Afro-Mestizo man who had occupied the gilded seat for the past three years.

Some may have noticed that the large painting of Simón Bolívar that normally hung behind Chávez was gone. The guests were also different. Chávez had developed what some considered the slightly peculiar habit of inviting people off the streets, party activists, cleaning personnel and such to the majestic hall inside the presidential palace. At formal receptions for foreign leaders, regular press conferences or meetings with local party activists, the palace was normally filled with people who resembled ordinary Venezuelans in terms of attire, skin colour and facial features. Those now filling the halls of Miraflores were by and large white or light-skinned people dressed in elegant dresses and suits. Many of them were very well known: directors of large corporations, leaders of the various branches of Fedecámaras, bank executives and representatives from the Catholic Church. They waited expectantly for the new president to announce the guidelines for the new Venezuela. Carmona did not disappoint. His council of legal experts assembled by his allies from the opposition parties and the business sector decided to dissolve parliament and dismiss the electoral commission, the Supreme Court, the human rights commission, the head of the central bank and the auditor general.

Venezuela's official name was changed back to *República de Venezuela*. The adjective *Bolivariana* which Chávez had added, was gone just like the portrait of Bolívar that hung behind the presidential chair. The constitution – the only one in Venezuela's history approved by referendum – was repealed. Carmona allotted himself the authority to remove the elected mayors and state governors from office and appoint new ones at his discretion, without elections being held.

As he read, the shouts of joy grew louder for each institution he announced was to be abolished through what came to be known as the 'Carmona Decree.' Throughout the ceremony, Carmona reiterated again and again that it was a 'democratic takeover,' and maintained that he ruled with a 'with a direct mandate from the people.'[22]

The affluent east of Caracas erupted in celebrations, the likes of which were rarely seen in Venezuela apart from during Carnival and the end of the baseball season, the country's national sport. The centre of the celebrations was Plaza Altamira in the wealthy district of Chacao, not far from where Antonio lived. Antonio described a state of wild euphoria. People had painted their cars with opposition slogans. The streets were filled with music. Towards evening it developed into a veritable party. The supporters' song for Venezuela's most popular baseball team, *Los leones de Caracas*, 'the lions of Caracas' was rewritten for the occasion. 'He's gone, he's gone, he's gone, he's gone,' was the chorus, referring to Chávez. Gone from the presidential palace and gone from Venezuelan politics for good. 'It almost feels like it's easier to breathe,' one of the TV presenters said, expressing the sentiment of Antonio and many of those celebrating with him.

'They Were Macho in Power But Now They Are in Hiding.'

According to the Venezuelan constitution, the vice president is to take charge if the president resigns or is prevented from carrying out his duties in any other way.

At this time, Venezuela's vice president was Diosdado Cabello. The Carmona regime had made it clear from the outset that the constitution was no longer valid, but Cabello was still viewed as a threat. That made him hunted game, and he went straight into hiding. On the morning of 12 April, with Venezuela awaking to the news that Chávez had resigned, Globovisión reported a rumour that Cabello had sought refuge inside the Cuban embassy in the affluent Caracas district of Baruta. The embassy was immediately surrounded by furious locals and *anti-Chavistas*. They attacked the embassy cars, leaving them overturned with doors torn off and smashed windows. Burning objects were thrown at the security wall surrounding the embassy. The local police force, under the command of the conservative mayor of Baruta, Henrique Capriles Radonsky, seemingly did little to intervene. Globovisión enthusiastically reported what they called 'a protest by civil society.'

A spokesperson for the group informed the journalists that Cabello was the object of their siege. 'To those of you inside, Diosdado Cabello and his entourage [...]. There will be no electricity, no food, and no water. By the time you have seen this broadcast, we will have cut off your power and water supplies.' The television crews also filmed the moment the power cables were cut, but made no critical enquiries as to why 'civil society' had attacked an embassy in pursuit of the country's legitimate vice president. Inside, the embassy staff feared for their lives. With the embassy now without power and water, there was particular concern for the children residing there, as they had also heard the threat that no food would be allowed in until Vice President Cabello was handed over.

It was not the first time a Cuban embassy had been besieged during a military coup in Latin America. During General Pinochet's seizure of power in Chile in 1973, after the death of President Allende in the bombing of the presidential palace, soldiers fired live ammunition at the Cuban embassy. Twenty-nine years later, the Cuban ambassador in Caracas was presented with an ultimatum by a growing mob, apparently with the blessing of the armed municipal police force under the control of the right-wing mayor, Henrique Capriles: Allow an armed police unit to escort broadcasters from the private media inside, search the embassy and apprehend Cabello or face a continued siege. With no food, no water and no electricity for the staff and their families inside, the ambassador was in a desperate situation. According to international law, their demand to enter the embassy in pursuit of a legitimate vice president had no legal standing. The ambassador nevertheless agreed to allow Capriles and the journalists inside, but not a police unit. 'This embassy is under siege, just as Cuba has been for the past forty years, and for forty years, we Cubans have never made a single compromise to any empire or anyone else who wanted to impose their will on us,' the Cuban ambassador said, then added one final message, his voice trembling: 'We will do as the Cuban people do when under attack: defend this patch of [Cuban] territory with our very lives. And this is not just talk. We Cubans don't do talk'[23]

His final point was one that all Latin Americans could appreciate, both followers and critics of the Cuban revolution: with Castro in power in Havana, the Cubans had kept their word and not caved in to the pressure from their northern neighbour, the world's most powerful nation. Apparently Capriles did not believe it was just talk on this occasion either, and unwilling to risk a bloody confrontation, he left the embassy. But he and his police force allowed the siege to continue. If the vice president really was hiding inside the embassy, there was little chance of him escaping, much less demand to be allowed to fulfil his constitutional duty to lead the government in Chávez' absence.

Not far away and in the same district, Justice Minster Ramón Rodríguez Chacín was caught unawares in the flat where he had sought refuge. Leopoldo López – mayor of the neighbouring district of Chacao and co-founder of the Primero Justicia party – accompanied an armed police unit, Capriles and the Baruta police force as they stormed the flat. All the major TV stations had been informed of the operation in advance. All of Venezuela witnessed Chacín as he was handcuffed and led out to a waiting mob who kicked, punched and spat at him. 'They were macho when they were in power,' López said as he proudly described his role in the minister's arrest to the journalists in attendance. 'But now they are hiding. But we will have justice.'[24] That same day, Tarek William Saab, a member of parliament and noted left-wing poet, was arrested at his home and driven away by armed police.

Carmona had already announced via press conference that those who refused to cooperate with his regime 'would have to face the consequences.' López urged everyone to assist the new regime in the opening phase. Similar scenes played out around the country, as several parliamentarians, state governors and mayors were hunted down, imprisoned or forced to flee. Amnesty International summed up the worst of the incidents, including 'the unconstitutional and summary removal of President Chávez, the illegal detention of his supporters and the arbitrary powers assumed by the de facto government.'

However the immediate effect of televising the arrests seemed to work. In publicising the arrests, the new regime succeeded in scaring off Carmona's opponents from parliament, government departments and other institutions. That way their positions could be taken over by the new regime with no resistance.

At the White House, a representative of the Bush administration called the takeover in Venezuela a spontaneous response by the military, one motivated by the regime's suppression of a peaceful protest.[25]

This was also the official version most often put forward by the Venezuelan and international media at the time. Perhaps still intoxicated by their victory, many began to loosen their tongues. Defence Minister Ramírez stated that the operation had been planned for months. General Lameda explained that 'the plan was to have civil society organise a huge protest and then bring in the armed forces when the pressure was at its peak.' Very few considered the consequences of what they were saying in front of the TV cameras and to the newspapers. After all, why should they? Since the state-owned broadcaster had been shut down, there was no opposition or scrutiny from the rest of the media, in fact, all major news outlets gave their whole-hearted support for the new regime. At the same time, orders to arrest ministers, parliamentarians and party activists had already been allocated to the various military garrisons. Those who had managed to escape had no means of reaching out to the Venezuelan people. The images of 'the murderers of Puente Llaguno' had dominated the airwaves that day, as well as the resignation letter in which Chávez accepted responsibility for the massacre. In addition – now that Chávez was under arrest and key figures in his government had been forced to flee – there was no need for discretion about their participation in the coup. On the contrary, with Chávez out of the way, a fierce competition arose to fill the key positions in Pedro Carmona's government. And those vying for a big role had to demonstrate that they had played a part, that they had risked something, or had made an important contribution to the regime change.

The media enthusiastically emphasised their vital role in the removal of Chávez. 'Thank you RCTV, thank you Globovisión, thank you Televen,' a representative from Venevisión announced when the key figures of the coup were gathered in the studio to celebrate their victory on the evening of 12 April. The newly-appointed defence minister of the Carmona regime, Héctor Ramírez Pérez, supported this view when on the same channel he expressed that 'the media was our greatest weapon.' The generals also explained that they had consciously used the media to implement the coup. Of particular importance was a declaration by the coup officers demanding that Chávez step down, which had been broadcast the previous day. The coup leaders assumed that a televised declaration by active officers demanding the removal of the president would force Chávez to cancel his planned visit to Costa Rica in an attempt to maintain control of the military. They had wanted to imprison Chávez, so it was imperative that he remained in the country. 'We had to keep Chávez in Venezuela. That's why we released that statement when we did, to ensure that Chávez would not leave the country,' they proudly admitted in the TV studio.

The international media received particular mention from Carmona, who thanked them for informing the world that his appointment was part of 'a democratic transition.'

On that evening in 2002, there seemed to be little doubt that Chávez was finished. About to go down in history as a bloody authoritarian and a cowardly buffoon who massacred innocent civilians and then retired.

The Chávez supporters were gone. Carmona controlled the entire city. The military supported the new president.

Among those who celebrated the fall of Chávez, few or none recalled the 1989 popular rebellion in Caracas and the power present in the city's *barrios*. However, there was still only a thin buffer zone, a few blocks of middle-class residential buildings separating Miraflores from the *barrios*. The distance between the majestic palace that served as the country's centre of power, and the vast, slum-covered hillsides, the most striking symbol of poverty and powerlessness, was short.

If the explanation offered by the media was true, that Chávez had lost all of his support, and that the entire capital was celebrating the resignation of such an unpopular president, this proximity would not be significant.

On the other hand, if Chávez was right, and the poverty-stricken majority still supported the Bolivarian revolution, Carmona and his jubilant supporters were surrounded by a powerful enemy – the slums.

An Inconvenient Prisoner

'My father asked me to tell you, if he dies today, it's because he stayed true to his convictions to the very last.'

Chávez' 21-year-old daughter, María Gabriela, had just spoken to President Fidel Castro on the phone. She had been barely able to speak through the tears. Minutes earlier on that morning of 12 April, she had received a call from her father, who had somehow managed to get hold of a mobile phone at the Fuerte Tiuna military base in Caracas where he was being held captive.

Chávez feared for the safety of his three children and when he learnt that their bodyguards had abandoned them because they were 'no longer the children of the president,' he advised them to find a new hiding place. He then gave her instructions to phone President Castro, believing him to be the only one with enough influence to get the message to an international audience that Chávez had not resigned. Shortly after, a Cuban TV journalist contacted her and broadcast their conversation live, enabling her to explain the situation concisely.

'What is happening in our country is a coup and they [the media] are attempting to cover it up with an alleged resignation … This is a right-wing dictatorship … ' María Gabriela asked for the situation to be presented to the Organisation of American States (OAS) and other international organisations, concluding with this plea: 'You must help my papa.'[26]

Carmona's inauguration ceremony at Miraflores was still underway when a friend of the Chávez family working at Fuerte Tiuna rang the daughters with news of their father. Hugo Chávez was being transferred from the base under the cover of darkness with a plastic bag over his head. The daughters feared he was going to be executed. But the move could also signal nerves on the part of the military leadership behind the coup. Perhaps they knew about the interview with the president's daughter on Cuban television. And even though Venezuelan media kept that information secret, it was now only a matter of time before the news reached Venezuela.[27]

At eleven o'clock on 12 April, María Gabriela's statement was released live on Cuban television, presenting the takeover in an entirely different light.

The wall of censorship raised by Venezuela's private media outlets lasted for twenty-four hours. Then the rumours that Chávez had not resigned began to spread throughout the country. *No ha renunciado, lo tienen secuestrado*, was the phrase soon heard everywhere in Venezuela: 'He has not resigned, they're holding him prisoner.' People wrote it on tablecloths and hung them from their windows, sent text messages and motorcycle messengers. But first and foremost, the message was spread by word of mouth – or what Venezuelans call *radio bemba*, 'lip radio'. At *Radio Bemba* there were no media owners to censor the decisive news.

Amateur video released in the days following the coup reveal the violence that *Policía Metropolitana* unleashed on the initial scattered protests. Live ammunition was fired at civilians, killing several of them while others were left beaten and battered. However when the size of the demonstrations increased, the police disappeared. Since the private TV channels did not report on the protests, little video evidence exists of how many people participated in the demonstration. Instead, repeats of soap operas and cartoons were broadcast, and news reports claimed that everything was under control.

Meanwhile, Chávez was constantly moved around by the increasingly pressured military leaders supporting Carmona. These were senior generals in charge of massive budgets and with the authority to set priorities for entire divisions and battalions. But their ability to execute military operations were dependant on the rank below, the officers who had direct control over the rank and file. This group consisted mainly of younger officers, many from the same background as Chávez, poor boys from the country and the *barrios*. 'The people's soldiers,' Chávez would later call them.

During the 1989 riots, many of these officers had refused to carry out orders by the Pérez government, which had commanded them to quell the protest with military force.

They were equally unwilling to take part in the military coup against Chávez. As the supporters of the deposed president took to the streets, they were prepared to refuse orders from their superiors again. They would not use military force to quell the protests by Chávez' supporters. However, during the initial twenty-four hours following the removal of the president, opposition within the military was hampered by the fact that many believed he had offered his resignation voluntarily, as stated by the inspector general of the army, Lucas Rincón, for one. In addition, the situation within the military was extremely complex. Attempting to organise a counter-offensive involved contacting officers with whom there could be uncertainty as to which side they supported. A personal lapse in judgement, proposing a move against the Carmona regime to the wrong officer, could have fatal consequences.

On 11 April, General García Carneiro had attempted to defend the presidential palace with tanks before being forced to withdraw. Having spent the first twenty-four hours eluding the DISIP intelligence officers, who operated on the instructions of the coup leaders, by the morning of the 13 April he had managed to organise and prepare a command group to recapture the presidential palace. At the same time, a large lorry had been procured, ready to drive to the gates of the prison outside Caracas where Chávez was rumoured to be held.[28]

However, the operation was aborted due to uncertainty as to whether Chávez was actually in that prison.

The overthrown president had now become a rather inconvenient prisoner. After abandoning their attempt to make Chávez sign a resignation letter, the coup leaders decided to transport him to a smaller base outside Caracas. From there they decided to send him to another military base on the small, unpopulated island of La Orchila, just off Venezuela's Caribbean coastline.

Just before setting off, Chávez got to chatting with one of his guards.

The young soldier explained that he was just an ordinary soldier doing his job, and that actually he had supported him as president. Chávez insisted that he had never resigned. On a small piece of paper, he wrote a message to 'the Venezuelan people and others it might concern.' 'I have not relinquished the legitimate power mandated to me by the people,' he wrote on the crumpled up note that the soldier later smuggled off the base before Chávez was sent to La Orchila.

Soon General Raúl Baduel, commander-in-chief of the paratroopers in the city of Maracay and one of Chávez' closest allies, read the short message to thousands of jubilant supporters. They had gathered outside the key military base to demand the reinstatement of the president.

At the same time, Baduel and the others who endorsed the demand to re-install Chávez received information that two ships and two helicopters with American registration were spotted off the coast and inside Venezuelan territory. This was bad news. The Bush administration had already backed the removal of Chávez at a press conference the previous day. Of all the Latin American leaders, both civilian and military, who had been toppled in US-backed coups and interventions over the years, none had ever managed to return to power. An opposition leader, Carlos Escarrá, proposed having Chávez extradited from Venezuela so that he could be indicted for crimes against humanity by the international courts. General Baduel, General García and the others who organised what they dubbed 'Operation Recover National Dignity,' expected to only get one attempt. They could not fail. They knew that it was extremely likely that if their rescue operation was uncovered, the coup leaders would execute Chávez or whisk him out of the country. But with news of American vessels near La Orchila, there was no time for further planning. They had to act quickly.

An hour after the crumpled note arrived at the military base in Maracay, a military helicopter manned with fifteen commandos from the presidential honour guard, an army doctor and a lawyer, was on its way to the island.

At the same time, the corridors beneath the presidential palace were filled with soldiers loyal to Chávez. [29] Amateur recordings from Miraflores showed the coup admiral Molina Tamayo, chosen for the key military position of *Casa militar*, nervously pushing aside a white curtain to look out upon the throng of people surrounding the palace.

Shortly after, they began fleeing through the back entrance.

Video recordings showed images of primarily white men and women from the country's economic power elite as they fled. Those who had applauded the establishment of the Carmona dictatorship the previous day were filmed making a wild escape to the car park. The elegant eveningwear that had given the ceremony an aura of glamour was now more of a hindrance as they hurried towards their respective cars so their waiting chauffeurs could take them to safety behind darkened windows. Men in suits forgot the usual Venezuelan *caballerosidad*, gentleman's etiquette, and ran with no regard for the women who straggled behind in their high-heels, struggling to keep their balance.

Most of the key figures involved in the coup, including Carmona and Molina Tamayo, managed to escape. Having lost Miraflores, Carmona established an improvised government headquarters at the Fuerte Tiuna military base. With Chávez as prisoner, Carmona still had the upper hand.

The Irish documentary filmmakers had remained in Miraflores and filmed the coup and Carmona's inauguration ceremony. They continued to film as Chávez' supporters retook the presidential palace. In the Carmona regime's rush to escape, they had emptied the safes and left them open, proving to many what the coup was really about: money. The large painting of Símon Bolívar that had previously hung in the main hall was discovered in the cellar, reportedly in a toilet – a symbolic fulfilment of the Carmona decree removing 'Bolívar' from the official name of the republic. The champagne corks and half-eaten canapés had not yet been cleared when the party came to an abrupt and sobering end. A group of politicians and businessmen who were believed to have played a vital role in the coup did not get out of Miraflores in time and were apprehended. The prisoners appeared disorientated and nervous, but brightened up a little when they were informed of their constitutional rights, promising them better treatment than the coup regime had offered members of the country's legitimate government the previous day. Perhaps it was more humour than humanism the prison guards had in mind when they set up a TV in front of their distinguished prisoners: They switched the channel to CNN – where Carmona insisted that the regime had complete control of the capital. 'Even though there has been a few scattered [protests], the situation is now under complete control. Absolute calm prevails across the country and everything is normal,' Carmona said, also claiming to be in Miraflores. On the evening of 13 April after Miraflores had been retaken, a helicopter of elite soldiers landed on La Orchila with a mission to free Chávez. The prison guards they encountered seemed totally unprepared when confronted by the commandos. No wonder they were taken by surprise. Isolated from the civilian population and *radio bemba*, the grapevine, the forces guarding Chávez on La Orchila presumably had no other source of information but the private TV and radio stations, where the massive protests against the coup, the military rebellion against the coup mongers and the retaking of Miraflores were all censored. Even before the rescue operation, Carmona was on the defensive, but at least with Hugo Chávez in irons he would have been able to use the deposed president as a hostage. The prisoner would have been a powerful negotiating tool against the Chávez supporters retaking Caracas. With Chávez freed and heading for the capital in a helicopter, Carmona had lost his last bargaining chip and only means of exerting pressure on his emboldened enemies.

The Return

14 April, 3.00 am:

Hundreds of thousands of people had come down from the poverty-stricken hillsides of Caracas to surround Miraflores, demanding the return of Chávez. They heard the droning of a helicopter and noticed a powerful beam of light piercing the darkness. Most of them had been encamped there since the previous day. By now everyone knew that Chávez was alive. No one was returning home until they had seen him with their own eyes.

The helicopter landed on the roof. For the first time since everything had exploded on 11 April, the noise that had ranged from chanting slogans to gunfire to the banging of pipes against the metal fence surrounding the palace was replaced by complete silence. Then a deafening applause as Hugo Chávez, moved to tears by the crowd of people, emerged from the helicopter. Wearing a tracksuit in the colours of the Venezuelan flag, he greeted his supporters with a clenched fist.

Chávez believed his alliance between the people and the military had saved the Bolivarian revolution and himself from suffering the same fate as Salvador Allende. *La alianza cívico-militar*, 'the civil-military alliance,' Chávez called it: a spontaneous mutual understanding between the soldiers assigned to guard the Carmona regime and the masses from the slums: they were on the same side. Together they ensured victory over the coup regime.

In his first appearance as reinstated president, Chávez stood holding a silver crucifix, asking the opposition to respect the constitution and democracy. He addressed the media in particular, urging them to end the propaganda of hate. He also warned his own supporters against seeking vengeance. Not everyone supported him in this. Some Chávez supporters began sharing an old Simón Bolívar quote: 'For each act of treachery there was a pardon, and for each pardon, there was a new act of treachery.' Most Chavistas had little faith that a forgiving attitude would shunt the economic elite and the right wing onto a democratic path.

THE OIL

The Oil War

In the autumn of 2002, as I was learning to live, speak party and eat the Venezuelan way, and still struggling to come to grips with what was happening in this strange country, the opposition was preparing for an offensive that would shake the ground under Chávez once again.

Already by the summer of that year, the former presidential candidate Andrés Velásquez had vowed that 'the government would not make it to December.' He called for the people to 'paralyse the country until Chávez steps down.'[30] His comments fell largely on deaf ears as he was in no position to mobilise any kind of effective strike. Taking such a radical step as paralysing the entire country demanded extensive planning. Luís Giusti, the former president of the state-owned oil company PDVSA, had a more effective strategy. In November 2002, he revealed what was really underway.

'If PDVSA halts production, the country will collapse in a week,' he declared to *El Universal*.[31] Giusti had been fired by Chávez but he was still considered one of the world's most influential oilmen, and at the state-owned oil company, it seemed he retained more real authority than the President did.

On 2 December, ten days after his declaration, *el paro petrolero*, a shutdown of oil production had become a reality.

Management, middle management, many of the engineers and a considerable number of the high-salaried employees laid down their tools and switched off the machinery. In a matter of days, oil production had been halved. After a week, it had fallen from three million barrels a day to two hundred thousand, before nearing a complete shutdown. The results were precisely as Giusti had announced to the papers when he spoke in favour of the action: 'The first thing to be affected will be the shipping of crude oil for export. Next shipments to the distribution centres which supply the country's entire transport sector with petrol and diesel will be paralysed.'[32] Eighty per cent of Venezuela's export revenues disappeared, the state was heading for bankruptcy and the fuel reserves were shrivelling. Total collapse drew nearer for every day that passed. The demand from the PDVSA leadership was simple: 'Not a drop of oil will be produced until Chávez leaves Miraflores.'

Would the PDVSA leadership single-handedly manage to topple Hugo Chávez once and for all?

In reality, there was no need for them do it single-handedly. For in the intense race against time with Chávez battling for his political survival, other powerful actors stepped forward. Uniformed officers continued their protest at Plaza Altamira in Caracas. They were a stark reminder that once again, the conflict could flare up on a military level. A weak government combined with economic chaos affecting people's everyday life always makes a good starting point for a military coup.

In addition, umbrella organisations for the opposition, NGOs, industry experts and even celebrities offered their full support for the PDVSA shutdown. The business sector again took a leading role. 'Democracy is at risk,' claimed the president of Fedecámaras, the Venezuelan federation of chambers of commerce, demanding the removal of Chávez.[33] CTV, the traditional voice of the trade unions across the country, also endorsed this demand.[*]

On 2 December, Fedecámaras, CTV and the opposition parties declared *paro nacional*. In Spanish, the word *paro* means shutdown but in Venezuela it is most often used to mean strike. However this was not a strike in the normal sense. Fedecámaras had announced that their businesses would halt production and shut the factories irrespective of what the workers wanted. This was a lockout.

The opposition also tried to get the teachers to go on strike. This was only partially successful, but state governors from the opposition parties managed to shut all the schools in their states. The major food companies stopped producing and shipping food.

---

[*] Even though CTV was the national voice of the trade unions, in practice it had been discredited by most workers. Support and membership were low and were heavily reduced when CTV came out against Chávez and supported the former power-brokers.

CTV president Carlos Ortega encouraged people to stockpile food and news broadcasts showed supermarkets packed with people desperately hunting for the few remaining bags of cornmeal, powdered milk, rice and other staples. Essential products like baby formula and a range of medicines disappeared from the shops while various types of medical equipment were lacking in hospitals. PDVSA also ensured that supplies to the country's gas cookers were cut off.

The consequences of the so-called *paro nacional* were felt across the country, but affected the various layers of society in different ways. For Antonio it was a question of activism and solidarity, fighting for a common goal. He could make do without certain goods and services – a small sacrifice for a greater cause. In any case, essentials items could still be acquired on the black market. Food made up an insignificant portion of Antonio's expenses, and even a tenfold increase on individual items would not have a big impact on his finances. Queuing for hours to get items on the black market was easily resolved by sending domestic workers to pick them up. The biggest sacrifice, Antonio remembers with a laugh, was getting hold of alcohol. A shortage of beer at the end of the baseball season and the run-up to Christmas was unheard of for Venezuelans, who love their beer and parties. For many, complaining about the lack of beer was a way of tackling the crisis with a sense of humour.

Among Caracas' poor, other shortages created far greater concerns. Millions struggled to get hold of food. As the price of food and other staples skyrocketed, in many cases as much as a tenfold increase, many factories and businesses also closed, depriving entire families of their only source of income. For some, *el paro* meant acute hunger.

The first countermove by the Chávez government was to distribute food from its strategic food reserves.

In Caracas, the person responsible for this was the mayor of *Municipio Libertador*, a man loyal to Chávez and charged with distributing food at the town hall near Plaza Bolívar. But the government's food reserves were limited compared to demand. People queued for days, with many choosing to stay overnight to get their hands on a small bag of cornmeal and a little cooking oil. In addition to worrying about not getting enough food for their children and exhaustion from spending hours in the queue, people had yet another obstacle to face: the Caracas police force was controlled by Mayor Alfredo Peña, the same man who had supported the coup against Chávez.

Queues outside the rationing stations for basic foodstuffs were sometimes peppered by teargas by *Policía Metropolitana*. In some cases, violent street brawls flared up between the police and the desperate people in the queues. For several months the entire pigeon population at Plaza Bolívar disappeared, reportedly scared away by the huge amounts of teargas launched by the police.

Another big problem was the lack of gas supplies. Only some upper and middle class families had electric hobs in their homes. Amongst the poor, a shortage of gas supplies meant they were unable to cook or to boil and disinfect water.

In some neighbourhoods, people resorted to burning rubbish for fuel. Others burnt their own furniture.

'Towards Total Chaos'

Alongside the chaos the people of Venezuela were facing, a rhetorical battle over who was to blame for the crisis was also playing out.

The private TV stations, which accounted for almost ninety per cent of the viewership, led the battle on behalf of the opposition. Commercial advertisements disappeared entirely, replaced with political adverts showing desperate people queuing outside petrol stations and closed supermarkets. The narrators and the words scrolling across the screen left no doubt: 'People are starving. We have no jobs, we have no food, we have no petrol. President, this is all your fault. Resign!' 'Only one person is responsible for all the terror, all the sadness, all the violence, all the stubbornness in this country. Only one person is responsible. Not one step back. Leave, resign now!'[34]

According to the president of Venevisión, Víctor Ferreres, seven thousand two hundred commercial adverts were supplanted by political broadcasts in support of the action to oust Chávez.[35] Soap operas and TV shows were replaced by round the clock coverage of demonstrations, press conferences and opposition statements. 'Chávez Resign Now!' was the demand that covered the front pages, inserts and headlines of most of the major newspapers.

Internationally, the situation was not much better for Chávez. Foreign firms operating in Venezuela, both in the oil sector and otherwise, supported the lockout by shutting down their operations. General Motors, Procter & Gamble and Goodyear joined the campaign. Ford put thirteen hundred workers on 'annual leave.' The Bush administration made threats and called for Chávez' resignation.

In South America, Chávez still stood alone in his defiance of Washington. Not a single government came forward to support Chávez' demand that he be allowed to fulfil his mandate. Venezuelan newspapers reported that the Organisation of American States (OAS) 'would activate the democratic charter (against Chávez) if the crisis is not resolved.' According to the front-page spread in the newspaper *2001*, this could lead to expulsion from the organisation or to direct intervention.[36]

The opposition called the halt in production a non-violent work stoppage. On the thousands of television features, the spokespersons were always mindful of using the adjectives *cívico y pacífico*, 'civil and peaceful,' when referring to the campaign.

But not everything was peaceful. Alfredo Keller from the opinion poll institute Keller & Associates was quoted by the national and international media, saying that the situation resembled a 'cold civil war with each side waiting in the trenches.' 'Without warning, the situation could explode into a real war.'

On 3 December it almost did. The opposition had asked for permission to hold a large demonstration outside public institutions in Caracas. The march, announced as *la gran batalla*, 'the great battle,' would be a 'crushing defeat' for the government, CTV president Carlos Ortega promised, a man who barely six months earlier had actively supported the military ouster of Chávez.[37] Clashes broke out on the streets. The following day the media reported: 'Two dead following ambush on opposition march.' *El Nacional* ran with the headline: 'Military police and *Chavistas* attack demonstrators.'[38]

At the time, I remember the president's seemingly desperate attempts to go on the offensive during his frequent public appearances.

He called his opponents 'traitors, fascists, and oligarchs' and insisted that the production stoppage was a lockout by big business, designed to pave the way for a fresh coup attempt. 'The oligarchy will never have power in this country again, no matter what,' Chávez stated, always mindful of affirming that the people were still behind him and that 'before long,' they would 'defeat *el paro fascista.*'

To me his tone and rhetoric seemed aggressive and out of control, as though the president believed he had lost the support he deserved and was shouting at everyone and everything, bitter at his imminent defeat.

According to the media, support for Chávez continued to fall. By the turn of the year, they were claiming that support for the president was between twenty and thirty per cent – down from eighty per cent only two years earlier. With opinion polls showing falling support and the country in total chaos, it was easy to get the impression that Chávez prioritised personal power, staying in power at any cost, above the welfare of the people.

At the time I believed the best thing Chávez could do for himself and the country as a whole was to step down voluntarily and end the crisis before further tragedies unfolded and he ended up in front of the international criminal court or being overthrown by his own people.

However, cracks soon began to appear in the image of the 'violent Chávez.'

One day after *El Nacional's* article on 'the ambush' of opposition demonstrators leading to two murders, it emerged that the two people killed, Óscar Gómez and Jairo Gregorio Morán, were not part of the opposition march, but unarmed Chávez supporters participating in a counter-demonstration. However many Venezuelans were left with the impression that they were opposition protesters shot by Chávez' police or military, as claimed on TV. A tiny correction was published in the newspaper, with the relatives of Gómez and Morán stating that those killed were *Chavistas*.[39] Relatives vented their fury at the murders of their loved ones, but also at the lies told by the media about them being opposition supporters killed by Chávez' men.

Just as he did in the weeks and days before 11 April, Chávez again donned his uniform.

In his speeches, he rained insults down on the opposition parties. The president encouraged the people not to give an inch to the 'treacherous oligarchy.' He could certainly come across as authoritative and energetic (or authoritarian and brutal) – but what was happening on the streets bore no resemblance to a president with a firm grasp on the situation.

In the centre of Caracas, several officers continued their protest for several weeks with an ultimatum for Chávez: Resign voluntarily or you will be removed by force in front of the entire press corps. *Policía Metropolitana* continued patrolling the streets of the capital. There was certainly something absurd about this situation, with the capital's largest and most heavily armed police force, one that had participated in the military coup only months earlier, still permitted to carry automatic weapons and patrol the area surrounding the presidential palace in armoured vehicles. In a rare break from the international media's usual editorial approach – with the opposition regularly presented as the victim – the news agency Reuters reported an explosion on the fringes of a pro-Chávez demonstration. One person was killed in the explosion and ten were wounded.[40]

Indications were that this could have been an attempt to assassinate the president. But this deadly blast did not result in any drastic measures by the government. No state of emergency was declared, there was no ban on demonstrations or expanded powers for raids and arrests by the police. The fact that the bombing campaign and such openly declared attempts to topple an elected government were not met with any reprisals would be unthinkable even in the most liberal society.

The question was why Chávez allowed this to happen.

Chávez supporters believed he was being naïve. A number of *Chavistas* expressed their frustrations that Chávez was failing due to his own leniency – that by preserving a futile hope that his gentle response to the coup, the bombings and the chaos would leave him on the moral high ground.

The media believed it was due to a loss of authority and legitimacy, and that the government was falling apart. Some claimed that his inability to act was because no one took orders from the president any longer, not even his own supporters, and that the president was doomed to defeat.

I was not sure which explanation to believe. One thing I was certain of, though, was that the enormous pressure on the president would mean the end of his rule. It was only a question of time, I thought – and a question of how much blood would be spilt before it was over.

The Battle for the Oil Platforms

Chávez' battle for survival played out on three main fronts.

On the first, he agreed to enter negotiations with the opposition under the auspices of the Organisation for American States (OAS). The OAS is an intergovernmental organisation with its headquarters in Washington, something that wins it little trust from

Latin America's left wing.* As long as the opposition was assured of victory, Chávez had little hope of reaching a compromise in any negotiations that did not involve him stepping down as president. Still, sitting down at the negotiating table would at least ease the international pressure a little. But with the state treasury, food supplies and petroleum reserves drawing nearer to rock bottom for each day that passed, times was running out for the president.

The second front was the military. The officers occupying Plaza Altamira made daily pronouncements that the majority of the army, air force and navy opposed Chávez' 'Castro-communist project,' and that at any time the president would be removed in order 'to restore peace and order.' For the time being, the battle for military loyalty between the government and the opposition was waged in public through speeches, rumours and rhetoric, and behind the scenes through orders, threats and promises of future promotions and positions of power.

Nobody was certain of who was loyal to which side and how many would consider changing sides if something happened. However, it was clear that the situation could turn violent at any time. In the *barrios*, people again worried about a military coup and a civil war.

Antonio also experienced the anxiety prevalent during this period. He and many other opposition activists were certain that Chávez was going to limit their freedoms and deprive them of their property rights if they did not put an end to the revolution. It was now or never. But there was a strong belief amongst opposition supporters that they would succeed this time. It was a question of how long Chávez would be allowed to continue tormenting the country in order to retain power, and how the masses from the slums, or 'the Taliban' as they were referred to by the media, and the

---

* According to the Latin American left, the OAS by and large had been transformed into an anti-communist apparatus during the Cold War. The OAS, for example, was lenient towards the most brutal right-wing dictators, whilst Cuba was excluded from the organisation after ousting the US-supported Batista dictatorship.

soldiers and officers who remained loyal to Chávez would react to seeing their leader fall. In the building where Antonio lived, many decided to buy weapons to defend themselves and their property in the event of a civil war, or if the masses from the slums arrived to pillage and plunder. Antonio simply stacked some cobblestones on his balcony above the building's entrance. Just in case.

The third and most important front was the workplace.

Perhaps Chávez would be able to buy time at the negotiating table and retain the loyalty of certain strategically placed senior officers, and in this way prevent the officers occupying Plaza Altamira from taking action against the presidential palace again. However, if he was unable to win over the labour force – where Fedecámaras and its allied unions were attempting to paralyse society – he would be doomed to failure irrespective.

Chávez staked everything on winning over the workers.

'The right to strike is one that workers have long fought for. We originate from this struggle, it is a mechanism which allows the workers to demand their rights when they are infringed on by the employers,' Chávez declared. He refused to consider what was happening in the oil industry and in other sectors of the economy a strike. Instead he claimed it was sabotage instigated by the oligarchy.[41]

This may have come across as wishful thinking on the part of the president. Even though the business sector had the biggest players, Fedecámaras and the PDVSA leadership supporting them, the CTV trade union had also joined the campaign. Both within Venezuela and internationally, the major media outlets were unambiguous in their depiction of this as a general strike. One Norwegian newspaper, for example, described the workers supporting the president as merely 'a fanatic minority.'[42] A minority so fanatic and insignificant – if the European media and news agencies were to be believed – that they were not worth mentioning in the almost daily reports about the crisis in Venezuela that December.

In Venezuela however, you could still find workers who did not support the campaign.

'We don't want to sabotage the economy and lose our jobs in order to bring down a president whom we have voted for, the only president who has ever cared about the workers,' one of them stated in an interview with the state-owned channel.

The battle to gain the support of the working class and control the means of production was where Chávez focussed his efforts. He knew that there was a weak point in the broad front of trade unions, business organisations, NGOs, opposition parties and military dissidents. The dozens of rallies announced by the private broadcasters ahead of the numerous demonstrations against Chávez had one thing in common:

They were all held in middle and upper class districts of Caracas.

In poor areas, where the majority of the country's workers lived, there was hardly any support for *el paro* to be seen. That was where the counter-offensive began.

Long before he was elected, Chávez had forged links with the organised industrial working class, a significant force in the heavy industry region of Guyana in southeast Venezuela. One of Chávez' sources of inspiration, perhaps his most important mentor on the radical left in the decade before he came to power, was Alfredo Maneiro, a former guerrilla fighter who had formed the Radical Cause party together in conjunction with workers in Guyana. Chávez knew where the shoe pinched for Venezuelan workers and was able to convince them to vote for him in the presidential election in 1998. But simply gaining the workers' sympathy was no longer enough for Chávez.

To survive, he would have to do get them to act.

In the early phase of *el paro*, Chávez called on the workers to ignore the work stoppage. Many heeded his call and went to work anyway, only to be met with shut factory gates, locked cash registers, factories lacking essential raw materials and resources, and machinery out of operation. Chávez had only two choices. One was to negotiate with the business owners who made his resignation a condition for any rapprochement. At best, Chávez might be able to get them to call off the campaign if he withdrew all of his reforms. The other possibility was to get the workers to take over the factories against the' wishes of the owners.

Venezuelan communists had been demanding this for over fifty years but they had never been anywhere close to succeeding.

With hostile military personnel on the streets less than a kilometre from *La Casona*, the presidential residence, and with death threats hanging over him, Chávez's freedom of movement was severely limited. However, he had managed to secretly visit a number of workplaces to test the mood of regular workers and key figures within the radical left wing of the trade union movement. When Chávez assessed the situation, he realised it was possible to encourage the workers to take control:

'Oligarchs know this; the Venezuelan working class supports the revolution. The workers stand ready across the country to take over and get production moving again. You have my full support. Wherever you take over, you will be allowed to retain control. If the oligarchy refuses to produce, the workers will do it without them. These will be worker-controlled enterprises.'

Many workers began organising in order to re-open the factories that owners had closed. The mood began to turn. For a while, the media promoting *el paro* was able to solve the problem virtually, by keeping their cameras away from areas where the lockout failed. In that way, opposition picketers from the urban middle class retained the sense that the majority was behind them and that the lockout was still effective, thus maintaining morale.

But big business knows a revolution when they see one. They had investments and capital to protect and could not afford to be fooled by the media.

Up until that point, Chávez had not nationalised a single business had been nationalised, no factory had been expropriated by the state, only a small minority had been affected by minimal tax hikes, and in any case, the state barely had the capacity to collect.

Business owners observed with horror as what had been a moderate economic reform policy by the president to that point, threatened to mutate into a genuine revolution. Furious workers who were desperate to regain their means of existence began taking control of factories.

Despite a media blackout that gave the impression that Chávez was already defeated and abandoned by his own people, business owners understood perfectly well the counter-ultimatum presented by the president and the workers:

End the lockout or lose your business.

Some business owners still believed that a combination of empty stomachs and an empty state treasury would eventually topple Chávez, and that a new government would be able to suppress the worker-led occupations before the movement spread. But most of them wavered. Chávez was advancing on several fronts.

When the oil and fuel depots began to run dry, the government's first course of action was to take legal action, demanding that any oil tanker transporting state-owned oil should be returned to the state. Unsurprisingly, this proved ineffective. The judicial system was manned by the same judges who had ruled that the leaders of the military coup who overthrew and kidnapped Chávez in April had acted 'with good intentions.' However Lieutenant Colonel Chávez had another card up his sleeve. Two weeks after the launch of the campaign, he ordered the military to seize control of the oil tankers.

At the same time, the president was making important progress internationally. Surrounded by conservative governments, Chávez paid close attention as the metalworker and unionist Lula da Silva just won the election in neighbouring Brazil. Lula had not officially taken office but still managed to send Brazilian oil tankers to Venezuela. This prevented a total collapse and gave Chávez and the workers who supported him time to organise the offensive on the oil fields. At the same time, workers and engineers defying the PDVSA management gained ground on the oil platforms. Many of them saw no sense in the production stoppage, that it was neither about working conditions or pay, but simply a way of reinstating a company management which they regarded as anti-national, corrupt and hostile to workers, a stoppage with the goal of toppling a president many of them had voted for.

By the middle of December, Chávez announced that the workers and engineers, whom he considered 'loyal to the fatherland and the constitution,' had re-started production on several oil fields.

Nevertheless, the situation was still tense one month later.

Many were uncertain as to who was telling the truth about what was happening on the oil fields: Chávez, who said that the 'saboteurs were defeated,' or the former PDVSA leadership, who still claimed to be in control. One of the most heated incidents occurred when an enormous oil tanker blocked the shipping channel outside the oil capital of Maracaibo. If production had re-started as Chávez claimed, it was to little avail as long as it was impossible to transport the oil. The tanker was loaded with tonnes of highly-explosive petroleum and the PDVSA management warned of the danger of explosion and of a fatal accident of immense proportions if the government attempted to board the ship in order to re-open the shipping channel.

In addition, the shortage of food afflicting the people was worsening.

The management of Venezuelan supermarkets maintained their claim that the warehouses were empty due to the workers' strike and that the little food they had in reserve had long since been sent to the shops, and that the famine which was threatening to break out among poor Venezuelans was not the fault of the supermarkets. Chávez was having none of it. 'The oligarchy is hoarding food in order to starve people into abandoning the revolution,' he railed – even threatening to send in the military if cornmeal, milk and cooking oil did not return to the shelves soon.

On 17 January General Luis Acosta Carlez visited one of the warehouse complexes for the food giant Polar, the country's largest distributor of essential foodstuffs. He had orders from Chávez to confiscate any food he found and distribute it in poor areas where the famine was at its worst.

General Acosta Carlez was confronted by a large group of reporters. They protested loudly as a soldier broke open a padlock on one of the warehouse buildings.

Endless rows of pallets with all kinds of food were visible inside the enormous warehouse.

The general selected a pallet with Venezuelans' favourite drink, *malta* – a sweet, non-alcoholic malt beverage; he opened a bottle and devoured it greedily – after all, *la malta* had not been seen in the shops for weeks. The sight must have been too much for one Globovisión reporter who could hardly contain herself, voicing her strong objections that the operation against the storage facility was 'a breach of human rights and the right to private property.' Her voice almost went falsetto as the general continued drinking, unmoved by her objections. Until finally, he slowly lowered the bottle from his lips and interrupted her with a load burp, right into her microphone. The scene was transmitted live and television viewers were treated to the sight of the general's quivering uvula as he burped. *Perdón señorita*, 'Sorry miss,' the general said in a smug and ironic tone.

'All of this will be confiscated. And given to the Venezuelan people,' he said pointing at the pallets of food behind him, to a chorus of protests from the journalists.[43]

The clip was shown almost every day for several months on Venezuelan TV and even ended up on CNN. Opposition supporters like Antonio seized upon the incident as further evidence of the brutal and uncivilised people ruling Venezuela. On the other hand, many poor people were furious at the big companies for trying to force Chávez from power by starving them, not to mention the media who supported them. They considered the general a hero and believed the humiliation of the journalists and the seizure of the food was an appropriate measure.

In addition to the production stoppage and the demonstrations, the opposition alliance Coordinadora Democrática (CD) had called on their supporters to block off the streets to contribute to *la ingobernabilidad*, the ungovernability, the chaos they hoped would topple the president. But support for this campaign was limited to the upper and middle-class districts. Any time opposition activists attempted to block off the streets in poorer districts and in the centre of Caracas, they were usually chased off by those living and working in the area. Despite the massive TV and radio campaign instructing people to *tranca tu calle*, 'block off your street,' several hundred times a day, the middle class gradually lost interest when they realised that by blocking off their own streets, they were inconveniencing themselves more than anyone else.

During *el paro*, millions of Venezuelans on both sides of the political divide had to survive without work and basic goods and services. Businesses of all sizes had lost significant revenue, market share, and in many cases went bankrupt.

The opposition's remaining morale was broken when the state-owned broadcaster announced the that while they were suffering through all of this, the president of Fedecámaras, the man who asked people to endure difficulties 'for the good of the nation,' was on holiday in Aruba – a paradisiacal Dutch island in the Caribbean.

Business owners realised that they had lost on both fronts, both in their power struggle with the president and with the enormous sums of money they had invested in halting production.

By February, it was all over as workers loyal to Chávez managed to take over the remaining oil installations, refineries, and tankers, and re-started production.

Hugo Chávez had survived. Again.

THE VOICE OF THE BARRIOS

Confession of a Closet *Chavista*

If you enjoy observing an intense political struggle of geopolitical significance at close range, while at the same time having access to tropical beaches and rainforests, living it up with a welcoming local people, and with the possibility of combining them all on one weekend for less money than you would spend on a night out in any northern European city, in 2002 there was probably no place on earth that could compete with Venezuela.

I had just realized that the date of my return flight was fast approaching, and I knew that I would have to find a way to return to Venezuela as soon as possible.

The pretence was to spend a year abroad from September 2003 to April 2004, as a part of my degree in social geography. However there was a risk involved. If something happened during the year and I had to interrupt my studies, I would miss both the autumn semester of 2003 and the spring semester of 2004 in Oslo. In which case I would be forced to return my student grant, which presumably I would already have spent. And safeguarding yourself against any unforeseen events in Venezuela, only six months after the oil shutdown and less than two years after the military coup, was impossible.

The political situation was difficult to assess. Naturally the fact that the president had survived attacks from some of the most powerful forces inside and outside of Venezuela had supplied a moral boost to Chávez and his supporters. On the other hand, from what I read in the papers after the oil lockout, the indications were that Chávez had only won a temporary reprieve that could quickly turn to defeat.

A dark economic landscape emerged after the production shutdown in the oil industry. During the first four months of 2003, with the economy still flatlining due to the drop in oil revenue and the lockout in a number of other industries, GDP decreased by a whopping twenty-four per cent. Even the most spectacular general strikes and financial crises in history have seldom led to this kind of drop. By and large, this has mostly been found in countries affected by war. Of the companies participating in the Fedecámaras lockout, between three and five thousand went bankrupt. Unemployment rose dramatically.[44] Venezuelan media claimed that oil production was still running at half throttle, despite the government claiming it was quickly returning to normal levels, around three million barrels a day. According to some Western newspapers, Chávez' popularity had dropped from eighty percent to around thirty. Judging by the media, Chávez was a weak president clinging to power.

Then there was the email I received from a Venezuelan academic in reply to my enquiry about the political situation in the country. I had asked for an assessment of the situation and its impact on my chances of studying in the country. 'I would not recommend anyone to travel to Venezuela in the current political climate,' Carmen Cabrera replied: 'At the moment we are experiencing a kind of 'dictatorial transition' and the opposition will not remain passive.' I was not quite sure what she meant by 'dictatorial transition.' But judging by the tone of her reply, I gathered that she was not a *Chavista*. 'It's difficult to predict what will happen in the coming months …' The three dots at the end emphasised her uncertainty. According to the constitution, the next presidential election would not take place until 2006 and Chávez did not seem keen on surrendering power of his own volition. If the president was going to be defeated in the months ahead, it was difficult to envision it happening by peaceful means. Nonetheless, I decided to study in Venezuela.

I gave up the large, public university, Universidad Central de Venezuela (UCV), as it required that I acquire an exchange agreement with the University of Oslo to study in Caracas. Instead, I chose a private Catholic university, Universidad Católica Andrés Bello (UCAB).

With a university place secured, I could spend more time and energy observing Venezuelan politics. I believed that studying sociology would be the best place to begin, in order to find objective facts and well-founded arguments in what was otherwise a rather polarised society. Equally important, I could finally take the first steps on the long, and as it turned out, sometimes painful attempt to interview Hugo Chávez. I also hoped that the social sciences faculty would be able to offer other opportunities. Left-leaning, liberal-minded people often have a tendency to be drawn towards such fields of study. Perhaps someone at UCAB could put me in touch with the right people, people with connections to the President.

However, UCAB was very different to what I had expected. I did not encounter a single *Chavista* at the entire university, at least not that I knew of. The closest I came was a professor who was suspected, or rather accused of being a *Chavista*, something he denied. His name was Henriques and he taught a course on economic development at the sociology institute. Because of his *Chavista* stigma, the student advisor at the faculty had advised me against taking his course: 'The professor is not particularly up to date, nor is his syllabus.' This was a stark contrast to the other professors; she unhesitatingly described them as 'fantastically clever.' My classmates normally greeted the other lecturers with an enthusiastic 'good morning,' but they barely mumbled a lethargic 'hello' whenever Henriques entered the lecture room.

And in fact Henriques did stand out. In contrast to the other professors, he kept silent when it came to Chávez, the opposition and Venezuelan party politics. 'Let's discuss the reading for today,' he would reply when the students cornered him with the latest news about what they considered the president's catastrophic policies. This differed from most of my other professors, who rarely let the course programme get in the way of going on a political tirade about the incompetence of the president. One of the lectures I remember best was actually supposed to be on Castells, the Spanish sociologist.

In the social sciences, Castells is known for his theories about the correlation between urban development and economic power dynamics. I had been looking forward to hearing about how the metropolis of Caracas, with its mix of flashy oil riches and beggarly slums, could be analysed through Castells' conceptualisations. But no. Castells uses Marxist theories, the lecturer explained, and since Chávez was 'dragging Venezuela down with communism,' he would prefer to devote his lecture to discussing Pol Pot and the Soviet invasion of Czechoslovakia in 1968 – 'in order to reveal the true face of Marxism.' None of the students batted an eyelid. When I left the lecture hall, I understood no more about the dynamics of Caracas' urban chaos than when I entered. However, I understood a lot more about the ideological entrenchment of the educated upper middle-class elite. Any hopes of the university leading me closer to an interview with Chávez quickly faded.

During my studies, I ran into one of my former Spanish teachers from the language school in Caracas. I asked for her take on the situation. I told her that I was interested in learning above all else and had little interest in choosing sides, so she took me into her confidence. 'Well, I am a *Chavista*,' she practically whispered. When the other teachers had talked to the students about *el loco comunista*, 'the crazy communist,' she had kept quiet or played along, expecting to be sacked by her boss if he found out she sympathised with the president.

The hatred towards Chávez was by no means limited to the country's educational institutions; it also applied to large segments of the urban middle class. The building in La Candelaria in Caracas, where I found an affordable one-room flat to live in while I studied, was no exception. For the most part, the opposition received at least twice as many votes as Chávez in this district.[45] Still, that had to mean that there were at least a few dozen *Chavistas* in the seventeen-storey building where I lived. Many more than in the rather posh district of El Marqués where I had stayed with my host family while I studied at the language school the previous year.

But if any Chávez supporters lived in my building in La Candelaria, much like my language schoolteacher, they must have been closet *Chavistas*, a rather silent, but considerable minority in Venezuela's urban middle-class areas.

In the queue for the lift the neighbours often castigated the President and the only person who protested was the security guard, *señor* Julio, an older, dark-skinned man, likely from a poorer neighbourhood of the city. He received many insults because of it – I even saw the middle-aged lady from the flat opposite me strike him with her umbrella one rainy morning as I hurried past on my way to university. I asked the guard why he would annoy the residents with comments supporting Chávez, when he had to spend twelve hours a day, six days a week with these people. He told me that he would be retiring soon and didn't care anymore. Otherwise, he probably would have kept quiet like so many others.

Caracas Dressed in Red

'The oligarchy is trying to claw back the power and the money. They want to keep the oil riches for themselves and for the foreign oil companies, like during the fourth republic when they were going to sell off PDVSA. Luckily the Bolivarian revolution put an end to their madness. Now the people rule Venezuela. And the Venezuelan people, the sons and daughters of Bolívar, nobody can stop them. Not even the Yankee empire. They have tried with a military coup. They have tried with threats. But this revolution is here to stay.'

Chávez waved his arms and shouted into the microphone at the top of his lungs.

The audience, perhaps as many as one hundred thousand *Chavistas*, listened enthusiastically. It was nearing four o'clock in the afternoon.

The previous day a pick-up truck with speakers mounted to the back had driven through the centre of Caracas, promoting *la marcha bolivariana*, 'the Bolivarian march.' I immediately decided to attend. I would finally get the chance to meet some genuine

Chavistas, I thought: People who would happily spend half the day, more for those travelling long distances, to celebrate *el comandante* come rain or shine, listening to hour-long speeches, only to later be labelled as 'riffraff' and 'drunkards' by the media. However I was not entirely convinced by that depiction of the protesters. Could a piece of bread, some cheap booze and a free red T-shirt be all that drove the Chávez supporters? Was it safe to write them off as a 'fanatic minority'? Anyway, if the people were finally turning their back on Chávez, as a number of opinion polls indicated, this might be my last chance to see who they were for myself.

The location for the mass gathering was Avenida Bolívar in the centre of Caracas, the same eight-lane thoroughfare on which the opposition marched towards Miraflores on the day of the coup, 11 April.

Now it was the red-clad *Chavistas* covering the *avenida*. Stretching all the way from the stage in the city centre, where Chávez stood four to five metres above the audience, ending more than a kilometre to the east. The side streets were also packed, and in the surrounding buildings supporters leant out from balconies and windows. Only those at the very front were able to see the president. The others had to make do with the large screens and speakers that had been set up along the avenue for the occasion. All ages, genders, and skin colours were represented, but there were fewer people of white European descent, as they largely (but not entirely) belonged to the city's middle and upper class.

They listened to their *comandante* in silence, but only an hour earlier a party atmosphere had prevailed. Every few hundred metres or so, the long procession was broken up by stages where there were salsa bands and volunteers throwing bottles of water to the dancing demonstrators. The people swinging and sweating under the afternoon sun appeared to be anything but a gathering of political activists. Around the same time as the bands packed up, I heard a rumour that the president was coming this way. '*El comandante* is coming, he's coming now.' The atmosphere quickly changed from laughter and dancing to quivering expectation. Following the advice of one of the supporters, I found my way to the top of a bridge so that I could look down on the road where Chávez supposedly was going to appear. Only a few minutes went by before the president arrived.

Dressed in a military uniform and wearing a red beret, he was standing – apparently unprotected and unconcerned – in an open jeep which slowly drove through the jubilant crowd. Chaos broke out around me. People ran, pushed and practically fought their way forward to get a glimpse of the president, hoping to shout something to him or to touch him. Some screamed, many cried. *Comandante te amo*, '*Comandante*, I love you,' a young woman shouted, *Que viva Chávez no joda*, 'Long live Chávez, goddammit,' a middle-aged man roared. It was a hypnotic, almost surrealistic experience, finding myself in the midst of this outpouring of emotions, one which I barely managed to wake up from as a supporter grabbed my arm to prevent me from slipping off the bridge and crashing to the road that lay four or five metres below.

Chávez was moving away from us but continued looking up at the bridge where I stood. He waved and smiled triumphantly. He was clearly comfortable with the homage, the chaos and the hysteria. For a moment, I got the sense that he was looking directly at me and it seemed that those around me felt exactly the same. Actually, almost everyone I have ever spoken to who has had a brief glimpse of *el comandante* in some kind of mass gathering felt that way. That is probably exactly how people experience an encounter with a true demagogue, I thought. What I wanted to know was whether it was simply empty charisma or whether there was something more to it.

Standing in the middle of the crowd, it was thrilling to be amongst this demonstration of Chávez supporters. But when I started moving around the edges of the procession with a camera around my neck and a notebook in my hands, not everyone was friendly.

Since foreigners were an even more unusual sight in Caracas than white Venezuelans, my pale skin meant I was often mistaken for a Venezuelan with European roots – a part of the European-descended minority, or part of the white elite who could not stand having a man like Chávez in the presidential chair. Now, many jumped to the conclusion that I was a journalist from the private, right-wing media. Few thought I belonged here. 'What are you doing here, *escuálido*?' one asked, using the slightly derogatory word Chávez supporters often call people from the opposition.* 'You'll probably write that we were no more than three or four idiots paid to march for Chávez,' another shouted. 'Tell your boss to stop forcing you to write lies about us,' he demanded then slipped back into the crowd before I managed to tell him that I didn't work for a Venezuelan newspaper. I recalled the TV images I had recently seen of a scuffle between journalists and a group of *Chavistas*, where a heated discussion ended in fisticuffs and bloodied noses.

I was close to abandoning my attempts at speaking to some of the demonstrators but instead decided to employ one of the oldest and most common tricks in Venezuelan society: flattery. When all else fails, it usually works.

Words like *mi amor*, 'my love,' or *corazón*, 'heart,' are all used in the rather obvious flirting that takes place between Venezuelans in a variety of situations, but first and foremost it forms a part of the Venezuelan vernacular used in everyday interaction between men and women. This is similar to how words like brother, sister, cousin or *pana*, the Venezuelan word for friend, are used between people of the same sex, even when they are complete strangers. Being

---

* Directly translated the word means delicate or frayed, but nowadays is not used in Venezuela with its original meaning. As a term for Chávez opponents, it refers to the opposition as a whole being a dismal and small group. Therefore when someone calls someone *escuálido* in Venezuela, it does not mean that this person is weak, but that she or he belongs to the opposition. The term came about as a retort to regular claims by the media and the opposition that Chávez supporters made up only a small minority of the voters.

generous with these terms makes perfect sense in a society where the spontaneous sympathy or antipathy you awake with the person you are dealing with – whether at the bakery, the office of a public or private institution, or even in the waiting room of the hospital – can have a massive impact on the outcome of any social situation.

I decided to take a chance and made an improvised attempt at charming someone with a flattering comment in the hopes of starting a conversation.

'Excuse me, I was wondering if I could take a picture of you and get your help: The opposition claims that women who support Chávez are ugly and envious. I was wondering if you could help me disprove that myth.'

I had long since tired of the extreme overemphasis on female beauty in Venezuela. If nothing else, the words that slipped out of me proved that no one is immune to cultural influences. However my opening salvo did yield the laughter I had hoped for and quickly broke the ice.

Her name was Omaira and she was about as close to the 'average Venezuelan woman' as you could get: forty years old, single mum with three kids, a woman facing a daily struggle to make ends meet. Her medium-brown skin colour and slightly narrow eyes were a clear sign that she had a combination of African, Native American and European blood in her veins, a trait she shared with the majority of Venezuela's poor. She lived in a small house in a *barrio* called Monte Piedad close to the centre of Caracas. She had spent the better part of twenty-five years as a textile worker.

Accompanied by Omaira and one of her daughters, it was much easier to make contact with the other demonstrators as we pressed our way through the crowd of people to get closer to Chávez. A man even approached me on his own initiative. He happily answered my questions about the president and the revolution.

The large dark-skinned man had a thick moustache and came from a village in the inland state of Yaracuy, a place where the improvement of public services and promises of land reform had won Chávez many supporters. 'If only the corrupt opposition and the gringos would let Chávez govern in peace, then Venezuela will be one of the best countries to live in,' he said, adding that 'Chávez is one of us. We trust him.' However the man quickly lost interest in me and instead focussed on Omaira, openly declaring his admiration for her. He promised us, Omaira in particular, that if we ever visited his village, he would slaughter a pig for us.

Chávez supporters here were about as far as you could get from the stereotypical left-wing activist or 'professional demonstrator' seen in Western Europe. Seeing someone in torn trousers was not a political statement here, but a sign that the person could not afford to buy a new pair. These were *el pueblo humilde*, 'the humble people,' a term often used in Venezuela. The people I was able to speak to worked at supermarkets, as mechanics, street vendors, builders or were stay-at-home mums. They were all devoted to the president. Many had never voted until Chávez came along. Few seemed to have been interested in ideology or party politics in their early lives. An old woman limping around with a cane in one hand and a small boy who must be her grandchild in the other, admitted that she had had not even voted for Chávez. 'You know, I am old,' she said, 'and I have never understood such things as registering and voting cards. There is nowhere to vote in my *barrio*, and it is so far and so difficult to get to the closest polling station. But I love my president. May God give him long life.' I realised that I had never seen so many poor demonstrators *supporting* their country's leader, while the rich were protesting against him. This was just one of many things that seemed to be turned on its head in Venezuela.

Talking to my new acquaintances pushed Chávez' speech to the background a little. But when I got the sense that it was getting towards the end – which is something you learn to detect after hearing a few of his speeches – I was all ears. 'The rulers doomed the people to starvation, destitution, illiteracy and humiliation while they lived in unrestrained luxury. The injustice and corruption they have left behind in our shattered fatherland cannot be defeated in five years, not in ten, perhaps not even in twenty. But the people have risen to demand dignity and respect,' he said, before repeating the oath which he and the five original conspirators had taken when they founded the secret Bolivarian movement MBR200 in 1982. 'I swear to the god of my fathers, I swear to the fatherland, I swear that my soul will not falter nor my arms rest until the chains of the mighty which repress my people have been broken.' After more than three hours in front of the microphone, he gathered his remaining strength and borrowed some concluding words from Che Guevara: *Hasta la victoria siempre*, 'Until victory, always.'

After the powerful and somewhat frightening messianic experience, I returned to my senses, with a beer in one hand, and emotionally battered.

Omaira was still there, as well as her daughter and the farmer from Yaracuy. The farmer soon left, but Omaira and I stood talking for a while. While the street sweepers battled the evening breeze to collect the enormous amount of rubbish on the suddenly deserted square, we had laid the foundation for a friendship that would become the closest thing I had to a family in Venezuela. Their family history, way of life and opinions would cast new light on the chaotic, sometimes surrealistic reality in Venezuela, as well as on the controversial president of this Latin American country.

'No Food and No Work'

The walk started at the presidential palace: a striking white building surrounded by lush greenery, tall slender palm trees and patrolled by honour guards wearing green uniforms and red berets. Continuing west, past a few buildings, and only five minutes from the political power centre of Venezuela I found myself in a borderland between the 'civilised' city centre and 23 de Enero, the slum where tens of thousands faced a daily struggle for survival. The transition was gradual, but there is a marked difference from one block to the next. At first the buildings, then the cars, and finally the people's skin colour gets a little darker with every block you pass. And then there was the noise.

Venezuelan *barrios* have their very own sound track. Mostly with a salsa, *merengue* and modern Caribbean *reggaeton* beat – almost always cranked up to maximum – intermingled with the barking of stray dogs and the erratic droning of mopeds accelerating up hills, not to mention all the shouting and whistling. Venezuelans are usually quite loud, and in order to be heard through the wall of noise in the city centre and in the *barrios*, you have to shout. Whistling is used instead of doorbells, with most people able to recognise a member of the family, a neighbour or a friend by their whistle.

Continuing on a couple of blocks and passing under a metro bridge, you find yourself surrounded by poor, seemingly half-finished homes at the foot of a steep hillside: the *barrio* of Monte Piedad within the enormous parish of 23 de Enero.

From here the *barrio* is an imposing sight. The structures at the bottom of the hillside and closest to the centre are old colonial buildings which fell into decay over the course of the twentieth century. Higher up, people live in so-called *ranchitos*, what Venezuelans call the small, improvised shacks made of everything from cardboard boxes to bricks and covered with sheets of rusted corrugated steel. These buildings house the majority of the country's impoverished urban population. From below, the entire hillside is a rust-red colour, dominated by brick and earthen escarpments, while a few pockets of intense green from banana plants and other vegetation clings to the ground wherever it can. At the top of the hill and visible for many kilometres, *los mega bloques*, the mega blocks: massive, colourful buildings which tower above 23 de Enero, making it stand out from the other slums.

Omaira lived at the foot of this *barrio*. The demonstration where we met was the first time I witnessed one of the massive mobilisations in support of Chávez. It did not seem as though the participants were motivated by a few bits of bread and some cheap alcohol, as *El Nacional* and the other media outlets claimed. However, apart from an emotional connection between the president and his supporters, I did not discover anything concrete about what *el comandante* had done to deserve their passionate support. A slogan I saw painted on improvised placards and walls was a direct acknowledgement that Chávez had in fact given them nothing at all:

Con hambre y sin empleo, con Chávez me resteo, 'No food and no work, I would do anything for Chávez.'

The slogan was often ridiculed on TV and in the papers. It was clear evidence of poor people's irrational idolization of a president who had managed neither to fill their stomachs nor provide them with jobs. Even official government statistics revealed that unemployment was higher in 2003 than when Chávez took office. This remarkable slogan was an obvious contradiction. But it only made me even more curious. After all, these same people had helped the president survive both the military coup and *el paro petrolero*. Nearly four years into Chávez' presidency and people were openly admitting that their living conditions had not improved – but they still seemed willing to offer the president everything.

I suspected that part of the reason for that could be found in the *barrios*, the urban slums that were home to the majority of the demonstrators I had spoken to. I needed to meet these people lived and hear their stories.

The Barrio

The first time I visited the area where Omaira lived in 2003, bullet holes were still visible in some of the buildings of 23 de Enero.

Climbing the steep earthen paths and stairs leading to the top of the hillside slum, you reach a cluster of buildings that have a story to tell from 1989, the year the poor inhabitants descended the hillside to force politicians to listen to them.

Back then, Omaira lived in one of the mega blocks. On 27 February 1989, she had just finished work and was on her way home when she found herself surrounded by chaos. Armed police were retreating from a crowd of people that had just looted a supermarket. Omaira had not been there to join the protesters, but she too was affected by the continual deterioration of living conditions. 'I was worried about not getting enough food. So I remember grabbing a pack of cornflour, a little rice and a bar of soap.' Looting was widespread in Caracas, as well as in the surrounding suburbs and in other large cities, where the doubling of food prices had spread fear and anger. The brutal crackdown by the army affected everyone.

Particularly the inhabitants of 23 de Enero.

Frightened by the number of soldiers and tanks entering the area, Omaira went to see a friend to borrow money for a bus ticket, so she could take her daughter to Birongo, her hometown. She was on her way up the hillside to the buildings at the top when it happened. From the main street where she had stolen groceries minutes earlier, bullets suddenly began pelting one of the tallest buildings in the neighbourhood. Soldiers fired automatic rifles and heavy artillery was launched from a number of armoured vehicles. They pierced the walls of the heavily-populated blocks of flats. Omaira watched in horror as two young boys, no more than six or seven years old, were killed as they poked their heads up from a balcony to see what was happening. 'It was the first time I saw someone killed,' Omaira told me. 'They were shooting to kill and wanted to frighten us into silence. They knew the people were protesting against a corrupt president whose reforms only served the rich, and they knew that the protests started here in this barrio.'

Omaira shuffled her feet. The sight of the children's bodies being torn apart by bullets had left her in shock. She froze in the line of fire but luckily someone managed to pull her to safety behind one of the buildings.

On 4 February 1992 – nearly three years after *el Caracazo*, the name given to the uprising and ensuing massacre in 1989 – history was repeating itself when Venezuela awoke to learn of Chávez' armed revolt against the Pérez government.

Once more the tall buildings were fired at by tanks and soldiers, allegedly to prevent the rebellious people of 23 de Enero from taking to the streets and offering the coup their support. Like the mass killing three years earlier, the government did not count the victims. But almost everyone in 23 de Enero knew someone who had been wounded or killed during the state's 'pre-emptive strike' on the impoverished homes of Venezuela's most unruly people.

'Everyone knows why the army used heavy artillery against the civilian population of 23 de Enero,' Omaira said. 'For the same reason they came here and fired on us during the military coup in 2002. They're afraid of us because they know people are organised here.'

23 de Enero was not quite like other *barrios*.

Today the image of Che Guevara is a normal sight in poor areas of Venezuela. However the mural on the bricked-up escarpment below Omaira's home, with Che looking across the small square between the liquor store, the hot dog stand and the lady who rents mobile phones, has a special story. For it was here that the Argentinian-born revolutionary lived when he visited Caracas in the late forties.

Caracas, or more precisely Monte Piedad, Omaira's *barrio*, was the last stop on one of young Ernesto Che Guevara's motorcycle journeys across South America. The motorcycle journeys, and his encounters with the continent's brutal social reality, shaped the young idealistic doctor into becoming an uncompromising revolutionary leader. A leader who would help seize power in Cuba, and continue as a guerrilla leader in Africa and Latin America until he was killed in the Bolivian jungle in 1967.

During his travels, he came to realise that only a revolutionary social upheaval could put an end to the injustice. But it was not going to start in Venezuela, he wrote in his famous *Motorcycle Diaries*. The people he met in Monte Piedad were far too busy with 'alcohol, dancing and women' for that to happen. Even now, the need to have fun above everything else was one of Venezuelans' most important characteristics. Venezuela is one of the world's top ten consumers of beer per capita. I remember more than a few occasions I passed the mural of Che Guevara on trips to the off-license with Omaira's friends and family, and sweating in my vest as I lugged the cases of beer up the hillside. One of the things I was quick to notice about many Venezuelan men, was how they measured their manhood by the number of female conquests. When a striking women walks down the street in Venezuela, most men will turn to watch her pass. For those trying not to stare, the infatuation with beauty which has dominated Venezuela over the past decade led to the country leading the world in the number of women with silicone breast implants, did not make it any easier. There was a standing joke told with a touch of seriousness, that bikini models for the country's biggest breweries, Regional and Polar, measured their success in the number of traffic accidents their billboards caused.

The Venezuelan characteristics which Che Guevara believed got in the way of the country's revolutionary potential, does not appear to have diminished over the years, at least not on the surface. But had he remained in Omaira's *barrio* for another decade, perhaps he would have discovered that beneath the surface there was far more than just a desire for merrymaking and sexual conquest.

On 23 January 1958, one of the most surprising events of the rebellion that toppled Venezuela's military dictator Marcos Pérez Jiménez took place there.

There are nearly eighty blocks of flats which tower side by side above Monte Piedad; the building were just being completed when poor workers and democracy activists occupied the entire complex.

The area was named 23 de Enero (23 January) to mark the end of the dictatorship.

However the newly-gained democratic rights did not lead to any profound upheaval of the skewed societal relations. A new political elite, one which had close connections to Washington, ensured that the filthy rich oligarchy would continue to line their pockets, and effectively prevented any attempts at turning the victory over Jiménez into an actual revolution. But the large-scale occupations in 23 de Enero – something unique in Latin American history – remained as a symbol of what the rebellion could have become.

A vivid symbol though, as 23 de Enero quickly established itself as a notorious breeding ground for radical opposition.

The self-governing neighbourhood organisations, cooperatives and locally-organised social programmes that popped up were seen as an obvious threat by the government. Radical left-wing parties were banned and the dictatorship's practice of killing, imprisoning and torturing radical left-wing opposition members continued throughout much of the democratic era that followed the fall of the military dictatorship. In 23 de Enero, however, social activism continued under the protection of urban guerrillas. The best known were *Los Tupamaros*, who kept the police and the army from entering the neighbourhood. *A plomo limpio*, 'Using pure lead,' as they say.

However no social organisation could offset the consequences of the neoliberal IMF package President Pérez implemented, not to mention falling oil prices. The effects were clear after he crushed the protests on 27 February 1989. A calm quickly settled after the massacre. But the crisis deepened: prostitution, children with protruding abdomens, homelessness, rising substance abuse, and shops reportedly selling dog food to people – with people carrying sacks of *perrharina* home after dark to avoid the shame.

Important social indicators had been trending downwards since the mid-eighties. Devaluation and hyperinflation followed the liberalisations undertaken by the Pérez government. Buying power was reduced so drastically that extreme poverty rose from fourteen to thirty-four per cent. The percentage of the population beneath the poverty line increased from forty-six to sixty-eight. Starvation was a genuine risk for many families. The flexibilisation at the workplace, another government measure, meant that workers – those who still had a job – now had to work even longer hour for their radically devalued salaries. Another new law made it easier for business owners to fire workers and replace them with temporary staff. Another law allowed every workplace law to be disregarded if both the business owners and the workers were 'in agreement.'

Omaira was one of many who noticed the physical changes to her body. She was asked to work fifteen hours a day at the factory with no extra pay, and had no choice but to comply. The alternative was unemployment.

'I actually liked working at the factory. It was always exciting when people arrived from Germany and other places, bringing the latest models of Adidas and other quality products, and taught us to make them. But after the flexibilisation, it was horrible. I remember leaving the factory half-asleep, exhausted after days working double-shifts. I barely had time to sleep, let alone spend time with my children,' she told me.

Neither Omaira nor any of the other poor Venezuelans I spoke to remembered getting any help from the authorities. Government institutions such as the police and the courts did nothing to investigate the thousands of murders that the army perpetrated in 1989. Instead they protected the gunmen and the government. 'If there were any human rights organisations or whatever they're called, people who do that sort of thing, we never saw them. The media was not particularly interested either,' Omaira explained. However one of the directors at RCTV, the country's largest TV channel at the time, said that in dealing with the 1989 crisis, law enforcement had acted 'professionally' and admirably. Politicians, political parties and AD-affiliated trade unions were unable to make any noticeable impact in preventing the deteriorating living conditions.

Salsa and Gunshots in the Caracas Slums

I had already made my first plunge into the *barrios* of Caracas by the time I crossed the threshold, or what served as the threshold in Omaira's home, for the first time. So I was quickly able to establish that her house, as it looked in 2003, was definitely not one of the worst I had seen. The walls were made of solid concrete. The living room, kitchenette and adjoining bedroom were a good deal bigger than most I had seen. It also had a high ceiling.

Omaira laughed nervously when she showed me in. She apologised for the mess. The only thing to counter the clean and tidy impression was the rusted gas tank connected to the hob, as well as a couple of large pots, stained brown by the gas flames and repeated deep frying. These were common sights in the kitchens of poor Venezuelans, as very few had enough cupboard space to store them out of sight. Otherwise there was not a speck of dust to be seen. There was nothing unique about her house being in that condition. Poor Venezuelans kept their homes well. Housewives and daughters made sure of this, by sweeping the floor, washing up and tidying up, usually a couple times a day. None of that 'shabby chic' or placing kitchen utensils, knick-knacks or furniture nonchalantly around her home. And no minimalism. Those who can afford golden figurines, religious symbols, TVs and stereos, always make sure to place them where they are most visible. The lighting in the living room consisted of a bare bulb hanging from the ceiling by a wire. It made for a slightly cold atmosphere, but this was compensated by tablecloths, decorations and a colourful mix of plastic and wooden furniture.

Still, there was no denying that this was the home of someone poor. The brickwork under the front door was uneven, worn and porous, something which must have made it easy for cockroaches to get in (though I saw none of that during my visit). The ceiling had a few leaks and the paint was starting to peel in places. Even though at first glance the house seemed spacious enough, movement was somewhat limited because half of the living room was occupied by sewing machines, rolls of fabric and cutting tables. Omaira apologised and explained that she'd had to start sewing from home on commission when the textile industry started failing. Like most other Venezuelan industries, its decline began in the nineties. Ever since then, her living room had served as a fabric room for her home business, which just about paid for her daily *arepa* (corn bread). The refrigerator was probably the only place in the house with free space, something that said more about the family finances than the size of the noisy appliance. The bathroom was a small room with a wobbly brick floor. A pipe poking through the wall in one corner served as a shower, while in the other corner there was a kind of toilet. There was a water drum in the middle of the room, next to a small bucket to rinse the toilet. Omaira's 100 litre plastic water drum (some people had tin or aluminium) was found in most poor people's homes. For some because they had no water mains – meaning it was used to shower as well – and for others, it was as a reserve tank when the mains were down. The emphasis Venezuelans placed on personal hygiene knew no class boundaries. Even poor Venezuelans liked to shower twice a day.

Omaira's home was a comfortable place for children to grow up compared with the living conditions of others in the *barrio*. Her biggest problem arose at the end of the 1990s. As Omaira put it: 'Suddenly, I was no longer a mother with her three kids, but a grandmother living with her teenage son, two grown-up daughters, a newborn grandchild and his on-again off-again father.' The solution they reached was the same as in other Venezuelan metropolitan slums: Scrape together enough money for some brick, a little mortar and a sheet of corrugated steel, then build upwards.

If you went out the back door, through a narrow garden and up an external stairwell, you found yourself on the roof of Omaira's house, a roof which after a little building work was now the floor of her daughter and grandchild's *ranchito*. The rectangular brick room was just big enough to be roofed over with a standard-sized sheet of corrugated steel, with space for a bed, a cot and a double gas hob. 'Nothing more romantic than making love to the sound of rain falling on corrugated steel,' at least according to Venezuela's most famous stand-up comic, El Conde del Guacharo. Perhaps he was right. In any case, it was far more romantic than having to climb down the precipitous brick stairs in the middle of the night to reach an outdoor toilet in the back yard that was often shared by four or five neighbouring families.

Like most Venezuelan *barrios*, the buildings were tightly packed. Having a personal life could be a complicated endeavour. No one could afford air conditioning, so to get some circulation, people had glassless windows covered with reinforced steel bars. This also meant that sound moved freely in and out of people's homes. With such extreme population density, whether you liked it or not, you knew what music your neighbours liked, their favourite soap opera, and you could judge the quality of their relationships based on the frequency of sex versus shouting and door slamming.

If the slumification of Caracas, Rio de Janeiro or any other major Latin American city with a similar topography had been filmed over the past forty years, viewing the development on fast forward would reveal that building development almost always went upwards. In such cities, you can often quite accurately predict how poor someone is by how high up the hillside they live.

It was less than ten minutes from Omaira's home to the heart of Caracas, which had many practical advantages. The Metro station got you quickly and cheaply to anywhere in the city and surrounding areas. Going up the slum was another matter. On public transport, most often jeeps or pickups with four-wheel drive, you only got as far as the asphalt or concrete road allowed. In many of the *barrios* in Caracas, you did not have to go far up the hillside before the roads became narrow dirt paths leading to gradually smaller and smaller *ranchitos*. In some places, the escarpments people built on were so steep that stairs were built into the hillside. For the elderly and the ill, it would be practically impossible to get anywhere. The lack of transport options meant that many goods and public services were scarce in the *barrios*. Water, electricity and phone lines were not a given in the uppermost and steepest areas, and it took both time and money to reach the city where the jobs were found.

The long arm of the law only reached as far as the infrastructure allowed police cars and motorcycles to reach. If you were lucky. The authorities' history of indifference towards the poor combined with heavily armed criminals who moved through the slums with great impunity, meant that the police were rarely seen in the upper regions of the *barrio*. The result of this was a harsh community.

Adults who had experienced the two previous decades of two-party rule by AD and COPEI remembered little more than continuously declining living standards for the country's poor. Most people blamed the former rulers. Over the course of Omaira's working life, from 1980 to 2000, unemployment had increased almost incessantly. Official figures showed a three-fold increase, from five to fifteen per cent.[46] 'The people of the *barrios* always get the lowest paid jobs, if that,' Omaira said: 'Most work as *buhoneros* and that sort of thing.'

A *Buhonero* was a Venezuelan street vendor. With deindustrialisation and recession, the number of *buhoneros* exploded, and since the 1980s the informal sector grew from being a fringe phenomenon to encompassing half of Venezuela's work force.[47] In the slums, the number working under the table was far greater than the national average.

Omaira's own informal business consisted of cutting and sewing together pieces of fabric for wholesalers who then sold the finished clothes to street vendors. The business provided few guarantees and little stability. In good times, her income covered her most basic expenses, and every now and again a little weekend enjoyment, something poor Venezuelans enjoyed with the same passion as their more affluent countrymen. 'In bad times, you need nice neighbours or close family so you don't sink into sheer misery and lose everything. Including your dignity,' Omaira said, describing what is normally classified as 'extreme poverty,' an existence where your caloric intake was not sufficient to maintain normal bodily functions over time. Let alone pay for electricity, water or a bus ticket to get you into town to look for work.

For men in the *barrios*, construction work was the usual alternative. In Venezuela, that meant temporary employment, terrible pay and a high risk of workplace accidents. A significant number of women worked as domestic servants, the lucky ones working as full-time maids for rich families. The unlucky ones just did the cleaning, and then usually for several homes. When she first moved to Caracas, Omaira worked twelve-hour shifts, often seven days a week, cleaning, babysitting and making meals for a middle-class family. This was still not enough to provide for her family.

Poverty and social issues created a heavy strain on the schools and the youth environments.

During the time I lived in Venezuela, I saw the small children of my close friends grow up to be teenagers in the city's *barrios*. Making sure that their kids completed their elementary education and stayed away from the crack, cocaine and marihuana that flowed in from Colombia in vast quantities, was a daily battle.

The suffering the drug trade added to the country's poor was immense. *Los piedreros*, crack addicts, were the easiest ones to spot, hooked on the cheap derivative of cocaine, almost a waste product, which Venezuelans called *piedra*, crack. Over a short period, *piedra* could turn users into filthy, emaciated vagrants, often with no teeth and a decreasing ability to speak. Cocaine, a little more expensive but still cheap, was mostly used in the slums by *los malandros*, the most common word in Venezuela for gangsters or criminals, but the middle class constituted the biggest market.

As well as addiction, being recruited into the gangs selling the drugs was a big problem. In a society with a constant shortage of most commodities, status symbols were extremely important, which made it easy to tempt young people into earning easy money as dope dealers. The first signs to worry about were usually new shoes, gold chains, mobile phones and new friends.

Selling drugs on a small scale did not earn you much money. However the smartest and most unscrupulous dealers could forge a career as *jíbaros*, distributors who controlled the sale of drugs in vast areas. With the money, a *jíbaro* could establish a network of benevolence, loyalty and protection amongst young drug-runners, neighbours and police. Often the local drug networks compete for territory. At times, it was bloody.

Violent crime was something I witnessed up close and personal. Only a couple of days had passed since a friend had tried to teach me the difference between the sound of a gunshot and fireworks, when a series of loud blasts made me run to the window one Sunday afternoon in the winter of 2004. The explosions sounded 'dry,' which was exactly how she described the sound of a handgun to me, as it lacked the trailing echo which normally characterises fireworks. I reached the window just in time to see three pistol shots fired through a car window a few metres away, and a boy falling off a motorcycle. I slipped on a T-shirt and shoes and raced down the steps. The boy had already been put in the recovery position and was surrounded by neighbours. He was squirming and sobbing in pain. The ambulance was on its way, but no one held out much hope that he would survive. Six shots to the torso was just too much.

The first time you see someone killed, it leaves a deep impression. For several days afterwards, I had a hard time getting the young boy's howls of pain out of my head. In the months that followed, every time I heard a shot – just about every weekend – an endless train of thought began, about senseless death and the families left behind. But maintaining such a high level of emotional involvement in the tragedies which regularly and without warning unfolded around me, it could not last. Over time, I became used to hearing gunshots. The usual resigned shrug, the sad smile and the automatic response that 'God only knows why such things happen,' had sounded infuriatingly indifferent to me in the beginning, but gradually became my way of dealing with it too. When the sound of gunshots blended with the salsa rhythms at a Saturday night party in the *barrio*, there was not much you could do but keep dancing. There was nothing romantic about it. That's just how it was.

'The Emotional Bond'

On the afternoon of 11 April 2002, as the coup generals finalised the military operation against Chávez and the opposition leaders redirected Antonio and the other demonstrators towards Miraflores, Omaira was sitting in a cafe.

In contrast to Antonio's experience, the ensuing forty-eight hours were a nightmare for her.

Without realising it, Omaira was part of the economic elite's plan to remove Chávez. The previous day she and the other workers had been sent home from the textile factory where they worked. Taking their orders from Fedecámaras, the owners of the factory agreed to shut down. They ordered the workers to participate in the anti-Chávez protest the following day. Fedecámaras made sure the same message was delivered to all the workers who were sent home: There will be no work and no pay until Chávez is removed. In 1998, many of the seamstresses there had collected money during their lunch breaks to help fund Chávez' election campaign. Now they were forced to demonstrate against him. Omaira refused. But she also ignored the call by a number of Chávez supporters to go to the presidential palace to defend the president.

Despite intense mobilisation on TV, radio and in newspapers, Omaira had never imagined that the demonstration would be any different to the other protests the opposition had held over the past months. She took advantage of the factory shutdown by meeting some friends at a cafe. The conversation had hardly begun when someone switched on a TV in the shop.

The images on the screen were disconcerting. There were rumours of a clash outside the presidential palace. In the growing panic, she could hardly think. People around her began talking about a civil war. Omaira feared for her children who were home alone, only a few hundred metres from the presidential palace. She quickly realised that public transport would not be during the chaos, so she hailed a taxi. The taxi was forced to take a long detour around Miraflores. On the way, Omaira saw soldiers and armoured vehicles on the streets. Roads were blocked off in places. A few flags and banners were scattered on the ground. For the most part, the streets were empty. The haze of tear gas that had briefly settled over large parts of the city centre had cleared. The sounds of gunshots, helicopters and people chanting slogans had given way to what Omaira remembers as a suffocating silence. Only broken by the sound of motorcycles and the occasional siren.

The first thing she did when she got home was to turn on VTV, the state broadcaster. But the programme was quickly interrupted. Previously, state governor Enrique Mendoza from the right-wing COPEI party had already announced on the private channels that VTV would be shut down.[*] On the TV, Omaira saw an armed police unit enter the TV studio. Then the screen went black. Now, she had only the private channels to go by. Omaira checked Venevisión, Globovisión, RCTV and Televen. They all claimed the same thing: Chávez had given orders to kill peaceful demonstrators from the opposition and later offered his resignation.

Like most people, Omaira saw the 'new Venezuela' on the private TV channels the next day. She did not like what she saw.

The people celebrating and signing decrees with Carmona at the presidential palace, and those sending police units to arrest Chávez supporters in the streets, they were familiar faces for

---

[*] Enrique Mendoza, from the former ruling party COPEI, in a TV interview that day stated: 'That rubbish called channel 8, we should take it off the air. It will be taken off the air.' The following day, also via a TV interview, he said that he could finally relax because Channel 8 had been shut down.

Omaira. 'These were the same corrupt people in power before Chávez, people who got rich at our expense,' she told me.

That day Omaira wondered what would happen to the president. She thought about how her life had been before Chávez, when those who had seized power were in charge of the country.

All her life, Omaira had lived with little money. Sometimes she went to bed hungry in order for her children to have enough food. As a child, she had once refused to go to school because the only thing she had to wear were *alpargatas*. *Alpargatas* are a kind of footwear, for a long time the only thing poor Venezuelans could afford to wear. For Omaira though, wearing *alpargatas* was a stigma that shouted 'I'm poor.' Omaira recalled how Chávez' predecessor, Rafael Caldera had once said that 'the poor will always wear *alpargatas*, that's how the world is made.'

'The poor were treated like second-class citizens,' Omaira explained. 'They called us apes, Negros, vagrants and such. Chávez explained to us that our sufferings were not determined by God or by fate, but that we are poor because a small minority of greedy oligarchs and corrupt politicians took all the oil riches for themselves and left us with nothing. They thought it was fine to keep taking more and more while we went to bed hungry. But not Chávez. He cares for us.'

Low wages and long workdays have meant that many Venezuelans from the lower class grew up with their grandparents. President Chávez was one of them.

Being born in a *barrio* meant your chances of making something of yourself in the future were slim. A rough economic period, either on a national level or for an individual family, could mean children failing to complete their elementary education. A parent losing their job or a father abandoning his family, leaving the household without its most important, perhaps only regular income, could force children to drop out of school and take on poorly paid odd jobs.

Neither Omaira nor her two daughters had completed elementary school when I first met them. Higher education was not something most poor people even considered a possibility. The Venezuelan university authorities have openly acknowledged that as of the beginning of the twenty-first century, only a tiny fraction of the country's university students come from a poor background. Coming from a public school in a poor area was usually enough to lose out in the competition for a place at a public university, to middle-class young people who had ballast from far better, often private grade schools.

On 11 April 2002, Omaira had difficulty accepting that the president had voluntarily relinquished the office he had been elected to serve. And what if they executed him? The mere thought of it made her cry. For Omaira, Chávez was not just a president. The fact that he had been willing to risk his own life during the coup attempt of 1992 and had gone to prison for defending poor people against the rich and powerful, she believed was proof that he meant business. He was the first president to regularly visit the barrios, including hers, one who took the time to talk to, listen to, and embrace people like her. After hundreds of hours of seeing Chávez speak, sing, laugh and rub shoulders with the poor in a way no Venezuelan ruler had ever done, she felt that she knew him.

'Chávez is like a member of my family now.'
The public idolisation of the president quickly became a much-debated phenomenon.

Analysts like Oscar Schemel and Vicente León from the Venezuelan polling organisations Hinterlaces and Datanalisis, used the term 'the emotional bond' to describe the relationship that existed between the president and the poor majority: There was a strong emotional connection to Chávez as a *person,* in addition to the sympathy for his politics and arguments.

On 12 April, the day after the coup, you had to have your eyes and ears about you, or better yet your sense of smell, to notice that something was happening on the hillsides around the city centre.

Omaira had not been alerted by the TV, radio, or newspapers – but by the smell of burning rubbish. With the media failing them, poor people began lighting bonfires in protest. Those inside the presidential palace may not have been frightened by the small pillars of white smoke rising from the *barrios* and the surrounding hillside of 23 de Enero. But for Omaira's family, the clouds of smoke signalled that she was not alone in her despair. A new hope was kindled. And with that, a desire to act.

Most major networks did not cover the protests that began in the barrios. They were small and quiet at first, then steadily grew larger and became more visible. Millions of Venezuelans in the *barrios* of Caracas and in several other cities could see the thin pillars of smoke from the protest fires rising into the sky on the 12 and 13 April. Having gone sleepless for the better part of two nights, Omaira grabbed a pot and a ladle from the kitchen and began banging away. Silenced by the censorship of the private media, the pots and the smoke formed the protest manifesto of the poor. Not the most precise means of communication, but effective enough to incite powerful forces.

Everyone wanted to do something, including Omaira. The decision almost cost her life. She had barely walked a hundred metres towards the presidential palace when a bus drove past. Inside were masked men with automatic weapons. She noticed them just as they opened fire on a crowd of people. Omaira's neighbour from across the street was shot in the stomach and had life-threatening injuries. Others had minor wounds from grazing shots, but no one was killed. Minutes after the vehicle disappeared, the streets were full again. Filled with the same people – frightened and aware of the risk – but just as many, and even more determined.

No one was prepared to give ground. At the same time there was a genuine fear that the military would be sent in with orders to kill, much like the last time people such as her descended from the hillsides in 1989. But this time the story would turn out differently. The turning point came when one of the guards on the roof of Miraflores waved an enormous Venezuelan flag. Another raised his hands and beat one fist against the palm of his hand, like Chávez used to do during mass demonstrations.

It was then that they realised that the military had not come to shoot them. The soldiers were on their side.

Latin America has experienced many military coups against democratically elected, popular left-wing presidents. But seldom have the people reacted with such determination. During previous coups, indignation was quickly transformed into hopelessness, and the protests died out and disappeared after the first wave of repression from the coup leaders. The most politicised and radical activists usually continued some form of protest, spray-painting slogans or murals – or attending political conferences, in exile.

Some also sacrificed their lives and provided the opposition with its martyrs. But the streets and the media were largely cleansed of resistance, and the majority of the people were pacified.

What was it that made millions of poor Venezuelans risk their lives for Chávez, when the people had given up during coups in other Latin American countries?

My conversations with Omaira convinced me that the emotional bond with the president was a key factor.

When I visited Omaira in 2003, there were four years remaining in Chávez' mandate. The opposition had failed in its coup attempt and *el paro petrolero*, the shutdown in the oil sector, but demands for the president to resign continued.

Less than a month after their stinging defeat in the oil shutdown, the opposition announced its latest attempt to return to power.

This time they were calling for a referendum.

The new constitution that Chávez implemented in 1999, allowed for a so-called 'recall vote.' When the president had completed half of his mandate period, the opposition could force a recall referendum if they managed to gather signatures from twenty per cent of the eligible voters, an arrangement that was unique to Venezuela.* Would the opposition manage to achieve through democratic means what they had failed to do with the military coup or the oil production shutdown, would they be able to end the Bolivarian revolution?

---

* A similar arrangement is found in other places, but always at a lower political level. In the state of California for example, the citizens can demand a recall halfway through a mandate to replace the state governor. Only in Venezuela can the people replace a national leader in this way.

A POLITICAL SURVIVOR:

The World's First Presidential Referendum

The Referendum Campaign

From February 2003 to June 2004, stands packed with tables, computers, printers and volunteer activists appeared everywhere in Venezuela. In Caracas, you could hardly walk more than a hundred metres without running into one of the many collection points, located on plazas, inside shopping centres, schools and churches and at the workplace. I too was regularly stopped by activists holding signature forms.

I was already used to my appearance causing many to categorise me as part of the white Caracas elite, meaning they automatically assumed I must be an anti-Chavista. If I walked by a stand, the activists did not ask if I wanted to sign – that was taken for granted – they asked if I had already signed or was ready to now. The activists were always friendly and smiling and though they were insistent, it was never enough to make you feel uncomfortable. The organisation of the signature campaign was impressive – and not just at street level. If you did not seek them, they sought you. At home in the living room on the private TV channels, at the shopping centre, the fitness centre or on weekends, at the beach, not to mention at the university.

Many of my university lecturers actively participated in the campaign and provided almost daily updates. The lectures were often spent discussing Venezuela 'post-Chávez' and the political dynamics that would take place in a few months' time when 'the tenant in Miraflores,' as the President was referred to by the media at the time, was replaced by someone from the opposition. Daily life was again filled with increasingly heated discussions between *Chavistas* and anti-*Chavistas*. Even at the night clubs in the Caracas party district of Las Mercedes, where the music normally only dealt with sex, love, broken hearts and fiestas – probably the last place I would have expected to discuss politics – booming from the speakers I heard: 'It's falling, it's falling, the government is falling.'

My friend Antonio also got involved. I often saw him wearing the yellow and black T-shirts of the opposition party, Primero Justicia (PJ).

PJ was one of the new right-wing parties founded just before Chávez came to power. Antonio, who had not donned a political T-shirt since his young days as a member of COPEI, the former ruling party, was now a keen supporter of Leopoldo López, the young PJ mayor in Antonio's district of Chacao.

Leopoldo López had gained popularity by resolving the endless traffic jams in his district, keeping the roads well maintained and free of rubbish and by increasing safety and having more police on the beat. Antonio was also pleased that the mayor provided a national face to the people of Chacao's opposition to Chávez. In his opinion, López had set a good example by going beyond his normal duties as mayor and becoming one of the opposition's most high profile figures in the battle to remove the president.

Antonio believed something big was at stake.

'This is about the freedom of our country,' he said. 'Are we going to become a military society or one that values freedom? If Chávez is allowed to continue, it will be a catastrophe for Venezuela. Chávez has filled his government with corrupt and incompetent officials, and he is leading the country towards oppression and communism.' But Antonio was optimistic: He had the corps of media commentators, the opposition politicians and most of the polling organisations on his side when he said that 'a large majority' had long since grown tired of the president.

However when I met Antonio one winter's day in 2004, he expressed some concern. After spending a long day in the baking sun at yet another mass demonstration against the president, sweating and still fired up by the speeches, the singing, and shouting slogans, Antonio talked about the one obstacle that could postpone an inevitable victory against Chávez: electoral fraud.

'This is not an honest government,' he said. 'They sabotage, lie and cheat as much as they can to hold on to power.'

I soon became acquainted with a word that dominated the newspaper headlines, radio bulletins, TV broadcasts and conversations on the streets: *fraude*. In Venezuela this word was synonymous with rigging elections.

The leadership of CNE, the Venezuelan electoral commission, was made up of representatives from the government and the opposition, as well as thousands of civil servants. CNE had purchased a new electronic voting system from the USA, considered one of the most secure systems in the world, including by The Carter Center, an NGO founded by former US president Jimmy Carter. Despite all this, the opposition and the media were doing everything they could to undermine the credibility of CNE with daily accusations of electoral fraud.

In the intense campaign against CNE, a new player appeared on the scene: Súmate.

Súmate introduced itself as a politically independent NGO 'founded to build democracy' with 'thirty thousand volunteers and the technical capacity' to aid the processes of participation. The organisation was founded at the end of 2002, but had only recently become well known. Its emblem was a pyramid with the colours of the Venezuelan flag. The young and attractive front figures, Maria Machado and Alejandro Plaz, were seen on TV and in the papers on a daily basis. Súmate promoted itself as 'the foremost guarantor of democracy.' The mere fact that someone had felt the need to establish an NGO to assure a fair electoral process could place CNE and the Chávez government in a bad light.

Alejandro Plaz and Maria Machado constantly reiterated that their goal was merely to safeguard democracy. They endorsed the opposition's demand for a recall election. In February 2003, Súmate submitted a list of 4.7 million signatures as evidence that more than twenty per cent of registered voters wanted a recall referendum to decide whether the president should be allowed to continue. CNE invalidated the signatures. According to Súmate, CNE was obstructing democracy. CNE's gave the reason for the invalidated signatures as technical shortcomings.

Several rounds of signature drives were held. In November 2003 – after a breathtaking campaign – the opposition declared that they had collected the necessary signatures: 3.4 million. But they seemed to have counted their chickens before they hatched. CNE was yet to rule on the validity of the signatures when *El Universal* used an entire front page to accuse CNE of 'Legal Trickery.'[48]

The media narrative of an unpopular president who used his lackeys at CNE to prevent a referendum was now firmly established.

CNE's decision appeared to confirm *El Universal's* gloomy prediction on this occasion. Half a million signatures were ruled definitively invalid by CNE, mostly because the names and identity numbers belonged to people who were either dead, underage, foreign citizens or had been entered multiple times. Another 1.2 million signatures were considered 'unsafe,' most of them because the personal information was filled in with the same handwriting. That left only 1.9 million valid signatures, well under the minimum requirement of twenty per cent of the eligible voters. The electoral authorities agreed to allow a new signature campaign whereby 878 000 of the 1.2 million signatures deemed unsafe could be verified.

Reactions were not long in coming. A united opposition shouted *fraude*. The media rolled in the heavy artillery. 'CNE has ambushed 3.6 million voters and blocked off every exit with a Berlin Wall,' *El Universal* wrote in an editorial, calling the electoral commission's decision 'a holocaust against the referendum.'* They ran six different articles under the title, 'Coup Against the Referendum,' a remarkable contrast to the paper's coverage of the violent removal of Chávez six months earlier, when the word 'coup' did not appear once.

---

* During this period, the opposition and the media operated with two different figures: 3.4 million and 3.6 million signatures collected for the recall election. Both figures were considerably over the twenty percent of the electorate needed to implement the requirement. El Universal, 04.03.2004.

The opposition demanded that CNE validate the signatures and refused to negotiate on the matter. Salas Römer, the multi-millionaire who had lost the 1998 presidential election to Chávez, urged people to boycott the verification process for the unsafe signatures in the spring of 2004.⁴⁹ Fedecámaras labelled the decision 'a mockery of the people's will' and 'an assault on the rule of law.⁵⁰ Soon the streets of Caracas and several other large cities were filled with tens of thousands of demonstrators demanding that the referendum go ahead. At my university, lectures were cancelled so that we could participate in the protest. Outside my flat there were explosions almost every day from what I assumed were teargas grenades and Molotov cocktails. I was caught in the line of fire one evening when I went out to buy some milk and bread, as a group of youths and a small patrol from the National Guard exchanged firebombs and teargas outside the bakery, only a block from where I lived.

The opposition quickly decided to crank up the pressure. Through the private media, they instructed supporters to block off the streets and shut the shops. A total of nine Venezuelans lost their lives during these confrontations. There was also increased pressure from the international media. 'The president, an unsuccessful coup-monger, is always uncomfortable with democracy,' *The Economist* wrote. They accused the CNE of 'stealing 1.2 million signatures.' *The Economist* was not alone in referring to the electoral commission as an instrument of Chávez, who was again accused of using 'any means' to stop the referendum.*⁵¹ The Bush administration openly supported the opposition's demand. The organisations mediating the conflict, the OAS and The Carter Centre, urged CNE not to let 'formalities' block the referendum.⁵²

---

* For example, NTB wrote that Chavez had personally refused to allow the referendum to take place. This was in line with the opposition's claim that the electoral authorities were simply an instrument of the president. NTB, 04.03.2004.

The Venezuelan press wrote of an increasingly isolated Chávez. 'Chávez is furious. World Opinion Makes Referendum Inevitable,' the front page of *El Nacional* read.[53]

The frenetic level of noise in Caracas grew even louder. For several months, flatbed lorries drove around with enormous speaker systems, playing recorded campaign slogans and music, encouraging people to add their signature in order to remove Chávez. But compared to the events that have marked the country since 2002, the signature campaign led the political conflict down a relatively peaceful track. However with newspaper headlines speaking of 'holocausts,' 'coups' and 'ambushes,' the peace appeared fragile.

'Chávez Must Die Like a Dog'

At an opposition demonstration, I received the clearest warning yet that the situation might well get worse. 'Goodbye Aristide, you're next Chávez!' several banners proclaimed, and I later saw similar banners in the international media.[54] During the previous days, while I was observing the clashes in the streets through my living room window, at the university and on TV, another rebellion was advancing quickly and with brutal violence elsewhere in the region.

Jean-Bertrand Aristide was the president of Haiti, the poorest country in the western hemisphere, about seventy miles north of Venezuela and only a one-hour flight from Miami. With massive protests in the streets, paramilitary forces had conquered eastern Haiti and were waging a bloody civil war to reach the capital of Port-au-Prince. President Aristide attempted to maintain control of the country from the capital with a badly equipped and underpaid police force.

Priest Jean-Bertrand Aristide was Haiti's first democratically elected president.

Similar to Chávez, Aristide was supported by the poor and was disliked by the elites who had thrived under previous conservative regimes. In 1991, Aristide was toppled by a military coup for the first time. Aristide supporters were later murdered in large numbers by paramilitary groups, who according to the paramilitary leader himself were trained and financed by the CIA.[55] Aristide returned however, winning the election again in 2000. According to Aristide, a diplomatic dispatch from the USA had recently demanded that he privatise the country's key national enterprises as a stipulation for being left to rule in peace, a demand he refused to accept and carry out following his election win. Now in 2004, Aristide was again under attack from the same paramilitary groups, while a new organisation, also supported by the USA, called Convergence Démocratique (CD), demanded the president's resignation.

Venezuelan media provided extensive and positive coverage of the campaign, one that ended when US Marines occupied the Haitian capital under the pretence of protecting the American embassy. They then entered the presidential palace, 'escorted' Aristide to the airport and deported him to an American military base in The Central African Republic.

Few doubted that the Bush administration wanted Chávez, who was now in control of the world's largest proven oil reserves, out of office just as much as it wanted to get rid of Aristide.

There was also a similarity in the way the US financed the opposition in the two countries. In both places, the National Endowment for Democracy (NED) was responsible for distributing the funds. NED's stated goal is to support democracy, but it has been criticised for supporting the anti-democratic undermining of governments that do not comply with US interests. In 2009, the NED had a budget of 135 million dollars to spend supporting political parties, trade unions, opposition movements and the media in selected countries. 'A large part of what we do today, the CIA did in secret twenty-five years ago,' NED's first president, Allen Weinstein said of the organisation's activities in an interview with the *Washington Post* in 1991.[56]

In Haiti, the NED financed civilian organisations which made preparations to assume power after the paramilitary militias had removed the elected president.

In Venezuela, Súmate – the organisation that called for the referendum against Chávez – also received funds from the NED.

Both in Haiti and in Venezuela, the recipients of the American money had distinguished themselves with their support for violent takeovers. Súmate's leader, Maria Machado, for example, actively supported the military coup in 2002.*

And again on this occasion – in the prelude to the referendum in Venezuela – it was revealed that the NED financing of Súmate was not only about supporting democracy. The evidence came from the leaked recording of a telephone conversation between opposition politician Teodoro Petkoff and one of his allies. In the conversation, he revealed that Súmate had lied about the number of signatures. Petkoff was furious because he believed that Maria Machado had known the entire time that the actual count was only 3.1 million, and had chosen not to inform her allies of the fraud. '*Coño*! Chávez was right then. This is *megafraude*,' he said, calling the whole mess 'a pack of lies.'⁵⁷

Petkoff's leaked comments gave the government the moral upper hand for a few days.

However due to the absolute silence from most of the private media, the effect was limited. People I knew from the opposition had never heard about the revelation. They were still convinced that a huge majority wanted Chávez out and the media continued to refer to Súmate as an independent advocate for democracy.

The persistent campaign against CNE's alleged *fraude* whipped up hate and desperation among opponents of Chávez. But in order for Chávez to end up like Aristide, someone would have to be prepared

---

* She signed the Carmona decree which formalised the implementation of a dictatorship in Venezuela.

to resort to violence, just as the paramilitary groups had done in Haiti. If that were the case, who would it be?

Chávez had managed to increase his support from the army. The military coup had given him the opportunity to sack many of the officers who supported the coup and the Carmona regime. That did not mean that they no longer posed a threat to the president. The insurrection against Aristide had been led by the military commanders he had personally sacked.

There were those who wanted the discharged Venezuelan officers to play the same role in Venezuela. The powerful Catholic church reached out to retired officers in an article in their magazine: 'This battle is fought not only with protests, whistles and placards: You may no longer have weapons and soldiers, but you have the ability to influence the military, and that could ensure the future of a peaceful Venezuela.' On the front page: 'Recall Election Fraud by CNE,' 'Decline of Democracy' and 'Chávez Cannot Continue.'[58]

Opposition politician Domingo Alberto Rangel believed that the best card the opposition had to play were 'the three biggest police forces in Venezuela' with a combined strength of twenty thousand heavily armed officers, who were all under the command of known anti-Chavistas.[59] The opposition's 'human rights lawyer' Ricardo Koesling was also in contact with the military. Recordings of his phone conversations broadcast on state TV revealed that his connections in the army wanted 'civil society to take the lead' before they acted. During the telephone conversation, Koesling could be heard instructing people to 'burn busses,' by 'inserting Molotov cocktails inside the petrol tanks,' 'distribute alcohol to the demonstrators [...] so that the people press forward' in an effort to create chaos in Caracas.[60] And the demonstrations did become violent. Masked demonstrators confronted the National Guard with weapons and homemade firebombs.[61] It appeared to be the same recipe General Lameda described during the 2002 coup: Start with violent street confrontations so the military can then move in.

Some of those who wanted to see Chávez deposed had found allies in Colombia.

On 9 May 2004, Venezuela awoke to the news that 130 Colombians had been arrested during a raid of two haciendas a few kilometres outside of Caracas.

One of the hacienda owners was Roberto Alonso, a conservative multi-millionaire of Cuban descent. Alonso managed to escape to the US before the raid. The Colombians who were arrested and questioned had been equipped with Venezuelan military uniforms and the same weapons used by the Venezuelan military. According to some of the Colombians, they had been under the command of Venezuelan officers. Documents and maps found among those apprehended, as well as admissions during the interrogations, indicated that they were a paramilitary group trained to attack the presidential palace and liquidate key government and opposition politicians. The group was reportedly recruited in Colombia by the infamous right-wing militia, AUC.*

AUC called its activities *contrainsurgencia*, 'counter-insurgency,' and claimed to protect Colombia's rulers against left-wing guerrillas and 'communism.' They had also declared Chávez as their enemy. Back in 2002 the AUC leader Carlos Castaño made headlines in the Venezuelan newspapers when he declared Chávez a 'military target.'

However, the extreme right-wing death squads were no longer restricted to the headlines. Now they been found at an estate only a

---

* AUC leaders have admitted killing between 24 000 and 30 000 Colombian civilians over the past twenty years, mostly poor farmers, trade union activists, indigenous people, and left-wing politicians. Along with extreme right-wing elements from the Colombian army and the country's infamous cocaine cartels, the AUC was also behind the near total eradication of Colombia's left-wing party, UP, at the end of the 1980s. Between three and five thousand members, almost the entire national leadership and two presidential candidates, were murdered, meaning that as the party raced ahead in the opinion polls, it barely had enough people remaining to stand for election.

few kilometres from the centre of Caracas and the presidential palace.*

The threat of paramilitary militias from Colombia bringing civil war from across the western border, and the recent coup against Chávez' like-minded president in Haiti led to increased tension in the streets.

The people I spoke to, both Chavistas and anti-Chavistas, were worried.

In July 2004, two months after the arrest of the Colombian paramilitaries, ex-president Carlos Andrés Pérez announced a death warrant for the president. 'Chávez must die like a dog,' he told *El Nacional* from his home in Miami: 'I am working to have Chávez removed ... He must be forcibly removed.'[62]

Omaira's normally easy-going manner was gone when I met her days after the Pérez statement. She was upset. 'How could that many Colombian paramilitaries get so close to our city? What would have happened if the intelligence services had not uncovered them? And how can the gringos allow that murderer in Miami tell people to kill our president?' God forbid,' Omaira's daughter said before repeating what she had told me on several occasions: she was willing to die for her *comandante* if necessary.

Many now feared an assassination attempt on Chávez. But even those calling for the murder of the president knew that would entail serious consequences. One of the most telling signs of the devotion Chávez supporters had for their leader was the graffiti which appeared in the rich east side of Caracas at the time: 'Kill Chávez and the east side will burn.'

---

* The media and the opposition brushed off the capture of the Colombians as a 'show.' Fedecámaras claimed Chavez had staged it all to draw attention away from the referendum. However Colombia's government, the Carter Centre and the OAS expressed their concern about the incident. Colombia's former ambassador to Venezuela, Gloria Gaitán, who had received political asylum in Venezuela, now asked Chávez to take the threats seriously.

The message was clear in every aspect. The Venezuelan upper class in east Caracas had a lot to lose, even after six years of Chávez in government. Up to that point, the lockouts of 2002 and 2003 had led to greater financial losses for local business owners than any of Chávez' reform. Taxes were still low, and with the increases to the minimum wage and consumer buying power, 2004 promised to be a good year for business. Not a single hacienda had been expropriated by the government; there were still long waiting lists for membership to the capital's exclusive golf clubs, and the city's rich youth turned up at the party district of Las Mercedes in cars even more luxurious than before. The prevalence of electric fences, armed guards and surveillance cameras in the more affluent residential and commercial districts showed how terrified these people were of losing their possessions. And not without good cause. The riots in 1989 came dangerously close to reaching the upper class districts. Many had seen their property looted after furious masses occupied the capital. 2002 had seen another close call during the popular uprising that followed the military coup.* Only Chávez' authority prevented the people's rage from turning into full-blown riots against the rich elite.

If the president were to be shot, it would provoke a rage of entirely different proportions amongst his supporters. Who would prevent them from burning the east side then?

I met several rich Venezuelans in Caracas who stated outright that Chávez should be killed. But there were many more who expressed their fear of what *las hordas Chavistas*, 'the Chavista hordes,' would do to them and their property if the president got a bullet through the

---

* There is a rumour that Chávez, when he was freed from prison, had to conceal his wounds in order to prevent furious supporters from attacking individuals, party offices and businesses which had a central role in the military coup. Chávez denied the rumours and assured people that he had been treated honourably. Still the fact that he felt the need to advise his supporters of this was telling.

head one day. That may be why the most unambiguous calls to murder Chávez came from the Venezuelan colony in Miami. Far out of reach from the furious Chavistas.⁶³

The situation was unpredictable. By November 2003 however, it seemed obvious to me that there were was enough opposition to Chávez to collect the required number of signatures. Accusations of secret plans by CNE were rampant in the media, and not one of my friends who supported the opposition trusted the electoral authorities. But the more I examined the allegations, the clearer it became to me that they were baseless.

'Yes, there will be a referendum,' I answered when some of my friends asked me how I thought it would turn out. However I took another moment to think before staking my prestige as an analyst on the follow-up question about who would win.

There was no doubt that the majority of the poor identified in some way or other with Chávez.

But after more than four years of the Bolivarian revolution, the statistics were depressing.

Unemployment had risen from fifteen per cent to twenty-five per cent. Since April 2003 alone, GDP had shrunk by a whopping fourteen per cent. Poverty increased by thirty-three percent and extreme poverty by fifty per cent between 2002 and 2003.⁶⁴ Very few saw any evidence of the election promise of prosperity for everyone. Social progress seemed impossible in the chaos afflicting the country. Experts believed that a further 6 billion USD in investments was needed to return the economy to the levels prior to the oil production sabotage. No one knew where such funds would come from. The question was, would the poor continue to offer their votes in exchange for something as abstract as dignity?

I recalled the slogan the opposition had launched through the media in November 2002, before *el paro petrolero*: '*Hallacas* without Chávez.' *Hallacas* is the Christmas dish prepared in every Venezuelan home across the country. The dish consists of cornmeal dough stuffed with a lightly-spiced meat and vegetable stew, which is then rolled in banana leaves and boiled. The motto, which was the hot topic among Venezuelans at the time, contained both a demand that Chávez would resign before Christmas, and a prediction that only when *that* happened, would food return to the supermarket shelves. Then and only then would there be Christmas. With *hallacas*, and without Chávez. As we now know, the result was the opposite. Christmas was still celebrated, but it was *with* Chávez, and, for many people, *without hallacas*, as it was impossible to find the ingredients. It seemed the poor would not be so easily subdued. But *that* was in 2002. Back then it may have been easier to think that as long as Chávez made it through the next crisis, he would be allowed to fulfil his election promises in peace.

But in November 2003, the situation in the country was worse than it was before the military coup and the oil production shutdown, and the opposition kept up the pressure.

I suspect that many of those who still sympathised with the president and his ideas realised that the continuation of a Chávez government would mean the continuation of chaos, job losses and a shortage of goods – the exact opposite of what they had hoped for when they voted the lieutenant colonel into Miraflores.

Ni de vaina, never in the world will the majority vote for another Christmas without *hallacas*, I answered after thinking about the question for a moment, and everyone knew exactly what I meant. Chávez was set to lose the referendum.

However, the statistics were one thing. There was an entirely different matter to consider: the offensive Chávez was mounting in the country's *barrios*.

When the Revolution Came to the *Barrio*

Meeting Omaira was always a celebration. This time for a particular reason. Omaira informed me that she and her daughters had enrolled in something called *Misión Ribas*.

Misión Ribas is a state programme for millions of Venezuelans who were excluded from or forced out of the educational system in the decades before Chávez came to power.

Omaira and her daughters were now well on their way to completing a further education which they had been forced to stop. Back when Omaira was sent to Caracas to work as a maid, her two daughters had worked in the textile industry to help contribute to the strained family finances.

'I never imagined we would get this opportunity. It is a tremendous joy,' Omaira said.

Misión Ribas is just one of the many social programmes – which the Chávez government dubbed *misiones*, 'missions' – introduced from the end of 2003. Other *misiones* arranged for literacy training, university education, basic health care, subsidised food and help for poor single mothers getting into higher education or employment. They were all free of charge, and many of them included grants.

'A lot has changed since I last saw you,' Omaira said, eager to invite me to her home again. She had made a number of improvements to her house. Everything was *gracias al comandante*, she said, 'thanks to the commandant.' Omaira, who seemed to have forgotten that I was a foreigner, tried to convince me to vote for Chávez. 'So we can keep him for a while longer. We cannot let the opposition take him from us now that good things are finally starting to happen.'

As far back as 2000, a significant number of Cuban advisors had been seen in Venezuela, both in the health and the education sectors. A bigger inflow of Cuban doctors, nurses, teachers and sports instructors began in 2003. Having sent eight thousand doctors and nurses into Caracas' *barrios* over the course of the year, by the summer of 2004 that number had risen to thirteen thousand countrywide.

The Cubans were first housed with poor families. Many of them lived in small shanties in the most heavily burdened *barrios*.

Then the building of small, octagonal brick clinics began in the slums, villages and remote jungle regions.

Misión Barrio Adentro, often just called *Barrio Adentro*, 'Into the Slums,' was the name of the project. The health services on offer were basic, but effective. Focus was placed on common and poverty-related illnesses. Another vital programme was the literacy campaign. It was led by Cuban teachers, and supported by Venezuelans, many of whom were volunteers. *Barrio Adentro* drew its inspiration from the Cuban revolutionary literacy campaign model of the 1960s. Now with the use of modern audiovisual educational materials.

Chávez was reaping the fruits of another recent victory, one of great strategic importance. During the oil shutdown, the PDVSA management were practically fighting for the limelight, using the commercial media to highlight their role in what became the second illegal attempt to oust the elected government. Less violent than the coup attempt, but even more expensive for a country that lost between fourteen and twenty billion USD from the shutdown. The amount of airtime dedicated to support and prepare the PDVSA executives and engineers behind the shutdown, now made it both politically justifiable and simpler for Chávez to identify and weed out those who had taken part and replace them with loyal employees.

Slowly – probably somewhat slower than the government let on – but surely, the new PDVSA leadership managed to increase oil production to around 3 million barrels per day, almost the same production level as before the shutdown.

At the same time, oil prices began to rise, in part due to the US invasion of Iraq and increasing demand from China.

The steadily increasing flow of dollars from the sale of oil was pumped straight out of PDVSA and into the funds that financed new social programmes, without taking any detours through the old state bureaucracy. Enormous sums were spent importing essential goods, and these were sold at heavily subsidised prices through *Misión Mercal*, a new national food outlet to battle hunger and malnutrition. To supplement the programmes for basic education, decentralised learning centres for higher education also spread to the poorest and most remote regions of the country. An important feature of *las misiones* was the grants. The large transfers of money financed students' monthly expenses as well as the steadily growing army of officials in charge of recruiting the millions of poor people who qualified for the various programmes.

Chávez insisted that they were not 'gifts' from the government, but the repayment of the state's 'social debt' to the people. It was a question of rights which the people had won for themselves and which were legally established in the Bolivarian constitution. Rights that were finally supported by the rising flow of dollars from PDVSA. Additionally, during this period the Chávez government managed to triple the social welfare budget that was paid out through regular transfers. According to Venezuelan central statistics, nearly sixty per cent of Venezuela's twenty-six million inhabitants made use of the new social programmes.[65]

The most symbolic initiative was the transformation of the PDVSA headquarters in Caracas into *Universidad Bolivariana*. This luxurious building, the very same building where the military coup leaders had organised the march on Miraflores, was emptied of oil bosses and filled with poor students, people who previously would never have beaten the near impossible odds of gaining entry into the established public and private universities. The message was this: From now on, the oil money is going to create progress and prosperity for the Venezuelan people, not foreign companies, corrupt politicians and anti-national PDVSA leaders. Only the opposition and its allies in the media seemed to worry about the lack of transparency in this mechanism that included the administration of enormous sums of money. Most poor people were happy that the oil money finally seemed to be flowing in their direction. And the government mostly countered any criticism by pointing out that when the opposition had ruled the country, there had been virtually no transparency and certainly very little concern for the poor in the management of the oil money. Omaira was almost offended when I admitted that I had not heard of all the social reforms and all the things that had happened in her *barrio over* the past few months.

'Maybe you are watching too much opposition TV,' she commented.

There might have been something to her explanation. The established commercial media had greeted *las misiones* with a combination of crass criticism and concealment. The first time I heard about the Cuban doctors, for example, was in an *El Universal* article that described a scandal of a child who had died as a result of alleged malpractice at the hands of a Cuban doctor. At the time, around one hundred Third World countries had requested help from Cuban health workers, who were internationally renowned for their expertise. But in Venezuela, Cuban health and educational workers were sometimes referred to in the media as Castro's agents or *matasanos*, literally 'killers of healthy people' – an expression describing doctors who do more harm than good. Amateurs was the most positive depiction I found of them in any of the articles.

Opposition politicians believed the education programmes was a 'Castro style communist indoctrination.' Representatives from private universities and businesses used the media to advise people not to participate. They said that certificates from these institutions would not be recognised. There were also attempts to stigmatise those participating in the government's social programmes as losers. This perception was firmly rooted in the upper and middle classes, but to an extent, also with a significant number of the more affluent poor in the big cities. People who lived in neighbourhoods between the *barrios* and the housing estates and considered themselves middle class, but in reality were never far from the breadline.

For the government, the fact that the established media hardly presented any factual information about the new opportunities available through the social programmes, was not only a political problem, but also a practical one. How do you get one and a half million illiterate people to sign up for a literacy programme if they do not know it exists? How do poor, pregnant women make use of the new local birth centres if they do not know where they are, or that their services are free? And what if they believed in the media's claims that the Cuban doctors were killers?

Chávez used his weekly Sunday broadcast of *Aló presidente*, as well as regular *cadenas* to promote the new welfare services. During this period, *Aló presidente* began climbing to the top of the television ratings. It was the first political programme to surpass the ratings of several of the country's most popular *telenovelas*, soap operas. During the live TV broadcasts, the national and local coordinators for the new welfare services often appeared alongside Chávez.

Representatives from the local population were given the opportunity to make suggestions, and offer their praise or criticism. During these TV meetings between the president and people from the slums and villages, a glimpse of Venezuelan social reality was revealed, one which had never before received much attention. Many of those who took the opportunity to thank the president had never stepped foot in a hospital or spoken to a doctor before. Women told of how they had been born on a dirt floor and how they always assumed that their children would be born the same way. Emotions were high. Some cried. Some, particularly a number of elderly people, believed that God must have been behind the miracle of *las misiones*. An older lady who had travelled miles just to give the president a hug, refused to let go of him, nearly forcing security personnel to step in.

I was particularly struck by the story of a middle-aged man who received his literacy diploma straight from the hands of the president. He was a dark-skinned man with a missing tooth, someone that many in the upper and middle class would refer to as *los desdentados*, 'the toothless,' one of the many insults for the poor. Judging by his demeanour, he had never held a microphone or been in the company of a leading politician before. Visibly nervous, he mumbled something about the humiliation he faced for not being able to write his name on a document. He went quiet, stared at the ground for a moment, looked up and continued with tears running down his face: 'What I want to tell you, *comandante*, is that I no longer bow my head. I finally feel like a real person, like a real Venezuelan.' It was the first time I had seen a Venezuelan man cry.

For a number of rich Venezuelans however, it was a shock to see these people on prime-time TV. A Venezuelan interviewed by the Financial Times expressed what many in the upper classes felt: 'The uglier they are, the more they support Chávez. Anyone without teeth [the most obvious physical sign of poverty in a country fixated on appearance] supports Chávez.'[66] At my university a fellow student told me how all the international media coverage of Chávez and all the 'ugly people that follow him' made her worry that Venezuela's status as the world's beauty contest superpower would be damaged.

In my conversations with Omaira and other poor Chávez supporters during this period, along with gratitude, I also sensed a relief that they had not been wrong to support Chávez during the military coup, the oil production shutdown, and the political chaos, despite the fact that until then they had received little in return. 'I knew we could trust that man. He fought the oligarchy, the gringos and all the rest so that he would get the chance to do something for the poor. Finally, it is our turn.' There was also a hint of revenge in his tone. A dig at the political elite, the experts, the journalists and the politicians, both inside and outside Venezuela, those who had ridiculed the Chávez supporters and presented them as exploited idiots, too stupid to know what was good for them.

'And where is the catastrophe that all the rich and clever people said would happen if Chávez wasn't overthrown immediately,' Omaira asked with ill-concealed malice. 'All we need now is to land a knockout blow on the opposition. You'll see.'

One Dollar on Chávez

On 17 June 2004, TV screens across the country were dominated by the shiny head and thick eyebrows of Jorge Rodríguez, the chairman of the electoral commission (CNE).

The opposition had finally agreed to accept another round of verification for the signature campaign. CNE had completed its report. 81 097 fraudulent signatures belonging to deceased individuals and confirmed Chávez supporters, had been excluded by the CNE. It was proven beyond doubt that widespread fraud had been used to inflate the number of signatures. The Chávez government suspected the banks of supplying Súmate with customer details, identity numbers, names, addresses, and signatures to assist their campaign. But there were still enough confirmed and verified signatures to satisfy the minimum requirement of twenty per cent of eligible voters.

The opposition and Súmate would have their referendum, Jorge Rodríguez declared.

The first presidential recall referendum in history was to be held in Venezuela in the late summer of 2004.

The mood in Caracas changed noticeably.

For several months the two sides had battled to show their superiority in the streets, creating an oddly aggressive yet festive atmosphere, with hard core political speeches, carnival-like processions and not least music. Competing techno beats with lyrics supporting either side were pumped out of huge speakers on the backs of lorries that moved slowly through the city.

No hay referendum, 'No to the referendum,' the red lorries blasted.
Si hay referendum, 'Yes to the referendum,' the opposition lorries countered.

When the CNE announcement was made, the latter had prevailed. It had probably come as a surprise to both sides. A number of Chavistas had been convinced by a government spokesmen's prediction that the opposition would be unable to gather enough signatures. The anti-Chavistas, on the other hand, had believed the conspiracy theories flouted by the media that Chávez controlled the electoral commission and would never allow a referendum to take place.

During the entire process, Chávez had said that he would respect the decision of the electoral commission regarding the signatures. Faced with the demand by millions of Venezuelans to revoke his mandate the president brought out his baseball jargon: 'We are going to hit a home run.' He promised to hit the ball all the way to The White House. 'Let's make a bet,' he proposed to President Bush: 'Which of us will last longer, you or me? One dollar,' with the last two words spoken in broken English and followed by a confident laugh.

The Referendum

The opposition parties were still not able to offer any coherent political project, well-organized political parties or a unifying presidential candidate. Hence the media remained the most powerful backer of the campaign for *el sí* – the yes side of the recall referendum.

'They will never accomplish anything,' Venevisión's frontman Napoleón Bravo concluded, the same man who had claimed he had seen Chávez' resignation letter during the military coup two years earlier. Bravo argued that the only time the economy had actually grown since Chávez came to power in 1999, was during the two days of Chávez' detention when the Carmona dictatorship had promised the business sector more favourable investment conditions. Accusations highlighting the decline and underinvestment of the military were also key issues. 'And in these conditions, Chávez has decided to declare war against the USA [...]

Idiotic,' declared Marta Colomina, a presenter for one of the four major channels, Televen.*

During the closing stages of the campaign, in an effort to demoralise the Chavistas, the opposition maintained that Chávez was already finished and had no chance of winning. This was a normal tactic in Latin American politics. Campaign strategists usually assume that creating a sense of defeat amongst the opposition camp can be as effective as rational political arguments in swaying the vote. The media published opinion polls giving the yes side around sixty per cent support, with Chávez only receiving forty per cent. 'Chávez is desperate now. There are also rumours that he is going to resign a few days before the referendum if the opinion polls continue to be against him,' Colomina said. She claimed that according to 'reliable sources within the government,' Chávez was going to replace the Vice President 'something Fidel Castro suggested or ordered him to do,' in order to prepare himself for electoral defeat. In addition to the endless opinion polls, politicians and experts that predicted election defeat for Chávez, for people with a more superstitious nature, RCTV brought in a fortune-teller. 'The lady wants a new queen,' she said after laying the cards on the table. In other words, Chávez was about to fall. 67

My friend Antonio was unshakeable in his belief that only massive electoral fraud could prevent Chávez from being voted out of Miraflores. He was not worried about the lack of a unifying opposition candidate. 'A new generation has arrived,' he said, alluding to the two young and successful mayors: Leopoldo López from his municipality of Chacao and Henrique Capriles Radonsky, from the neighbouring municipality of Baruta – both affluent areas of Caracas. They both represented the right-wing party, Primero Justicia (PJ).

---

* Of course Chávez had never said anything to indicate that he wanted to go to war with the USA.

According to Antonio, there were plenty of good candidates to choose from. He was far from impressed with Chávez' *misiones*. 'Of course we need to help the poor, but you have to teach them how to fish, not give them fish.' For Antonio, *las misiones* were simply cheap populism. He believed they testified to the government's desperation when confronted with the majority support for the opposition.

Both international and Venezuelan sources gave the impression that Chávez was going to lose. I had changed my mind. Quite possibly, a majority had been behind Chávez the entire time, although the margin had definitely been tight at times. And *las misiones* had only increased his support. Some of the moves by the opposition towards the end of the election campaign indicated that they may not have believed their own representation of the parties' relative strengths. For one, the opposition suddenly promised to protect the very social programmes which they had brushed aside as Castro-communist infiltration. This was an indication that their election strategists realised how popular the reforms were with the people. Also telling was the revelation that the opposition and the media had concealed opinion polls which gave the no side a clear majority, polls which they had commissioned themselves.

The election campaign for the Chávez camp, *el Comando Maisanta*, made its final preparations for the decisive referendum. Chávez called forth the fighting spirit of *las tropas* and *batallónes*, the troops and battalions of his million-strong volunteer army who went door to door to secure the vote in their favour. Now *Comando Maisanta*'s biggest challenge was not convincing the poor majority that the revolution had to continue, but getting people out to vote.

The people's tenacious contempt for politicians had been firmly established during the fourth republic[*]. Even dedicated *Chavistas* I spoke to at the time were not accustomed to voting, not

---

[*] The Fourth Republic lasted from 1958 to 1998.

even for a president they wholeheartedly supported. Another problem was that over the years, the state had limited electoral participation by having far fewer polling stations in the country's *barrios* than in middle-class and upper-class areas. The poor people in the slums of Caracas had to make use of terrible roads and public transport in order to cast their votes. While rich families could simply leave their children at home with the servants, (who were often not given time off to vote) a significant number of women in the slums were unable to vote because they had to stay home with the kids.

Chávez knew the everyday reality of the country's poor. He instructed his battalions of volunteers to do everything they could to ease the practical restrictions on voter participation. Childcare, collective transport to polling stations in the *barrios* and remote villages of the country, and crash courses in the voting procedures for the new electronic voting machines; these were just a few of the initiatives to ensure maximum participation. In the period before the referendum, the electoral register increased by three million people, in part due to the government's *Misión Identidad*, which provided Venezuelan documents and voting rights to previously undocumented immigrants. Election day arrived on 15 August. At some polling stations in the country's *barrios* where turnout was normally low, people queued for up to ten hours to cast their vote. This was despite CNE significantly increasing the number of polling stations in poor areas where they knew voter turnout was going to increase.

It did. Turnout was a whopping seventy per cent, considerably higher than the fifty-five per cent average of previous elections. The greatest increase was with the poor.

Uh ah, Chávez no se va, 'Hey ho, Chávez will not go.' This was the refrain of the referendum salsa which the popular Afro-Caribbean orchestra Grupo Madera recorded in honour of the president. And Chávez did not go. At midnight, the electoral commission announced that fifty-nine per cent of the voters voted no. Forty-one per cent voted yes.

After the polling stations closed, Chávez supporters gathered around the presidential palace to await the results. After more than two years of constant destabilisation and chaos, the Chávez camp erupted with joy. The celebrations which ensued surpassed those of 1998, when Chávez broke the former elite's forty-year monopoly on power.

But not everyone was happy with the result. The opposition alliance Coordinadora Democrática (CD) had hired the American polling organisation Penn, Schoen & Berland Associates (PSB) to carry out exit polls on voting day. PSB used personnel from Súmate to collect the figures. And Súmate delivered. Their figures predicted a crushing defeat for Chávez, by a whopping eighteen point margin. The word *fraude* returned to the front pages.

The opposition refused to accept defeat and the private media refused to recognise the result. For several months, the supposed electoral fraud by CNE and Chávez was the primary theme of the private media. Opposition leader Henry Ramos Allup promised to present evidence to support these accusations, but as of 2016, that has not happened. In the meantime, there were fanatical conspiracy theories about a Russian satellite – others believed it was an Arabic satellite sent by Al Jazeera – which transmitted electronic signals which swapped the vote counts for the yes and no side.

All international election observers concluded that the voting had been free and fair and logistically well executed.[68] Former US president Jimmy Carter had observed the election and labelled the opposition's use of exit polls sabotage: 'Not only did they create a false expectation of victory which could have led to the destabilisation of democracy, it was a clear attempt to influence the outcome of the referendum.'[69]

Antonio was certain that the vote was a fix. He mentioned several possibilities, including seeing Haitians in the queue outside the polling station who were 'paid to vote for Chávez,' the possible rigging of the electronic voting system, and the dishonest nature of Chávez. In addition *nobody* – in Venezuela 'nobody' often means 'practically no one' or 'very few' – he had spoken to planned to vote for Chávez.

Most of my middle and upper-class friends reacted the same way as Antonio. In some ways it made sense. For example in Chacao, the district where Antonio lived, the Chavistas were a clear minority. The opposition received eighty per cent of the votes there. In the decades before Chávez came to power, when the potentially explosive topic of class was excluded from the political debate, there had never been any major systematic difference in party preference between the rich and the poor or between rich and poor districts. And considering that the private media mostly silenced the enormous support for Chávez in the poor neighbourhoods, it was no wonder Chacao's inhabitants asked themselves where Chávez got his fifty-nine per cent from – almost five million votes – when he barely got twenty per cent in their district. Previously, before Chávez brought the class divide to the forefront of Venezuelan politics, such a difference in voting preferences would have been statistically impossible.

But with Chávez in power, a deep political divide emerged, matching the enormous social rift which divided Venezuela's rich elite and the poor majority. The latest vote was a reflection of that.

At the polling stations in Omaira's district, Chávez received between sixty-three and seventy per cent of the votes – while in other *barrios* and villages the figure was as high as eighty per cent. This was the new political reality. Antonio, my fellow university students and the rest of Venezuela's middle and upper class could still not accept it. Much less understand it.

SOCIALISM FOR THE TWENTY-FIRST CENTURY

1 May 2004, in front of a packed crowd on Avenida Bolívar in Caracas, Chávez for the first time announced his goal of achieving socialism in Venezuela.

I was there to find out which of the two political camps had the best support amongst the Venezuelan working class. It was clear that poor Venezuelans, and those without work or simply selling cheap Chinese goods on the streets, supported the president. But having heard the phrases *huelga* and *huelga general*, 'strike' and 'general strike,' used against Chávez time after time, it was by no means a given that his support also stretched to organised workers. To counter CTV – the established federation of workers which supported the opposition – workers supporting Chávez established a national Bolivarian federation of labour unions.

Both the opposition and the Chávez government were attempting to fire up their respective supporters by presenting the 1 May as a duel, a show of strength.

The opposition march was an unusual mixture. Around half of the supporters wore T-shirts with the name of their respective unions on them, all affiliated to CTV, the traditional federation of labour unions allied to AD, the former ruling party. The participants were largely dark-skinned and made up what remained of AD's power base from the working class. The rest were groups of political activists from right-wing parties, who showed all the tell-tale signs of being from the richer east side. The enthusiasm of the opposition marches I had witnessed a few years earlier was gone. The demonstrators, numbering only a few thousand, had barely reached the city centre when they packed up and went home, each to their own districts. Only two blocks away, the crowds of red-clad Chavistas were still streaming onto Avenida Bolívar.

Chávez was the clear winner in the fight for the support of the working class that day. I was about to head home when the president made a surprise appearance on the big stage.

It was often difficult to tear yourself away when listening to Chávez.

On this particular occasion, I chose to stay and listen. There was something intriguing about how the faces and movements of the normally nonchalant and noisy Venezuelans transformed when Chávez addressed them. Chávez almost always had at least one surprise announcement when he spoke in front of large crowds. This time, the president said that it was time to take a closer look at socialism. He encouraged his supporters to read Marx and to prepare themselves for more profound changes in society. *Karl Marx*, I wondered aloud. Nineteenth century economics as a reading tip for Venezuelan street vendors and builders who for the most part have not completed their elementary education. A thousand pages of complex economic political jargon from a century and a half ago, for a people who had such little interest in reading as most Venezuelans did? Even some of my fellow students, Masters-level sociology students, admitted that they had never read a book, and those who had, openly confessed that their favourite books were self-help books on the lines of *Ten Steps to Success in Life* or *Seven Keys for Conquering the World*. How could he possibly believe Venezuelan workers, some of whom had just recently started to learn how to read and write, would go out and read Karl Marx? But Chávez had no doubts: The working class needed an ideology to 'defeat the oligarchy.'

Up to that point, Chávez had been confrontational towards the existing powers that be, but at the same time pragmatic. He had referenced role models as varied as Tony Blair, Simón Bolívar and Che Guevara. His gradual approach to change up until then did not follow any traditional ideological manual. If Chávez initiated government intervention in a specific economic sector, it was usually only when business owners strategically used their power to hurt the government politically. Or where nationalisation and regulation presented opportunities to create more jobs or offer better services than those which had been previously privatised. Apart from that, Chávez had been cautious with the economy. With Chávez´ endorsement of Marxism and socialism, would the process of reform be altered to follow purely ideological guidelines? Was the ultimate goal of Chávez' power struggle with the economic elite to create a new society founded on Marxism? My first impression was that the endorsement of socialism was just another whim from Chávez and of no great significance. The crowd responded far more enthusiastically to the twenty five percent increase in the minimum wage, announced by Chávez during the same speech than to his words about Karl Marx

Hardly anyone outside of Venezuela knows about this speech and most journalists, writers and academics mark Chávez' launch of socialism the following year.

In 2005, he declared his intention to establish 'Socialism for the twenty-first century.'

He encouraged the left wing from around the world to develop new content for an ideology which suffered an enormous loss of legitimacy after the fall of the Berlin wall. The initiative was successful, both in drawing some of the world's most important left-wing intellectuals into the discussion about a new socialism and in making Venezuela the centre of that debate. Soon Marxists and radicals from far and near would turn up in Caracas. One day someone would come from Italy, the next day, Japan or Brazil. Many were invited to press conferences and private conversations with the president. In 2006 Caracas was filled to the brim when it hosted the World Social Forum. An entire generation of young, radical left-wing activists from all over Latin America and the rest of the world were able to see the Bolivarian revolution at first hand.

Chávez was starting to look like a global political leader.

His first three years in power were primarily a battle for survival. All the same, he had managed to make important inroads internationally. Chávez was the only head of state to vehemently oppose the US invasion of Afghanistan in 2001. But his increasingly harsher criticism of what he called 'imperialistic aggressions' from the USA found resonance in large parts of the world. Soon he spoke for a growing international anti-war movement and a world wary of George Bush. In 2006, he stepped up to the podium at the UN

General Assembly in New York – the day after President George W. Bush had spoken – made the sign of the cross and said that he smelt sulphur, referring to Bush as 'the devil.' The enormous applause from the national leaders in the assembly room indicated that he had said what many of them felt, but dared not say in public.

Left-wing supporters from around the world were intrigued by Chávez' clear denunciation of imperialism. Several important left-wing intellectuals gave their open support, including the Spaniard Ignacio Ramonet, founder of the ATTAC movement and editor of *Le Monde Diplomatique*, the North American dissident Noam Chomsky, the British-Pakistani author Tariq Ali, and the popular mayor of London, Ken Livingston. In Latin America, the Uruguayan author Eduardo Galeano and Nobel Peace Prize winners Rigoberta Menchú and Adolfo Pérez Esquivel offered their support. And the Marxist priest and poet from Nicaragua, Ernesto Cardenal – a powerful authority on the Latin American left – had this to say about the impulsive political shift by Chávez in Venezuela: 'Today we have a revolution. It is taking place in Venezuela. It is a quiet revolution. The majority of the media do not speak of it, they simply call President Hugo Chávez a dictator. But it is a real revolution. [Venezuela] produces oil. But the USA produces ninety per cent of the world's information,' implying that most of the international media's negative coverage of Chávez was a reflection of US economic and geopolitical interests, rather than a true reflection of what was actually taking place in Venezuela.[70]

Chávez also altered the political reality outside of his own political camp. The notion of Latin America unification in the spirit of the independence hero Simón Bolívar was so well received by a broad spectrum of the continent's population that not a single Latin American government wished or dared to openly confront the idea at the time.

Caracas was now teeming with foreign correspondents who had been dispatched to the capital following the military coup in 2002, all on the hunt for a front page story on 'Hurricane Hugo,' his latest nickname. Most often Chávez' reforms and initiatives were presented in a negative light. Still, the intense interest from the international media helped him to get his message across: The neoliberal monopoly on power and US dominance in Latin America was over.

THE BOLIVARIAN CRUSADE IN LATIN AMERICA

A Funeral Procession in Mar del Plata: Defeat of the FTAA

With the referendum victory in 2004, Chávez consolidated his position in Venezuela. This empowered him to intensify his international offensive. The next major pan-American summit at the Argentinian seaside resort of Mar del Plata would be a demonstration of power.

On 4 November 2005, Mar del Plata was turned on its head.

This was the location for the fourth pan-American summit, where all thirty-five American countries, excluding Cuba, were represented by their leaders. One of the guests, US president George W Bush, appeared to have brought his 'war on terror' to this medium-sized Argentinian coastal town. The venue and neighbouring 20 blocks were blockaded by three rings of security, guarded by Argentina's federal police, National Guard and provincial police, comprising a total of ten thousand armed officers. Helicopters patrolled the skies, along with the Argentinian F16 variant, the A-4AR Fighting Hawk, as well as US surveillance planes. Orders were given to shoot down any aircraft which entered the 200 kilometre no-fly-zone around the city. Naval vessels blocked off the city's seaway.

Gone were the times when international free trade summits were simply a matter of luxury hotels, extravagant food with leading politicians and business leaders surpassing each other in maxims about the blessings of a free market economy in front of an obliging press. The surprising anti-globalisation protests which took place during the World Trade Organisation (WTO) negotiations in Seattle in 1999 changed that tradition.

The official topics of the summit in Mar del Plata were jobs and democracy.

But everyone, including the hundreds of international correspondents, were aware that the pan-American free trade agreement, the FTAA (Free Trade Area of the Americas), proposed and developed by the USA would dominate the agenda. The FTAA agreement entailed the dismantling of trade barriers, increased privatisation and the deregulation of national economies across the region.

The idea of incorporating Latin America into the US economy was proposed as early as 1889. American President William Taft expressed his vision in 1912: 'The day is not far distant when three Stars and Stripes at three equidistant points will mark our territory: one at the North Pole, another at the Panama Canal, and the third at the South Pole. The whole hemisphere will be ours in fact, as by virtue of our superiority, it already is ours morally.'[71]

A hundred years later, with Bill Clinton now president, the USA would try to realise the idea through the FTAA. Since 1994, the proposal was discussed at all three Summit of the Americas. The free trade area would be the largest in the history of mankind: a collective agreement spanning two continents, with its soon to be one billion inhabitants merged into the largest economy in the world, with Washington as the undisputed centre of power.[72] Securing the agreement would be a historic victory: a realisation of USA's long-term goal of complete economic and political control over Latin America. The collective agreement also contained clauses detailing sanctions which would make it impossible for future Latin American governments to gain control over their own resources and economies. In that way, the FTAA would also be 'the end of history,' an irreversible victory for capitalism and the free market, just as market ideologist Francis Fukuyama had postulated. The neoliberal development philosophy which it is based on, presupposes that deregulation and privatisation lead to increased economic growth. The growth which private agents provide, as long as they are given sufficient protection from governmental intervention, would travel down the socio-economic ladder, following the so-called 'trickle-down' principle, the free market's take on an old Norwegian proverb, Since the early seventies, this message was spread by the IMF, the World Bank and the US Treasury, and it was eagerly embraced, both by Latin America's economic elite and its governments, including military dictatorships and elected governments. In 1989 it was referred to as *The Washington Consensus*. But as the media warned ahead of the Mar del Plata summit – without hiding their concern at the development – the Washington Consensus which Bush presented at Mar del Plata was no longer as marketable as it had once been.

The task George Bush had at the Argentinian seaside resort was to secure the agreement by collecting the signatures of the continent's leaders. But not everyone wanted that to happen. According to most major American newspapers, Latin Americans had begun to blame rising poverty and social problems on the policies of classic liberalism. The reason was simple. Contrary to the promises of increased growth, the IMF was forced to admit that 'the past twenty-five years [between 1982 and 2007] the per capita income in Latin America had increased by a mere ten per cent, as opposed to eighty-two per cent between 1960 and 1980.' According to figures from ECLAC, the UN Economic Commission for Latin American and the Caribbean, 136 million Latin Americans or forty-one per cent of the region's population were impoverished in 1980. After twenty years of privatisation and deregulation, that figure had increased to forty-four per cent of the population – with the total number living in poverty rising from 75 million to 211 million.

Globally, decades of IMF and World Bank privatisation programmes had resulted in a comprehensive redistribution from the poor to the rich. In 1960, the twenty per cent of the world population living in the richest countries had thirty times more income than the twenty per cent living in the poorest. In 1997, the figure for the richest had increased to 60 times that of the poorest.[73] As former chief economist of the World Bank, Joseph Stiglitz was tasked with administering the neoliberal policies. However he later offered this crushing condemnation of neoliberalism: 'A reform strategy which promised to create exceptional prosperity has failed in an equally exceptional manner.'[74] The period which many academics, journalists and politicians in the USA called *the heydays of market liberalism*, was now referred to as *la larga noche neoliberal*, 'the long night of neoliberalism,' in Latin America. Instead of combatting poverty, the neoliberal governments were combatting the poor,' Noam Chomsky concluded, perhaps with the Pérez government's 1989 *el Caracazo* massacre in mind.

The streets of Mar del Plata had been filled with demonstrators since early morning. The protest would grow larger and more intense over the course of the day, with the droning of helicopters and the chants of radical left-wing activists intermingling. Radical Argentinian trade unions and socialist parties had mobilised protests outside the venue. During the morning everything had been peaceful. Then a group of masked protesters broke away from the crowd. They attacked shops and banks using cobblestones and Molotov cocktails. It took the police forty minutes later to organise a counter-attack, and during the ensuing street battle, twenty people were wounded and sixty arrested, while disappointed trade union activists, workers and students saw their protests completely overshadowed by the sight of broken windows and tear gas. They withdrew when the clashes began.

The situation was typical of what had become a regular pattern in the years following the Seattle protests. The antiglobalisation protests were an important feature of this period, but just as sure as the free trade summits would be met with young people in hoodies, clowns and trade union activists, it was equally certain that safely inside and behind the police barricades, the politicians would pass their neoliberal resolutions, unfazed by the clamour outside.

This time however, another factor came into play: Hugo Chávez.

Chávez wants 'to kill or demoralise' the free trade agreement and 'threaten to steal the show,' the *Washington Post* and *New York Times* warned in the days leading up to the summit.[75]

The Venezuelan president had barely landed at the airport in Mar del Plata when the international press had their suspicions confirmed. The international news desks had been right about their worries. Chávez did intend to 'steal the show.'

Among others, Argentinian footballing legend Diego Maradona and Bolivia's future presidential candidate, the coca farmer Evo Morales, had joined Chávez at a 'counter-summit' in the city. A special train was brought in to transport the celebrity protestors and their fans from Buenos Aires to Mar del Plata. Included on the passenger list were the musicians, Manu Chao, the filmmaker from the former Yugoslavia, Emir Kusturica and the Argentinian Nobel Peace Prize winner, Adolfo Pérez Esquivel.

Whilst inside the summit venue the leaders of the thirty-four participant countries conducted corridor diplomacy and outside the anti-globalisation demonstrators attacked banks, Chávez gathered his people at a World Cup stadium a little outside the city centre. Forty-five thousand people were in attendance. He informed them that if the FTAA agreement was approved, it would ensure the continued plundering of Latin America's resources by giving big companies more power at the expense of the region's democratically elected governments. He summarised nearly two hundred years of US interventionism in Latin America and warned of 'one hundred years of war in the region' if the US attacked Venezuela. He then called Maradona to the platform. 'We Argentinians have dignity. Let's kick out George Bush,' the footballing legend shouted, wearing a special T-shirt for the occasion with the words 'war criminal' above a picture of the American president.

However Bush did not stand alone. It was not just the majority of the Latin American governments who were safely inside the conservative leader's camp. The day prior to the meeting, the *Washington Post* predicted that the majority of the newly-elected left-wing governments – the paper must have been referring to Uruguay, Argentina, Brazil and Chile – were going to close ranks in order to pass the free trade agreement. 'The leaders who are going to meet Bush this weekend, are generally more sympathetically inclined to the USA than their voters [...] It seems the continent's politicians are open to making these kinds of economic agreements which the USA hopes to achieve,' the *Washington Post* wrote – exposing a hope that the agreement would be approved by governments acting against the wishes of the very people who had elected them.

Negotiations for the free trade project started off well. The US government knew very well that Bush was one of the most unpopular presidents ever in Latin American. So it made sure that leaders from a little further south would take the offensive in pressing for the FTAA agreement. Mexico's president, Vicente Fox, from the neoliberal right-wing party PAN, did not disappoint. As leader of Latin America's second largest economy, Fox put his weight behind the requirement that the FTAA agreement would be approved over the course of the current summit. The Mexican delegation 'did the hard work for us', American diplomats told an Argentinian reporter during the negotiations, and it is seemed likely that the agreement would be approved.[76] The discussions were intense and lasted hours. But a block of five countries, Brazil, Uruguay, Paraguay and the host country Argentina, united around Venezuela and refused to waver. An agreement for the world's largest free trade area had failed. After the failure of his endeavour, a humiliated George Bush tried to smile as he was photographed with Chávez and the other thirty-three leaders. He boarded Air Force One and disappeared before the closing declaration had been announced. A spokesperson from the State Department was left with the awkward task of explaining to the press how the defeat was actually a kind of victory.

The Argentinian left wing, from revolutionaries to social democrats and Peronists, was overjoyed with Chávez' contribution to the achievement. Thirty years earlier, during the right-wing dictatorship, thirty thousand Argentinians had been murdered simply for believing and standing up for what Chávez was now able to say from the podium – and he was met with approval.

But what might be the most interesting analysis of Chávez' role in the battle for the FTAA agreement came from the opposing political camp – from the conservative Colombian newspaper El Tiempo. The analysis was particularly interesting as Latin American press were generally negative towards Chávez. But this victory was impossible to deny. According to El Tiempo, 'the entire discussion for and against FTAA [...] was an attempt to isolate Venezuela commercially.' In other words, a difficult starting point for Chávez. But the Venezuelan president 'gained ground where he is able to work his magic,' the paper wrote: 'In the streets, with the people, and with the left wing who consider him their messiah.' Chávez also proved to be a master of negotiations, according to the paper. 'He made a qualitative and quantitative leap forward with his regional leadership,' taking a leading role which had previously belonged to Brazil's President Lula. The article ran with the headline 'Leadership of Hugo Chávez Crosses Latin American Borders at the 4th Summit of the Americas.'

Red Sunrise

Mar del Plata was only the beginning for Chávez, a small battle in his war for a new Latin America. He was convinced that Bolívar's ideals of a unified and political and economically independent Latin America would finally be achieved.

Under the rule of the Spanish empire and the weak governments which followed the end to colonial rule, the region was drained of its resources. Perhaps the largest and longest blood-letting in the history of the world. The Uruguayan author Eduardo Galeano coined the metaphor in his famous book 'Open Veins of Latin America.' In Incan Peru, entire palaces of gold were disassembled and sent to Spain in pieces. In Bolivia entire mountains collapsed, having been riddled with mines and emptied of silver and other metals. Chilean copper supplied the cables which gave the world electricity; large swathes of the Amazon, the world's largest rainforest, was burnt and ploughed up to grow food. The food was sent from a continent where people still went to bed hungry, to the well-nourished elite of Europe. Adam Smith once concluded that the colonisation of America led to the perfection of the global trade system which would otherwise never have been achieved.[77] Latin America's *human* resources had also been consumed to achieve that perfection. Millions of used-up corpses were left in the mines, plantations and freighters after digging, ploughing, harvesting and transporting the continent's resources to colonial masters and consumers in Europe and the USA.

But Latin America still possesses enormous deposits of gold, silver and other metals and minerals which are needed to support manufacturing and other industries. And more importantly: the world's largest sources of fresh water, the world's largest proven oil reserves, concentrated in the Orinoco region in Venezuela, and the most biodiverse region in the world, the Amazon – the key to future advances in medicine, food security and other scientific branches. For Chávez, it was not just about stopping the bloodletting. He wanted to use the resources as a weapon to establish Latin America as a regional 'power block.'

'The sword of Bolívar is sweeping across the continent.' From the middle of the 2000s, the slogan spread from Caracas to more and more cities, political parties, social movements, placards and brick walls in South America. *La patria grande*, 'The Great Fatherland' is a term coined by the Argentinian author Manuel Ugarte and the title of his book. Normally *la patria grande* refers to 'a kind of imagined community' associated with an unfinished project to unite Latin America politically, something which began with liberation leaders during the wars of independence such as Símon Bolívar and José de San Martín.[78] Chávez wanted to transform the imagined community and potential political unit into a concrete reality. As far back as 2004, the year before the summit at Mar del Plata and before elections brought new allies to power in Bolivia,

Ecuador, Nicaragua and Honduras, his objective was clear. An international alliance was founded to make it possible.

One of the instruments was ALBA, or *Alternativa Bolivariana para las Américas,* the Bolivarian Alternative for the Americas, which later became the Bolivarian Alliance for the Americas. The idea for ALBA came into being in 2001 when Chávez and Fidel Castro were in Havana to establish a strategy to counter the FTAA. They played with the letters of the acronym ALCA, the Spanish equivalent of FTAA, and by changing one letter they made ALBA, the Spanish word for sunrise. On 14 December 2004, the founding document for ALBA was signed in Caracas. Forty-nine documents established the basis for the alliance: Member countries would exchange of technology, cooperate in the fields of agriculture, industry and transport, and finance teleSUR (Latin American's first continental media enterprise, with Argentina, Cuba, Ecuador and Uruguay as investors) and other forms of independent media. A key part of the agreement offered Cuba favourable conditions for the import of Venezuelan oil in exchange for providing Cuban doctors, medical equipment, teachers and educational material to the Venezuelan social programmes. The founding principle behind the development of ALBA can be summed up as cooperation and solidarity instead of competition. The results would be measured by looking at the concrete improvements in people's living conditions, not the trade figures of each country's export firms. Free trade was acceptable as long as it offered the people prosperity, but not as a goal in itself.

Chávez had another principle in mind: He was convinced that lasting unity between the nations could not be achieved through agreements signed by men in suits in air-conditioned rooms. 'The people must participate, the integration must come from below.' In 2005 Caracas hosted the first international summit for workers who had taken over abandoned enterprises. Through ALBA, the Venezuelan capital became the heart of an integration process which attracted labour activists from across the region. Meetings between production cooperatives, worker-run enterprises, social movements and small and medium-sized family enterprises were arranged.

Chávez attended many of the meetings. This helped supply a certain political clout to the project and was the source of inspiration for the activists. Organisations from countries outside the project were also allowed to join ALBA.

In 2004, the leaders of Latin America's indigenous peoples met in the Ecuadorian capital of Quito. The fate of the indigenous people is usually considered the greatest casualty of the continent's history. Despite this, the various indigenous groups still make up around fifty million people, according to some calculations. They live in large swathes of the continent, and despite their suppression, some are still able to achieve considerable power over the core businesses, with many of them growing quite rich from strategic natural resources. With the coming of the new millennium, the winds were changing for the indigenous population; shame many had felt over speaking Quechua, Aymara or Mayan was on the decline. The leaders who met in Quito, coordinated an offensive with a powerful network of organisations which covered large parts of South America. By an overwhelming majority, participants of the summit agreed to join the Bolivarian integration project. They took Chávez at his word and immediately began developing a list of ideas and concrete measure to make the ALBA collaboration an effective instrument for the struggles which the indigenous populations faced.

When the World Social Forum took place in Caracas in 2006, ALBA was one of the main attractions. The forum reached a historical climax as an international meeting place for radical ideas and popular movements. Using the slogan 'another kind of integration is possible' ALBA was put on display to activists from around the world. After several years spent focussing on defensive battles against neoliberal trade agreements, the left wing was hungry for an initiative which put them on the offensive. ALBA was their flagship. Within a few years, Bolivia, Ecuador, Honduras, Nicaragua and Haiti joined the alliance. Chávez formulated it as such: 'ALBA is an axis which is being extended in every direction. Bolívar's dream has begun to spread the heart of our country and our people.'[79]

When Simón Bolívar drove the Spaniards out of South America at the beginning of the 1800s, the Spanish colonial power retreated to its final bastion, the islands of the Caribbean. Bolívar had no intention of allowing them to become entrenched there, as it would give them control over Latin America's most important seaway.

In 1828 he organised a large-scale naval attack to free the Caribbean colonies from the Spaniards.

But what would have been the largest sea battle of the independence wars, one which would sound the death knell of the Spanish colonial power, never took place. Bolívar was betrayed. Someone had infiltrated the high command during the planning of the attack. The warships, fully loaded with artillery and soldiers, remained sloshing in the harbour of Cartagena in Colombia. The Spaniards managed to hold on for another seventy years and the Caribbean remained a location of piracy, great powers rivalry and geopolitical races, just as the region had been for hundreds of years. Up until the USA conquered Cuba and Puerto Rico in 1898, the Spaniards last entrenchment in The New World, imposing its hegemony over the Caribbean. By 2000 – nearly two hundred years after Bolívar's failed attempt – Chávez decided to make a new push to link the Caribbean to South America and its continental unification project.

With his usual sense of historical parallels, Chávez ceremoniously declared that the time had come to incorporate the Caribbean into the Latin American community, just as Bolívar had imagined. His plan was this: Chávez knew that many of the Caribbean states could not chance a close political alliance with Caracas. Not only were they too small for that, but their fear of a US backlash was too great. They remembered what happened in Grenada and the Dominican Republic, and in Jamaica where the USA went in heavy as punishment for its rapprochement with Cuba, and finally Haiti, where President Aristide was toppled as recently as 2004. The fleet which set off from Venezuela's Caribbean coastline however, was not loaded with soldiers or ideology, but with oil. Chávez made the Caribbean governments an offer they could not refuse: PetroCaribe – an alliance not dominated by ideology but one to supply oil at favourable rates. Participating countries would pay up to forty dollars a barrel, but every dollar above that was put on credit, with an interest-free deferment of up to twenty-five years available. Alternatively, the oil could be exchanged for products, without any money changing hands.

One after the other, the Caribbean leaders arrived at Simón Bolívar International Airport in Venezuela. Chávez welcomed them with military parades, salutes, and flashes from the cameras of the state broadcaster. A military greeting from Chávez, followed by a firm thump on the shoulder or a hug; then a few words about Simón Bolívar and how important the Caribbean was and is for the independence of Latin America. Then on to important matters. Chávez never asked which party the leaders of these island states belonged to or which ideology they followed. The important questions were: 'How can we help you, how much oil do you need?' Many of these leaders seldom travelled much further than the neighbouring islands, occasionally to the capitals of their former colonial masters and every few years to an international summit. When on rare occasions they met foreign colleagues from outside the region, they were used to having to spell out the name of their country and explain where it was. For them, the attention they received from Chávez must have been quite overwhelming.

For his part, the Venezuelan president made no attempt to conceal his strategy: He wanted Venezuela to be the motor for the new independence project. Fuel was needed to get the rest of the region on board. For five hundred years, the resources of Latin America had been used to build up the fortunes of the European royalty, oil the wheels of the Industrial Revolution, and later allowed oligarchs and foreign firms to accumulate massive fortunes. As God had been generous enough to store two hundred million barrels of oil in the Orinoco region, safely hidden from the colonial bloodsuckers, Chávez believed it was his historical responsibility to wield this resource gift as a means to liberate Venezuela and Latin America from the dominance of foreign superpowers and companies, so that the region and its people would finally control their own fate. The only formal commitment the member countries had to make was to ensure that the money freed up by the favourable payment terms went to the good of the people.

DISTRIBUTING THE OIL BOOM

The 2006 Election

Early in 2006, with the presidential election set for 3 December, Chávez had less than one year of his mandate remaining.

The eyes of the world were already on Venezuela. The controversial paratrooper who had stuck it out in Miraflores since 1999 had no intention of stepping down and launched his candidacy with the support of the governing parties MVR, PPT, PODEMOS and PCV, the communist party. It would be the eighth time Venezuelans went to the ballot box since Chávez rose to power. The question the world now asked, was whether the president would spend another six years in power.

Within the Chávez government however, an entirely different question was considered.

It had only been a year since a united opposition chose to boycott elections for the National Assembly in 2005 based on claims of electoral fraud. The Carter Center, the Organisation of American States (OAS) and observers from the EU had all dismissed the accusations of fraud directed at the electoral commission following the 2004 referendum had been dismissed as groundless. But the opposition and the media continued to claim that Chávez had carried out some kind of 'electronic raid,' stealing millions of votes through his 'marionettes' at the electoral commission, hence swindling their way to power against the will of the people. Only a year earlier the opposition had boycotted the parliamentary elections with similar claims of alleged fraud. The opposition had demanded that the digital fingerprint machines, which prevented voting multiple times using false identity cards, be removed from polling stations, despite external observers offering their assurances that the fingerprints could in no way be traced to individual voters. To encourage the opposition to participate, the electoral commission yielded to their demand, despite it being contrary to electoral law. However the opposition leadership still decided to withdraw from the election. The OAS, at the time led by Cesar Gaviria, the liberal, US-backed former president of Colombia, stated that in retrospect, the opposition's demand regarding the voting machines and its decision to boycott the election were both incomprehensible.

Chávez however, understood perfectly well what was at play. Through dubious opinion polls and analyses, for years the media had created a false perception of reality amongst the opposition, leading them to believe that Chávez was so unpopular that he would be toppled at any moment. This was an effective method of getting opposition supporters to participate in extreme measures such as violent demonstrations, as well as supplying much-needed motivation for the signature campaign and the referendum in 2004. But after this defeat, the opposition was struck by the downside of their propaganda: the enormous expectations they had created made people's shock at the election result even greater. The ensuing regional elections were a disaster. The opposition lost the key states of Miranda and Táchira to Chavez allies, as well as key metropolitan districts like Greater Caracas and Maracaibo.

With opinion polls in free fall and the campaign machinery weakened by frustrated activists, demotivated by defeat after defeat, the opposition knew the ruling alliance would win an absolute majority in the National Assembly. Since 1998 the opposition had concentrated all of its political activity around one goal – removing Chávez as quickly as possible – there was no sense participating in an election where they were doomed to fail.[*]

An election boycott based on accusations of fraud combined with violent riots, however, would serve to weaken Chávez' image internationally and could even be a pretext for intervention by US

---

[*] For many years the Venezuelan opposition consistently maintained the logic that voter turnout and recognition of the people's votes was only expedient if they won the election. In the past, opposition parties represented in parliament were not fundamental supporters of democracy. The fact that none of the parties offered any protest about the 2002 coup was a clear indication of this.

and conservative Latin American governments. Up to that point, it had been relatively easy to get the international media to publish fierce criticism of Chávez. Thus, the opposition had good reason to assume that the facts about the highly secure electoral system, and the international observers would not stand in the way of a good story about a battle for freedom and democracy against the power-hungry Chávez regime. But neither the accusations of fraud which followed the referendum in 2004 nor the election boycott in 2005 provoked the reaction the opposition had hoped for. The complete lack of evidence for their accusations was one factor. But perhaps even more important was the fact that Chávez no longer appeared as vulnerable domestically, enjoying strong support from the army and from the people. To organise a successful intervention against Chávez under such circumstances was simply too difficult and too risky.

The government could not take for granted that the opposition would participate in a presidential election they knew they were likely to lose. The question was whether the opposition had a plan B and whether it would be violent.

However on this occasion, the opposition chose to participate in the election. That decision surprised both Chavistas and anti-Chavistas.

The umbrella organisation Coordinadora Democrática (CD) announced that a decision as to who would take on Chávez would be made at a grass roots level through internal elections. The candidates were: Julio Borges from the right-wing party, Primero Justicia; the newspaper editor Teodoro Petkoff, a former communist turned neoliberal finance minister in the nineties; and the governor of the oil state of Zulia, Manuel Rosales. However the internal election was later cancelled in favour of closed proceedings, with Governor Rosales emerging victorious.

Backed by the largest state budget in Venezuela, Manuel Rosales was the one candidate who had enough personal resources to invest in the election campaign. Cancelling the open vote was likely motivated by a desire to use opposition resources on the presidential election, not on a three-way internal battle.

Rosales had another advantage: He was light-skinned, but not white. He looked more like the average Venezuelan, not an upper class snob. This was the first time a strategy of appealing to the poor majority was implemented in a coherent way with the full weight of the opposition's political machinery behind him. The Rosales campaign was radically different than anything I had ever seen from the opposition (including the 2004 referendum, local and regional elections that same year, and elections for the national assembly in 2005.)

Right-wing strategists had spent a long time concentrating their efforts on radicalising the middle-class opposition to Chávez. Merely convincing them that the opposition had better policies than Chávez was no longer enough to motivate a few hundred thousand affluent people with a lot to lose to risk their lives in a protest to topple the elected government. For people to go to such lengths they had to be driven by hate and panic. The opposition achieved this by resorting to classic anti-communist fear propaganda. 'Chávez is going to take your car, your home, even your children.' Soon they were going to impose a ban on bikinis, claimed one of the many spam emails I received at the time. But if the opposition wanted to return to power through democratic means, this strategy was no longer useful. The election statistics and demographics were merciless: Even with a runaway majority amongst the upper and middle class, it was impossible to defeat Chávez without gaining the votes of at least two million voters from the lower class who still made up the majority of the population. This meant the opposition was faced with what was fundamentally a political dilemma: It would be impossible to find two million poor Venezuelans who wanted a return to market liberalism, who were terrified that Chávez would implement radical reforms, or who were losing sleep over fears the government would expropriate their private property. Fears like these had made the middle class take to the streets, yet were practically non-existent amongst the lower class. If there was any dissatisfaction amongst the poor voters that the opposition needed to win over, it was due to the exact opposite – that the promises of redistribution had not gone far enough. It had been two years since Chávez launched *las misiones* and there were still districts and villages where the social programmes had not been implemented. Unemployment figures were beginning to improve but those who were still without work were not happy. They were the voters the opposition needed to reach.

The campaign strategists for Rosales knew that they could not have their cake and eat it too, so they were forced to change tack. They decided to completely abandon the propaganda of fear. No more attacking the government's welfare projects by labelling them 'communist' or anything else that could make the voters suspect that Rosales would reverse Chávez' social policies if he won the elections. Another striking change was an end to accusations that CNE was merely a tool for electoral fraud that had given Chávez' dictatorship a veneer of democracy. Rosales instead asked people to vote for him, and disregard any fears of having their votes stolen or being registered and punished by the government.

This change of course could easily have caused the opposition some trouble. All it would take is for someone to ask how the opposition could justify a military coup, an election boycott or encouraging international sanctions against Venezuela, now that it openly acknowledged that the country's electoral system did not allow for any fraud, implying that previous accusations were false. But neither the Venezuelan nor the international media were in the habit of asking critical questions of the Venezuelan right-wing. This question was never asked.

This allowed Rosales to concentrate on the main theme of his new strategy: attempt to weaken Chávez' core vote by openly courting the poor.

A number of opposition leaders admitted for the first time that previous governments formed by their parties or their coalition partners, had ignored the issue of poverty. Teodoro Petkoff, a former presidential candidate for the opposition, went as far as acknowledging that Chávez had given the poor a voice and had moved social issues higher up the agenda. Even previous arguments that the government's social programmes were wasteful and vulgar populism were abandoned. Rosales did his best to avoid discussing *las misiones* but when forced to answer a direct question during an interview on state TV, he promised that they would not be stopped.

Rosales staked everything on two concrete promises: to stop the shipment of 'oil gifts' to allied nations in Latin America, and to transfer profits from the oil industry directly into the accounts of Venezuelan families.

By 2006, Bolivia and Nicaragua had joined the growing camp of left-wing governments in Latin American. In Bolivia, the socialist coca leaf farmer Evo Morales was elected in 2005. In Nicaragua, the former guerrilla turned president Daniel Ortega walked away with another victory. Chávez immediately offered his assistance, offering oil in exchange for commodities from the two countries. Venezuela would also send aid to alleviate emergency situations in the two countries, which were both far poorer than Venezuela. Cuba continued sending teachers, health care workers and athletic trainers to Venezuela in exchange for an increasing flow of oil, up to a maximum of one hundred thousand barrels a day. In addition, Chávez launched PetroCaribe, extending a helping hand to the Caribbean island sates whose vulnerable economies struggled to cope with rising oil prices.

According to Manuel Rosales, these were gifts, pure and simple, money which rightly belonged to the Venezuelan people.

Newspapers and TV channels showed images of impressive, newly-constructed housing estates in Cuba, supposedly paid for with Venezuelan money. 'While Chávez gives away our money to build homes in Cuba, the Venezuelan people live in shanties,' the opposition candidate stated. Rosales was able to create some indignation, selling himself to the poor as a genuine patriot. The opposition really was in desperate need of a little patriotism, as for many years, the US flag was the one most often seen at anti-Chavista demonstrations.

With Rosales in government, the money from the oil industry would no longer go to Cuba or poor countries, but directly into people's bank accounts. This was Rosales' most important election promise: Twenty per cent of the profits from the sale of oil would be deposited into the accounts of every family at the end of each month. 'This would amount to one million Bolivars every month,' Rosales said, the equivalent of well over 300 USD and more than the monthly minimum wage at that time. The opposition candidate launched his scheme with a special bank card he called *mi negra*, 'my black.'

His political advisors had come up the idea and the bank cards were developed with the assistance of the banking and finance sectors.

One month before the election, Rosales declared that he had distributed the black bank card to 2.5 million poor Venezuelan families. Many of them were former Chavistas, he claimed.

Now all they had to do was vote for Rosales and the money would start rolling in. Tax-free, automatic deposits every month, no effort needed by any of the recipients.

Faced with this rhetorical about-turn by the opposition, one that finally synchronized its electoral strategy with the expectations of the poor majority, it was even more surprising that Chávez made socialism the key plank of his election campaign. Until that point, Chávez had largely focussed on concrete reforms in his election battles. The president knew what the people wanted. He had a flair for the pragmatic. Why did he now believe that an abstract message like ideology – one that according to opinion polls, the people were highly sceptical of, even affirmed Chavistas – could compete with Rosales' black credit card and the promise of oil money paid directly into their bank accounts? Or as the opposition media framed it with their attempt at populist rhetoric: 'Socialism? How do you eat that?' There was also the unavoidable issue of voter fatigue, no matter how well the government performed. At such a moment, an ideological shift to the left, substituting pragmatist electoral promises for ideology, right before the presidential election seemed like an overtly risky, almost inopportune step by Chávez, with Rosales now staking everything on seducing the poor.

Still, Chávez coasted to victory with sixty-three per cent of the votes, increasing his support from 4.6 million votes to 7.3 million.

To the surprise of Chavistas and anti-Chavistas alike, the main opposition leaders, including Manuel Rosales and Teodoro Petkoff, the former candidate who withdrew in favour of Rosales, acknowledged the election results shortly after CNE made them official.

The media were more reluctant. Carla Angola from Globovisión, one of Venezuela's most famous TV journalists, was shocked and indignant and attacked Petkoff during an interview for simply accepting that Chávez would continue in power for years. She was given her due by the veteran politician: 'Do you want us to demand another military coup?' he asked and hinted that the credibility of the media and the opposition would suffer needlessly if they openly refused to accept the will of the people.

The 2006 presidential election was probably the point when the opposition and the rest of Chávez' opponents began to realise that they were not facing just any charismatic leader who came to power because of unfortunate historical circumstances – but an incredibly shrewd election strategist.

The candidate the opposition had selected, Manuel Rosales, was neither politically nor economically an heir presumptive, one who had been handed power or paid his way to the top of the right-wing leadership, but a man who had shown enough nose, guts and elbows for politics to forge a career from the bottom up.

However in the final run-up to the election, he committed two serious errors. The first one occurred during an interview by a TV station in Miami, the capital of the ultra-conservative Latin American upper class. Perhaps sensing that he was on home turf got the better of Rosales as he completely abandoned his election strategy of appealing to the poor and blurted out an eye-popping statement: 'Chávez has only 33per cent support. They are parasites who live off the government and are subsidised by the state.' It was like there was a flashing sign in front of him telling him to 'party like it's 2002' – back when opposition politicians competed over who could make the most derogatory statements about the poor.

His other big mistake was committed as he was recorded exchanging cheek kisses with an older black woman. For Chávez and poor Venezuelans, this was an everyday interaction. However Rosales revealed how uncomfortable he was with that kind of close contact, when he wiped his face with an anti-septic wipe just after the hug – with the camera still rolling. This quickly became a Kodak moment and inspired hundreds of satirical sketches on the state-owned TV channel about the extreme trials 'the oligarchy's minions' had to go through to pretend they did not look down on the poor.

But the 2006 election was not won or lost on election strategies or opposition blunders.

Instead, the story of Chávez' historic landslide victory that year should actually begin in the deserts of the Middle East in the early noughties, when Hugo Chávez made his controversial trip to visit the world's leading oil exporters.

The Resurrection of OPEC

Chávez' presidential tour in 2000 was not his first overseas trip. However it did give notice of the Venezuelan president's unique ability to provoke the media, transnational companies and state leaders all over the world, in particular, Washington.

This time he managed to provoke a reaction even before his departure. A press release detailing his itinerary was enough to set them off. The president would be visiting the ten nations of the Organisation of the Petroleum Exporting States (OPEC).

When OPEC was founded in 1973, its members – all Third World oil exporting countries – managed to increase the oil price to over thirty dollars per barrel by limiting supply. But in the 1980s, prices went downhill, taking the organisation with it. It was a vicious circle. The oil exporters attempted to compensate for falling oil prices by increasing production, which led not only to lower prices but also quickening the depletion of their oil reserves.

As long as one exporting nation believed that the other would simply increase production, none of them were willing to take on the cost of reducing production, particularly not when prices were so low. In 2000, the price of oil was under twenty dollars per barrel. OPEC was an empty shell lacking any ability to exert influence.

Chávez now wanted to resurrect the market power of OPEC. It was a formidable task. Not only was OPEC unable to agree on oil policies. Member countries were also divided along political and religious lines, with a number of them in open conflict to achieve dominance in the Middle East. Two of its most important members, Iran and Iraq, had spent most of the eighties at war.

Chávez' first stop was to meet Mohammed Khatami, the Iranian president and the country's first reformer since the Islamic Revolution in 1979. The two must have hit it off, as the meeting laid the groundwork for industrial and technological exchanges which went far beyond oil.

From there Chávez set course for Iraq, a country which the USA had subjected to an extreme regime of UN sanctions, imposed because of Saddam Hussein's alleged weapons of mass destruction. One of the sanctions created a no-fly zone. The US government had given itself the authority to shoot down any military or civilian aircraft entering Iraqi airspace. The only way for Chávez to get there was by car. Crossing the border region was already difficult enough in an area of vast mountains and deserts. On top of that, following the wars in the 1980s which had taken the lives of half a million people, the two warring nations had only officially agreed to a ceasefire. Both sides held war prisoners, and there was still tension along the border.

When the Iraqi dictator invaded Iran in the eighties, Saddam Hussein had the support of the USA. Now he was their enemy. The mere idea of travelling to Iraq was enough to invoke the anger of the American government.

Before Chávez had even set out on the strenuous car journey, he received the following message from the US State Department: 'We believe it is a dubious distinction to be the first democratically elected president to visit the Iraqi dictator.' An American Middle East expert who was quoted by a number of media stated: 'I think he was looking for a chance to spit in the face of the USA.' The US State Department also advised Chávez how to act during his visit: 'During any meeting with Iraqi civil servants we expect Venezuelan officials to explain to them the basis of [our] confrontation with Iraq.'

Chávez' response was brief: 'What am I supposed to do if it upsets the Americans? We have our dignity, and Venezuela is an independent nation.' Years earlier, when the US Secretary of State, Madeleine Albright was confronted with claims that the UN sanctions imposed by the USA had caused the deaths of 'more children than those killed [by the US atomic bomb] in Hiroshima.' Albright replied, 'It's worth it.'

Chávez made it very clear that he had not travelled through mountains and deserts to justify US allegations or the deadly sanctions against Iraq. He was in Iraq to talk oil.

Venezuelan and Iraq are two of the founding members of OPEC, formed nearly forty years earlier. Chávez was willing to do just about anything to make OPEC an effective organisation again, even if it meant provoking more anger in an already hostile Washington, including getting the two former enemies, Iraq and Iran, to agree on a joint oil policy.

The Americans had reason to be upset with Chávez. Breaching the sanctions regime imposed on Iraq could lead to other nations doing the same, and it made for a disruptive element in their preparations for invasion. The theme of the talks made it even worse. If Chávez succeeded in resurrecting OPEC and contributing to increasing oil prices, as the world's largest importer of oil at that time, the USA would be most affected. What's more, with a revitalised OPEC, Iraq's stated aim of discarding the American dollar as the unit of currency for oil exports could also be taken up by other member countries.

From Iraq, Chávez continued his journey to the rest of the OPEC countries. They too were divided along political and religious fault lines, between Islamic monarchies and secular republics, and between populations of Shia Muslims, Sunni Muslims and Christians. The message from Venezuela was the same everywhere: you all have a shared interest in working together to achieve greater national control over their oil reserves and achieving a higher oil price. Chávez had also made them an offer none of them could refuse. He promised to end plans by the previous government to increase oil production in Venezuela from three million barrels a day to over ten million, if the rest of OPEC agreed to decrease output.

Chávez later announced that in September that year (2000), Caracas would host OPEC's first summit of heads of state since the glory days of the seventies. The OPEC leaders had not met in twenty-five years, but now they agreed to take the first step towards re-establishing discipline and confidence in maintaining production quotas. Aided by increasing demand from the rising economic might of China, oil prices began to rise.

One summer's day in 2006 – six years after the historic OPEC meeting in Caracas – with Chávez and Rosales competing for the hearts and minds of Venezuelan voters, I was queuing up to buy ice cream at the exclusive Sambil shopping centre in Caracas.

I had not been to a shopping centre or indulged in anything other than *arepa* or other typical Venezuelan fare for a while, and the Italian ice cream I remembered buying at the same shopping complex four years earlier was burnt into my mind. However, something was different.

When I went to Sambil for the first time in 2002, there were hardly any poor or dark-skinned people there, apart from the security guards and the people serving fast food, cleaning and clearing tables. However in 2006, the *barrio* was represented on both sides of the exclusive ice cream counter. Sporting new trainers and mobile phones and with a big splash of perfume just for the occasion, they waited impatiently for the delights which previously, people of their social class had mostly only served to others.

So great was the influx of people from the slums, some of my friends from the upper middle class began shunning Sambil. 'It's full of *chusma*,' a former classmate despaired, using another derogatory term for poor people. Luckily for them a new, more expensive and even more exclusive shopping centre soon opened in the same district. There was no public transport there, making it outside the reach – for the time being – of the new moneyed (calling them nouveau riche might be laying it on too thick) dregs from the *barrios*.

As I devoured my ice cream on this day in 2006 outside the shopping centre, I noticed that the traffic was at a complete standstill. There were far more traffic jams now, and they had grown worse over the past few years. I heard someone cursing about Chávez. The main reason for all the traffic was of course that more people were able to afford cars. Cámara Automotriz de Venezuela (CAVANEZ), the Venezuelan Automotive Union, reported that between 2004 and 2005, car sales increased by seventy per cent in a single year. In 2006 nearly three hundred thousand new cars were sold. Observing the cars in the four lanes outside Sambil, not only were there more of them, but they were very different to the ones I had seen in 2002, with far fewer rusting American boats from the seventies and eighties and an impressive number of towering new SUVs beginning to dominate the streetscape.

What I noticed in the streets and at the shopping centre was the fruit of favourable changes in the oil market combined with a long-term strategic process which Chávez had set in motion when he criss-crossed the Middle East deserts six years earlier – a process which was about to derail the well-organised populist campaign being run by Rosales and the opposition. A higher oil price was responsible for much of the rapidly increasing prosperity in Venezuela. And even though China's growing energy needs played a strong part, the renewed ability of OPEC to limit supply was an important reason for the rise in the world oil price. First it rose above the thirty dollar peak achieved during the oil crisis in the seventies, to then rise above the historic level of fifty dollars a barrel. In 2006, the price of oil was well on its way to the hundred dollar mark.

In Venezuela GNP rose faster than ever, by nineteen per cent in 2004, and by ten per cent in 2005 and in 2006. According to the World Bank, this made Venezuela one of the fastest growing economies in the world and the fastest growing economy in Latin America. Higher oil prices had ignited the boom, but growth had still increased by 11.4 per cent in sectors of the economy unrelated to the oil industry. In 2006 currency reserves reached an all-time high of thirty-seven billion dollars. Unemployment had decreased from sixteen per cent in 1999 to eight per cent in 2006. The minimum wage had risen from 183 dollars a month in 1999 to 238 dollars in 2006.[*]

Although the country was growing richer, the slums did not simply disappear.

---

[*] The reason the figure is presented in dollars is so that salary growth is not swallowed up by price rises as a result of the devaluation of Venezuelan currency. Hence the salary growth in dollars reflects an increased buying power.

There were accusations that Chávez had been hugely ineffective in getting anyone out of the *barrio* (while some may have left, others moved in). These claims were repeated on a daily basis by the Venezuelan and international media – as proof that the revolution was a fiasco.

But for anyone who was interested, finding tangible proof that the slums were no longer the same, was not difficult.

With people swapping their leaking corrugated iron roofs for new ones, the colour of Omaira's *barrio* began to change, from rusty-brown to silvery-grey. It could mean the difference between a house filled with rainwater and damp, destroying the floors and walls and leading to rodents, insects, bacteria and illness, and a house with proper hygiene. Many homes were freshly painted. Some homes were extended – horizontally where possible, vertically if not, so at the very least, each family had a separate room. Omaira built a new kitchen and bathroom.

Traffic in the *barrio* also increased. The narrow street outside Omaira's home had been wide enough a few years earlier, when traffic was so scarce that two cars rarely met. Now cars were constantly having to stop, with noisy negotiations and excited gesticulations as drivers tried to agree on who should yield. The car park in 23 de Enero, a few hundred meters above Omaira's home where I often visited friends, was usually full. Mostly with old American cars, but luxury SUVs and other new cars had become an increasingly common sight. My girlfriend, who worked at a casino and lived in the *barrio* a little further west, had bought a brand-new Chevrolet.

Children raced in and out of the houses – still poor but better dressed. They had better food and more of it. People who previously went through periods where they had little more than boiled cornmeal or rice with margarine and maybe a bit of salted cheese (in hot countries, salt is a way of preserving the cheese, and adding only a few grams of cheese gives a bit of flavour, meaning the food does not taste like cotton) could now afford meat, chicken, beans and vegetables. As caloric intake increased, malnourishment decreased.

Fast-food outlets were popping up everywhere: KFC, McDonalds, Burger King and Venezuela's only successful fast-food chain, Pollos Arturo's were increasing both in number and in reported profits.

Mobile phones were another booming industry. I noticed that the curiosity Venezuelans had previously shown for my rather basic mobile phone now gave way to patronising smiles. From 2005, most of the people I knew, whether poor or rich, had newer or better mobile phones than me. 'Jeez man, you can't walk round with that crap,' a friend admonished me. With the best intentions. 'You won't get any ladies with that phone,' he said shaking his head resignedly.

The guys in the *barrio* started buying mopeds. Silicone breast implants, insanely popular in Venezuela, but previously reserved for the rich, became a more and more common sight, also for women from the lower and middle class. And they kept getting larger. Faced with competition from the girls in the *barrio*, the rich upgraded theirs from 300 grams to 400 or 450 grams.

Spiralling upwards, buying power also increased the demand for more manpower. The first time I flipped through the want ads in Últimas Noticias in 2003, the *vacancy* section usually only had two or three posts. Now it was several pages long, often with hundreds of job offers.

My friend Antonio struggled to find seamstresses for his wife's small design company he financed with the surplus from his main business, so he asked me to find someone in the *barrio* where I lived. It was a sign of the times that none of the people I asked were interested: Either they already had a job, or they were full-time students.

With the Venezuelan government making regular, hefty increases to the minimum wage, it was now the second highest in Latin America. Farmers and fishers received interest-free loans, cheap tractors and fishing boats. Poor unemployed people in the cities and villages started cooperatives for the small-scale production of goods and services. The Metro in Caracas added new lines. Large-scale infrastructure projects such as train and Metro lines were undertaken to link up surrounding cities and villages with the capital.

The media did not report all of these changes, either before, during or after the election.

But it was in the economic and social spheres, not the rhetorical duels between Chávez and Rosales, where the presidential election of 2006 was decided.

But the question was, would it last. The dark clouds on the horizon were barely noticed, with the airwaves simultaneously dominated by politically motivated denials of increased prosperity and talk of booming oil prices driving economic growth figures and consumption. One of the encroaching dangers was an old enemy of the oil-dependent Venezuelan economy: inflation. At its worst point in the nineties, it reached over one hundred per cent. For the time being, inflation was still increasing slower than wages. But between 2005 and 2006, inflation rose from fourteen to seventeen per cent, and the government's economic policies gave no indication that it would stop rising.

Economic redistribution can be a risky sport, when not accompanied by increased productivity: for every extra Bolívar [the unit of Venezuelan currency] to land in the pockets of the poor, a high percentage was spent on consumption, as by definition, the poor have more unsatisfied needs. This is in contrast to the rich, who put a relatively large share of their wage increases in savings (often in US dollars in foreign banks).

The problem was structural: the production of goods and services was increasing slower than demand and prices were driven mercilessly upwards. Equally unnoticed – at least by most people – and perhaps equally worrying, were the decreasing water levels of the country's hydroelectric dams that started to occur as the economy grew. The massive Guri Dam facility, once one of the largest hydroelectric power plants in the world, supplies both Venezuelan heavy industry and the population with a sufficient amount of kilowatts. But income equalisation and the consumer boom affected the energy arithmetic: Poor Venezuelans bought fridges, freezers, fans and DVD players (most already had TVs); the middle class bought microwaves and computers; the upper class bought electric garage door openers. You could no longer find a home without a mobile phone charger in the wall socket, there were an increasing number of private and public businesses, new shopping centres, cinemas and night clubs purchasing air-conditioning units, while new electric machinery for industry and agriculture was constantly on full blast. While electricity usage increased more rapidly with every new electrical item, energy production stood still. In 2006, the rainy season still managed to fill the power stores but the water levels reached a new low for each year that passed.

Some opinion polls gave Chávez over seventy per cent backing in the months following the election. But inflation, the threat of food shortages and power outages always evoked gloomy associations in Latin America. And in the Venezuelan case, these problems were looming on the horizon, even with the price of oil close to one hundred dollars a barrel. While there were isolated voices, many of them neoliberal economists, warning of the dangers of an economy dependent on such a high oil price, the government was confident that peak oil theory, whereby oil steadily grows more scarce and more costly to extract, meant there was no possibility of prices decreasing. In addition to all of this, time was against Chávez. Fewer and fewer people remembered the events of *el Caracazo*, being forced to eat dog food, and the general degradation people suffered in the time before Chávez, and the memories were growing more distant. Confronted by new issues in society, simply blaming the bickering opposition for their policies during the fourth republic – back when everything had been far worse – became more difficult year by year.

Optimists from the opposition, the brightest of them, already recognised the scent of an impending collapse.

Would Chávez and his strategists recognise the danger signs in time, or was the Bolivarian revolution headed for the precipice?

TAKING ON
BIG OIL

A Letter for *el Comandante*

Like most powerful people in international politics, Hugo Chávez also has a family.

The first family members to join Hugo on the national political stage – with the same distinctive narrow eyes, strong nose and copper-brown skin – were his brother Adán Chávez and his father Hugo de los Reyes Chávez. The elder Hugo became an important political figure in the Barinas plains during his later years, while the president's older brother Adán was an active communist. Chávez' second wife, Marisabel Rodríguez, a journalist who later became a parliamentarian before the two divorced – was now in open political conflict with her ex-husband. After the military coup in 2002, his daughter, María Gabriela Chávez, began appearing with the president at official events.

In 2006 a series of coincidences led to us meeting.

The lecture theatre, though it looked like a normal classroom, was full.

There must have been thirty students in the room, laughing, joking and shouting to each other. Not in English, the language the lecture was supposed to be taught in, but in Spanish, or *Caraqueño* – more specifically the *Caraqueño* spoken by the poor people in the slums and in the west of the city.

Motorcycle helmets, make-up, and a few pens and notepads covered the desks. The atmosphere inside the lecture hall was a stark contrast to the streamlined exterior of the building, where the bright-blue sky reflected off twenty stories of glass. This was La Universidad Bolivariana de Venezuela (UBV), the university Chávez had established at the former PDVSA headquarters, so that poor Venezuelans would have access to higher education.

None of the students in front of me looked very interested in ending the chatter to listen to me. But I had no choice. A young Spaniard employed by the university, Iñaki Gutiérrez, had thrown me into the deep end, when he introduced me to the students, not as a guest as I had expected – but as a guest lecturer in English. 'An expert with a perfect British accent,' was how he put it.

Gutiérrez was a law professor who studied in a number of European countries and in New York. For a time he worked as a human rights advocate in the Caracas slums, but now he taught Law and English at the Faculty of Law at the Bolivarian university. He was what the Venezuelan and American media usually referred to as a 'revolutionary tourist.' I had expected to meet a lot of them in Chávez' Venezuela: young radicals and hippies from the US and Europe with dreads, Che Guevara T-shirts and a desire to finally be part of a more concrete version of the slogan 'Another World is Possible.' But until recently, I had been under the impression that these potential revolutionary tourists were still not aware of Chávez. In any case, I had not seen a single one during my first few years in Venezuela. But by 2006, they had begun to arrive. You would run into them at alternative clubs and bars; places where there was less salsa and merengue and more reggae and rock, less make-up and plunging necklines and more ripped jeans and Converse trainers. They were also at some of the pro-Chávez demonstrations.

And at the Bolivarian University, there was also a French girl, a Scot and an Argentinian on staff.

In addition to these anonymous international idealists, there was also a popular American-born lawyer with Venezuelan roots by the name of Eva Golinger. In fluent Venezuelan Spanish, intermingled with the distinctive American 'r', she shared what she uncovered after sifting through hundreds of CIA and US State Department documents relating to Venezuela, made public through the Freedom of Information Act.[*] Many of the revelations, which reveal US support for the military coup in 2002, and their continued financing of groups in Venezuela which participated in the coup, she

---

[*] A law in the US providing access to official documents which previously had been wholly or partially declared secret.

publicised in her best-selling political book from 2005, *The Chávez Code*. Poor students from other Latin American countries, lured to Venezuela by the offer of free university education, were also a normal sight. In addition to the Bolivarian university, Chávez, with Cuban assistance, had built one of Latin America's largest international universities for medical studies. The students came to Caracas from all over Latin America, as well as from a few African countries, where medical studies were practically inaccessible for those without rich parents, to then return home as doctors and born-again Chavistas.

As a representative of this new internationalisation of the Venezuelan project, Gutiérrez was an intriguing person in himself.

But the main reason I had come to the Universidad Bolivariana de Venezuela, was to see Chávez' university flagship from the inside. Before the English lecture, Gutiérrez had told me the story of Venezuela's 'educational revolution' as we hurried through the university corridors. He told me all about the new options, which as well as law, ranged from petroleum engineering to medicine, public administration, pedagogy, architecture and political economy.

There was a striking difference between the students here and those I had seen when I walked around the campus at Venezuela's largest university, UCV, only a stone's throw away.

At UCV, the young students were usually easy to distinguish from the professors in their suits. In the crowded corridors of the Bolivarian university, it was far more difficult. Many of the students were older than the lecturers, some over sixty. Many of the lecturers were young idealists who wore jeans and T-shirts and who had just completed their degrees. And then there was their skin colour. Venezuela has not had any official racial segregation since the colonial period. Both at UCV and UBV, the entire spectrum of Venezuelan skin colours was present, from dark-brown, like in the West African countries where America's slaves were taken from, to my own colour. But the average student at UBV was strikingly darker than at UCV. The reason was simple, as Gutiérrez explained: 'In Venezuela, class and skin colour go hand in hand. Public and private universities almost exclusively admit upper and middle class students. The poorer half of the population are excluded and have long made up less than ten per cent of the student population at these universities.'

Chávez made many efforts to get UCV, the largest public university in Venezuela, to enrol more applicants from poor backgrounds. Like at other public institutions though, deep-rooted power structures and conservative bureaucracies often obstruct change of any kind. Despite large subsidies from the public purse – said to be the size of the Dominican Republic's entire state budget – neither UCV nor any other large public university would agree to any reform that ended the quasi monopoly the privileged elites had on higher education. The argument from the UCV chancellor Antonio Paris, an active Chávez opponent, was that there were no more places for students at the university, and that the government's request would negatively affect their merit-based entry system. According to Gutiérrez, UCV's system was anything but merit-based. Privately-schooled students were heavily favoured. Many former, current and rejected applicants have also described the corruption – where those with money were able to buy themselves a place at the university. In any case, the leadership of UCV and ULA, the two largest public universities in Venezuela, thwarted the government's attempt to open the sector up to poor students, successfully wielding the constitutional guarantee of academic independence.

With that, Chávez did what he so often did when met with similar obstacles within the state apparatus: He allowed the old institutions to remain, and instead of making any controversial interventions, he founded brand-new parallel institutions. UBV was founded from the bottom up, a collaboration between left-wing intellectuals and trade unions, again with Cuban support, and financed by the oil industry.

In 2003, Chávez issued the decree that founded La Universidad Bolivariana de Venezuela. Other locations would soon appear in several large cities in Venezuela, as a part of *Misión Sucre*, named after Antonio José de Sucre, one of Simón Bolívar's most trusted generals. The university is made up of smaller units of higher education, satellites designed to serve the educational needs of the country's poor. In 2006, the number of *Aldeas Universitarias* was approaching five hundred locations in small towns and villages throughout the country. Through *Misión Sucre*, the poor village population was able to gain access to higher education where they lived.* Upwards of five hundred thousand registered students indicated that demand was high. With *Misión Sucre* and six new universities, the number of Venezuelans in higher education increased from 370 000 to 1.12 million in 2006 – more than tripling the number of students.

'The Bolivarian revolution is about giving people the tools to free themselves, to exercise power and create a modern, functioning and representative government. Education is a fundamental part of that,' Gutiérrez said gravely – he sounded practically devoted – convinced that he was part of something big.

In the lecture hall he displayed his more humorous side, when he introduced me to the students as a guest lecturer.

My thoughts shifted between Gutiérrez' words and the boisterous students in front of me.

Poor Venezuelans were not used to being in classrooms. Growing up poor in Venezuela, with lots of TV and little homework, resulted in extremely limited patience and difficulty focussing on one person or subject for more than a few minutes. Few were aware of the social codes and norms of behaviour at an institute of higher education. On the other hand, many of them

---

* At times, the Venezuelan state has been largely absent from the villages. For Chávez' nation-building project, it was fundamental to take public services to the peripheries. Only in that way could the depopulation of rural areas and overpopulation in the urban areas be stopped or at least slowed.

knew exactly what they needed to do to get by in the slums. There it was a matter of acting tough so that you did not get pushed around. Don't be nice without a reason, as in some situations that can be interpreted as a sign of weakness; speak loudly and do not wait for your turn if you want to be heard – if you don't interrupt people, they'll interrupt you – highly effective behaviour in the *barrios* but not exactly conducive to an ideal learning atmosphere at university. I got the impression that the students were weighing me up to see whether I was someone they should listen to or not. The obvious solution in that kind of situation was to be firm and establish my authority.

But there was something I had to take into consideration: one of the students was Hugo Chávez' daughter.

When Gutierrez told me, I thought it was a joke at first. Children of Latin American presidents studied in the USA or Europe – not in their own country, certainly not at a public university, and never at a newly-established public university filled with poor people from the slums. Even Latin America's communist guerrilla leaders preferred to send their children to Harvard, Oxford or Madrid. But somewhere in front of me was María Gabriela Chávez. Gutierrez had not pointed her out to me. But of all the female students, one stood out. She had light-brown skin, her facial features had the usual Venezuelan mix of European, African and indigenous features, but there was something about her narrow eyes and the natural authority she exhibited when interacting with the other students that gave her away.

My English lecture went well. I managed to strike a balance between being authoritative and cheerful. The students were surprisingly receptive and showed me the positive side of coming from the *barrios*: gratefulness. These students knew they were lucky. If they worked hard, a university place could be a way out of poverty. This attitude was in sharp contrast to what I sometimes witnessed at UCAB, the private university I had studied at before. There, many of them talked about education as something their papa paid for so they could put a Master's degree on their CV. UBV was still a new initiative, but at that time few people seemed to take it for granted.

After the lecture, I stayed behind for a while to chat.

One of those wondering why a Norwegian was living in Caracas, was María Gabriela.

Curiosity, I told her, before going on to explain how I eked out a basic existence as a freelancer writing articles about Latin America for Norwegian newspapers. We continued chatting as we walked towards the exit. It was now or never, I thought.

'And of course I would like to interview your dad.'

Oil Soup by the River: Trickle Down, Chávez-style

Bringing up the interview like that was not exactly by the book. But apparently the president's daughter was okay with it. She gave me an email address for the president's office and told me to submit an application. I sent off the application and soon received confirmation that it had been received. A few months later in 2007, I received an informal approach from an acquaintance who worked for the government and had contacts at the president's office.

'They're looking at your application, Eirik. But you're number one thousand in the queue.'

I suppose I could boast that I had identified the Chávez phenomenon long before anyone else when I travelled to Venezuela in 2002. But I submitted my interview request at a bad time. Never had a Latin American president been so coveted by journalists as Chávez at that moment. In 2000, 116 articles were published about Chávez in the Norwegian media, a relatively high number for a president from a medium-sized Third World country. In 2007, the figure had risen to 6,753. That was an increase of 5,880 per cent, making Chávez the fourth most talked about international leader by the Norwegian press. Over the past fifty years, few Third World presidents have had such a powerful global impact as Chávez.

Naturally with that kind of stardom, not only did normal journalists want to interview the president, but Hollywood stars like Sean Penn, Harry Belafonte, film director Oliver Stone and Danny Glover, the African-American hero from the Deadly Weapon films. One by one they arrived in Caracas to feel the pulse of the Bolivarian revolution and shake hands with Chávez – or more often than not, give him a hug. And then there was the supermodel, Naomi Campbell. Her first appearance with Chávez was outside a new housing estate for the poor. Before the cement had dried, she and the president drew a heart on the step outside the entrance. 'H' for Hugo and 'N' for Naomi, they wrote inside the heart. Naomi had the task of interviewing Chávez for the famous British magazine, Gentlemen's Quarterly (GQ.) 'A rebel angel,' she called the president in the article, describing him as 'fearless' but fair.

With competition like that, it was going to be a long wait to move forward one thousand places in the queue.

In the meantime, in the summer of 2007, I moved to the *barrios*.

Not so much because I wanted to be closer to the social deprivation or break bread with the poor or anything noble like that. My reasons were mostly financial. Whilst the accumulated annual minimum wage increases of twenty-five and thirty per cent had driven up demand and caused the rental market in Caracas to spike, my income stayed exactly the same and any savings I had were quickly disappearing. So a one-room flat in a middle-class district of Caracas was beyond my reach. I could not afford to pay three hundred dollars a month, waiting for a phone call from Hugo Chávez that might never come.

Leaving the capital was out of the question, making the *barrio* my best alternative.

I decided on Monte Piedad – close to the centre, the Metro, the presidential palace and Plaza Bolívar. And with Omaira and her family as neighbours.

In Monte Piedad, I would have a better chance of observing the social developments that Chávez had implemented in Venezuela. At a bare minimum, I would gain a better insight into the massive national health care project, *Misión Barrio Adentro*. A married couple I knew let me stay with them for free on a mattress in their kitchen. This was not a normal house though, but a B*arrio Adentro* clinic, built to admit patients from the surrounding area. The doctor and her family lived on the floor above.

The doctor was married to a good friend of mine. Like many other Venezuelan doctors, she used to earn good money working at a private clinic that offered cosmetic surgery. She explained to me that for the most part, she implanted silicone implants into women's breasts, as well as performing rhinoplasties on women with indigenous and African roots – and some men – to give them narrower and more 'European' noses.

Venezuela was a land of contradictions. For example, the first women I noticed with silicone implants when I arrived in the country was a young woman studying to be a nun. Neither she nor her girlfriends thought there was anything unusual about that. My friend married a doctor who had traded silicone implants (obviously not her own), good money and comfortable surroundings in a fashionable private clinic, in favour of long workdays in the slums, on call twenty-four hour a day. All to serve *el comandante* and his Bolivarian revolution. Venezuelan revolutionaries were certainly unlike other revolutionaries.

The house was small and the only exit was on the ground floor, through the clinic's waiting room. Sometimes people would think I was the doctor and describe their afflictions to me before I had a chance to explain. There was almost always people there. Old and young, men and women. Mostly from the surrounding *barrio*, but some also travelled from the neighbouring district.

The kind of doctor you visited could be an important indicator of your social status in Venezuela. 'Going to the Cubans', as it was called, was not entirely unproblematic. If you were middle class, visiting one of them might feel like you were sinking to the same level as the poor. In addition if you were an anti-Chavista, you would be renouncing one of the opposition's primary claims, namely that the doctors in *barrio adentro* were no good – or even worse, that they were an invasion force for the Castro brothers. That is, if you were seen in such a clinic. If you were spotted by a fellow anti-Chavista, you were expected to make some kind of excuse, that it was your last resort and anyway, the treatment was terrible. Otherwise your political loyalty would be questioned. If on the contrary, as an anti-Chavista, you were seen by a Chavista from your circle of friends, family or place of work, you could look forward to hours, days and weeks of political jibes at your expense. Because there was almost nothing a Chavista enjoyed more than someone from the *opposition*, someone who had bad-mouthed the Cubans for years, to personally visit the *barrio adentro*.

For that reason, some patients pulling their baseball caps even lower when they entered the clinic where I lived.

The doctors would never ask anyone who they voted for. In any case, there was never any time for that. There were a lot of patients – often in acute condition where every second counted. Young men usually had the worst wounds, from workplace accidents or more often than not, motorcycle accidents. Occasionally they came in bleeding, with knife or gunshot wounds. If laboratory examinations or surgery were required, the patient was referred to the nearby *Centro Diagnóstico Integral* or *Clínica Popular*. These treatment centres were what the government called *Barrio Adentro 2*, and could best be described as a cross between a clinic and a hospital, with more specialists, more advanced equipment and a larger selection of medication. It was all free, even there. Later there was *Barrio Adentro 3*, with even larger and more advanced hospitals.

A few serious cases are etched into my memory. I remember in particular a guy who had been found in a ditch. He had taken so much *piedra*, crack, that he had lost the ability to speak and could not tell us his name. Both the doctor and the nurse were appalled. 'How could he ruin himself like that?' they asked and seemed particularly struck by the fact that someone with 'such beautiful green eyes' could end up like that. Another one to make an impression was a young girl who came in to get free HIV medicine. She was happy for the doctor to tell other people about her case so that they would not suffer the same fate as her. With the new HIV medication, in theory you could live a long, healthy life, but only if you belonged to the small minority of the world's HIV victims who could afford them. The girl in Monte Piedad was provided with the medicine free of charge through *barrio adentro*. Her goal was to go to university and get a good job so that she could look after her mama when she got old.

Most people had far less complicated illnesses that could be treated there and then. There were a lot of infants with fever, or children and adults with stomach bugs and parasitic diseases. Many of the illnesses were linked to poverty and a lack of clean water, hygienic conditions and adequate nourishment. The Cuban doctors were known around the world for being particularly proficient at treating these precise kinds of illnesses. Young pregnant women coming in for their routine health checks was also a common sight. The cases varied a lot from patient to patient. But they had one thing in common: Without the *barrio adentro*, they would not have free health care where they lived. For a lot of people, the clinic where I lived was the difference between life and death.

For my part, there were also a number of disadvantages to living there. I could be woken in the middle of the night by people whistling and shouting *doctora*. Sometimes the patient was seriously ill or wounded. Other times they only wanted a headache tablet. None of the locals had ever had access to free health care in such close vicinity. So the unwritten rules about what kind of afflictions justified waking the doctor and her family, and ones which certainly did not, had not been firmly established.

But the patience of *la doctora* was impressive: 'You cannot work in *barrio adentro* unless you are strong in your belief. Doctors generally have to deal with a lot of pain, suffering, fear and death. In the *barrio adentro*, we have to face poverty and the problems of the *barrio* on top of that. But we also encounter an enormous gratitude and love from the local community.'

I had witnessed that gratitude. A lot of the people thanked God, some kneeled; a number had problems keeping the tears at bay when describing the support they received at the clinic. And at times when people in the *barrio* believed the revolution was under threat, if was often *la doctora* and *barrio adentro* they mentioned. The mere thought of losing that treasure made people furious. In practical terms, their gratitude also came in the form of food, with some bringing a packed lunch, an *arepa* or a piece of cake for the doctor and the nurses. Even the local homeless population and the drug addicts took on the task of guarding the clinic at night to make sure that nothing happened to the doctor or her family. The doctor explained her motivation for taking on such a tough job: 'For us this is about something bigger. We are foot soldiers in a revolution which is about offering a people who have been suppressed for five hundred years a dignified quality of life. We don't do this for money or for status, but because we have been taught that healing is not a commodity; healing is something people have a right to, whether they have money or not. There is a lot we can put up with because we are doing what is right. I am here for God, for Chávez and for the people, for the children who for the first time will grow up in a country where the state ensures that they get the care they deserve, from the day they are born.'

One night I was woken by the irritable droning of what must have been at least ten mopeds. I tried to switch on the lights, but noticed that the power was out in the entire *barrio*. I could not see what was happening outside. Then the motorcycles stopped. They could not have been far away, because I could still hear the motors idling.

Then I heard shots, first a cluster of five or six shots, then another and another, until finally the motorcycles raced off and disappeared.

When the lights came back on right after the shooting, I thought nothing unusual about it, until the next day when I was chatting with one of the nurses. An evangelical Christian lady in her late fifties, she was leaving the clinic when with a smile, she asked me if I had heard the shooting the previous night. To my surprise she seemed unconcerned. According to her, *Los Tupamaros*, the former urban guerrillas who had made peace with the state when Chávez came to power, were behind the whole thing, the shooting, the motorcycles and the power outage. 'You know, sometimes *los malandros* [the gangsters] get a little too cocky and start openly selling drugs to young people in the area, then Tupamaros comes to set things right. The criminals here have weapons and think they are tough, but they are just a bunch of snot-nosed kids. Sometimes *Tupamaros* shuts off the power and attacks *los malandros* in the dark. They give them a good thrashing and fire bullets into the air to frighten them, just enough so they soil themselves,' she explained in a surprisingly cheerful tone. I was used to hearing her talk about medicine and the Bible.

Apparently it was not that unusual. There was certainly crime in Monte Piedad and the rest of 23 de Enero. A number of my friends from nicer neighbourhoods stopped visiting me when I moved there, because they were too scared to enter the area. But if the only thing you noticed was a little dirt, a few bangs and the droning of motorcycles, you had little reason to complain in a city like Caracas, where large parts of the population were severely affected by crime. In *El 23*, I had never had any problems. This was still one of the safest *barrios* in the capital, and many, including evangelical Christian nurses in their fifties, gave Tupamaros much of the credit for that.

The small clinic was situated between a car park, a new basketball court and the river, El Guaire. It was a filthy river that Chávez had promised to clean up years ago, but which was still muddy and putrid – something the media and the opposition reminded people of from time to time. The car park was a hang-out for a number of drug addicts. On the weekends, I often saw a group of homeless people and *piedreros*, crack addicts, boiling their *sancocho petrolero* by the river.

Cooking *sancocho*, soup with meat, chicken or fish and vegetables, over an open fire along the riverbank is an old tradition Venezuelan families still practice on weekends, particularly on holidays like Easter and Carnival. However *el sancocho petrolero*, oil soup, is a slightly different tradition. It is cooked in rusty oil barrels using rubbish or food left outside restaurants. It got its name back in the eighties when the number of homeless people skyrocketed in line with poverty. The rotting tankage had people competing with rats and the vultures that constantly soared above the cities and urban areas of Venezuela. For the country's poorest people, the rusty oil barrels that the soup was cooked in, were all that remained of Venezuela's enormous oil revenues after the foreign oil companies, the PDVSA meritocracy, the corrupt state and the oligarchy had taken their share.

In December 2007, I went over to the homeless by the river one day to have a chat and see how they made the soup. The oil barrel was gone, replaced by a proper aluminium pot. The chicken was not from a rubbish dump or a trash bin outside a restaurant, but from the new state-subsidised food retailer, Mercal.

I chatted with the three men for a while, and naturally I could not refuse when they asked me to try the soup. It was surprisingly good and something of a minor revelation to me. Obviously it was not the sense of living some socialist paradise that I was struck by, surrounded by thick tropical weeds, the trickling of the filthy river mingling with salsa beats and traffic. But the *sancocho petrolero* upgrade from a half-rotting waste product to something you could actually eat without getting ill, was tangible evidence of the promised 'trickle-down effect' that the poor people of Latin America had been vainly waiting for through two decades of neoliberal governments, had finally reached the very rung of the social ladder in Venezuela. Certainly not due to privatisation or the dismantling of the state, as the IMF and the World Bank believed and imposed upon the country in the 1980s and 1990s. On the contrary, this had happened with half a decade of initiatives of the exact opposite nature: nationalisation of the oil industry; doubling of the social budget; large scale welfare reforms; price controls; increased minimum wage; massive support for local grass roots movements; higher business rates. Or 'Castro Communism,' 'radical populism' and 'misrule,' as the reform policies were referred to by critics.

This was a good period in Venezuela. However, there was no guarantee the prosperity would last. I remember one day in particular, when the people fully came to understand the forces which Chávez had unleashed when he began reforming the oil industry and redistributing the wealth.

The fans were droning intensely, competing with the salsa music and the rhythmic sound of metal on metal as muscular bodies raised and lowered the heavy metal bars. I had also made an upgrade: from the improvised 'outdoor training centre' on a small plaza in the centre of Caracas where I trained with other young men from the poor neighbourhoods with weights made of rusty reinforced iron and concrete, to the nearby fitness centre. Outside on the plaza, there was better fraternisation, fellowship, jokes and *piropos* (chat-up lines and compliments directed at random passers-by) amongst the scraps of iron. I had to pay to go to the fitness centre but it had a shower, toilet and changing room and was delightfully free of exhaust fumes. Plus a small food counter. I was chatting with one of the staff over a glass of pineapple juice when a woman came running over and pointed at the television which was on mute.

    While someone searched for the remote, the woman explained.

    'Haven't you heard? Venezuela is being sued by the oil companies because of Chávez. They're demanding twenty billion dollars and they've already frozen twelve billion dollars of PDVSA money. We're bankrupt, the entire country is bankrupt. This is what we get for handing the power to a communist ape.'

'You're Working for Chávez Now'

Chávez had already dropped the bomb the previous April, in 2006.

He announced that on 1 May, International Workers' Day, the Venezuelan state was going to wrest control of the oil industry from the transnational oil giants in the country.

The vast Orinoco Belt in the east of Venezuela was the primary target. It was the world's largest proven oil field, according to the American government agency, the US Geological Survey. Altogether, the foreign oil companies, including British Petroleum (BP), Exxon Mobil, Chevron, ConocoPhillips, Total and Statoil had invested around USD 17 billion in getting heavy crude oil extraction started in the region, according to the New York Times. Chávez was now going to use expropriation to get his hands on these vast oil reserves. Armed expropriation, was how many international media outlets portrayed it. Control of the oil fields would fall to PDVSA, by having the state-owned oil company become the new majority stakeholder. This would mean buying out the foreign companies, effectively forcing them to decrease their stakes. Nationalisation occurred far less dramatically than the catastrophic media headlines indicated. Chávez assumed control of the oil fields to the sound of jubilant workers, salsa music and the jingle of money running into the oil companies' coffers as compensation for the takeover. Most of the foreign oil companies continued to be minority owners.

All the same, nationalisation was a significant break with Venezuelan oil policies of the past. The American business magazine, *BusinessWeek*, described an environment which was 'a far from the 1990s, when Venezuela welcomed the big oil companies to invest.' A month after nationalisation and Chávez had already turned the oil industry on its head.[80] 'Oil companies are no longer running the show,' the magazine wrote.

After nationalisation of the Venezuelan oil industry, many did not want to go on record to *BusinessWeek*. 'But one executive confides that this has been a brutal year. The low point came on Mar. 31, when he was required to attend a ceremony at the Miraflores presidential palace, where Chávez took pleasure in bringing representatives of the world's oil elite – companies such as Chevron, Shell, BP and Repsol – to heel.'

The occasion had been the signing of documents which gave the Venezuelan state control over oil fields which had previously been at the disposal of foreign companies, with the compensation to be negotiated in the future. 'It left a bad taste in my mouth,' the unnamed executive told *BusinessWeek*.

Nationalisation also encountered strong reactions within Venezuela.

The media warned that Venezuela had evicted companies with the knowledge, technology and capital to extract the oil – thus frightening off future investors. On its own, PDVSA would never be able to do the task at hand. Many of the people expressing themselves had a background working for foreign oil companies and for PDVSA.

I was in Norway when Chávez announced the nationalisation, putting the final touches on my dissertation about the Venezuelan oil industry. Unfortunately, when I had travelled to Venezuela the previous year to write about the national takeover, I had been too early. After six months of waiting, I had been forced to return to my university in Oslo with the situation still up in the air. Still, I had eleven research interviews under my belt and had presented a series of lectures about the oil industry at Universidad Central de Venezuela (UCV), but there was no indication when the anticipated nationalisation, the original topic of my dissertation, would take place. But now the moment many people had been waiting for ever since Chávez had risen to power – some with hope, others with fear – had finally arrived.

One of the people I interviewed during my field work, was the deputy minister at the Venezuelan oil department, Bernard Mommer.

Within international oil circles and the business media, the Oxford educated, French-born Belgian – who has held Venezuelan citizenship since 1987 – is believed to be the architect of Chávez' nationalisation strategy. According to Mommer, nationalisation was a necessary, though not particularly radical step, which allowed Venezuela to regain control over the country's most important source of revenue. 'Venezuela received practically nothing in return for its most valuable and non-renewable resource, apart from temporary employment for underpaid workers,' Mommer said, describing the situation in the oil industry before Chávez assumed control. So this was about money. Or to be more precise, *billete verde*, greenbacks, Venezuelan slang for American dollars – the currency of the international oil market. A lot of *billete verde*.

Mommer had expected no sympathy from a European journalist (I was writing a story for the Norwegian weekly *Morgenbladet* on the subject too) and asked me not to pass judgment until I had considered Venezuela's oil history and analysed some basic statistics on the division of profits from the sale of oil between the state, foreign companies and oil importers.

In 1975, President Carlos Andrés Pérez nationalised the oil industry and founded the state-owned company, PDVSA. This was during Pérez' first term in government. At the time, there was an element of economic nationalism in the manner Pérez and his AD party ruled the country, although many Chavistas would reject this as mere posturing or opportunism. The fruits of nationalisation, however, were very real. In the record year of 1981, oil sales reached a peak of twenty billion dollars, of which fourteen billion, or seventy-one per cent, went to the Venezuelan state.[81]
But there were massive gaps in the nationalisation programme. Pérez' oil law allowed foreign companies to operate in some of the more demanding heavy oil fields, under so-called service contracts.

They received tax rebates – officially to make the oil fields with higher operating costs more profitable.

During his second term as president, when he implemented the IMF's shock liberalisation policies, he announced a plan to vastly expand foreign investment in the oil sector, dubbed *la apertura petrolera*, the oil opening. Taxes and royalties were also reduced. Tax was lowered from fifty and sixty per cent to thirty-four per cent, and on some fields as low as one per cent. Ostensibly to make the more difficult oil fields viable. But Mommer told of fields where oil, the world's most lucrative raw material, was extracted at a loss to the Venezuelan state.

The result was a drastic reduction in PDVSA's revenue, and accordingly, a reduction in the state's revenue.

In 2000, twenty-nine billion dollars of Venezuelan oil was sold, nearly 10 billion dollars higher than the record year of 1981. With the same division of profits as before, that is a 70/30 split in favour of the Venezuelan state, it should entail revenues increasing from 14 billion to 20 billion dollars for the Venezuelan Central Bank. But years of liberalisation policies had meant that the state's share of oil revenues was reduced from seventy-one per cent to thirty-nine per cent. Instead of increasing to twenty billion, the state's revenues were reduced to eleven billion.[82]*

When Chávez sent in the army to take over the oil fields, there was none of the predicted drama. In Norway, most people seemed to

---

* When I began researching for my dissertation, the PDVSA brand was still seen in The Netherlands, Germany and Sweden. In the USA, PDVSA opened a subsidiary called Citgo, which in collaboration with 7-Eleven, operated 14 000 petrol stations. PDVSA's investment programme, *la internacionalizacion*, the internationalisation, was the largest investment of capital from the so-called Third World in Europe and the USA. But according to PDVSA accounts, no earnings were ever reported. Instead, the operating expenses from the foreign subsidiaries were transferred to PDVSA in Venezuela, while the profits were transferred in the opposite direction. Mommer explained that the result was a large-scale reduction in PDVSA's income basis, from which tax and profit dividends to the state were calculated. He vowed that the drain on the state budget would soon be tightened.

have forgotten the doomsday predictions their country once faced. Back then, it would have been absurd to think that all hell would break loose just because a country, pursuant to the constitution, asserted its right to extract oil from its own territories. Particularly when oil companies would continue to make healthy profits in the country.

Not until the autumn of 2007, when everyone at the fitness centre crowded together in front of the TV, did I realise that I had been mistaken.

The newsreader explained that Exxon had won a ruling from a British court in its demand to freeze twelve billion dollars of PDVSA capital. The reason given for the decision was a fear that the Chávez government would attempt to hide the assets abroad, now that all indications were that the Venezuelan state would be ordered to pay the twenty billion dollars Exxon was demanding. News of Exxon's lawsuit and the court ruling to freeze PDVSA's capital did exactly that. And with good reason. Twenty billion dollars constituted two thirds of the country's entire currency reserves and was more than the state's spending on health, education and food combined. If the decision was upheld, it would likely mean bankruptcy for PDVSA, the company responsible for eighty per cent of Venezuela's export revenues. An economic crash would ensue, causing a massive wave of bankruptcies, unemployment and huge cuts to the welfare budget. Venezuela imported around seventy per cent of its food at the time. The disappearance of hard currency would lead to a shortages and send food prices sky-high. It would mean malnourishment and starvation for the poor. And there was no reason to doubt Exxon's legal capacity. In 1989, the company was responsible for the largest man-made environmental disaster in history when the Exxon Valdez oil tanker sank off the coast of Alaska. Exxon was fined five billion dollars, which most believed was far too lenient, but when the company appealed, it had the figure reduced by ninety per cent, to a dismal five hundred million. And that was in a US lawsuit, against the most powerful government in the world. How much could Exxon win in a US-friendly and market-orientated court, against a Third World country like Venezuela?

When Chávez announced the nationalisation of the enormous oil reserves in the Orinoco region in 2006, there was little vocal resistance from the opposition. One or two experts, most of whom were part of the former oil technocracy, warned that PDVSA would not be able to extract oil without the foreign companies, and that Venezuela would be shunned as a consequence of the hostile investment climate Chávez had created. But the sense of ownership the Venezuelan people had for the oil was deeply rooted. Few politicians wanted to risk the political cost of going against such a popular initiative. The ruling changed that. With Exxon on the attack, appearing to have international and legal backing to bankrupt the state, the media portrayed Chávez as the attacker and Exxon the victim. Chávez was blamed for the looming economic disaster.

From the moment the ruling against PDVSA was announced, Chávez stressed that he considered it an economic and politicised attack on Venezuela and the revolution, not a neutral legal settlement based on paragraphs of legal interpretation.

'This is a multinational imperialistic company attempting to damage our flagship [PDVSA]. But this ship will continue to sail [...] PDVSA will not sink. Venezuela will not sink. The revolution will not sink,' he stated.[83] Chávez did not consider it a dispute about the rights and wrongs of international business law, but a pure power struggle for Venezuela's oil, dressed up with clauses and legal texts. For that reason, he responded with pure power, issuing President Bush an ultimatum: Stop the attack on the Venezuelan oil industry or attempt to make do without Venezuelan oil.

Venezuela was still the USA's fourth largest oil supplier. International media ridiculed the threat – Chávez had hinted at it before, though without following through. But in Caracas you could sense the patriotic atmosphere whipped up by the clash with Exxon and the courts. The streets soon filled with red-clad oil workers, marching with banners in defence of 'the new PDVSA.' In contrast to the prevailing business philosophy of selling off, outsourcing and cutting everything but core activities, Chávez had directly linked PDVSA with the growing number of social projects offering new welfare services to the poor and to some extent, the middle class. Every *barrio adentro* clinic, every Mercal outlet selling subsidised food, and every new school, nursery and university were supplied with banners, brochures and staff to let people know that these services were only possible because the new PDVSA had taken over the oil industry and was using its resources for the good of the people. While this strategy may have lacked efficiency, politically, Chávez' unspoken yet clear strategy proved to be a success. The people in the *barrios* took Exxon's offensive against PDVSA personally. An attack on the benefits they were finally enjoying after seeing the oil money flow out of the country via foreign firms and a small but increasingly wealthy upper class. For the first time in decades in Venezuela, perhaps in Latin America, people took to the streets to defend, not protest against, a state-owned company and the government's plans for how it should be run. But as both international and Venezuelan commentators pointed out, practically in chorus: PDVSA was headed for collapse, and with that, Chávez' Bolivarian revolution would end up as bankrupt as the oil company that financed it.[84]

While the war between PDVSA and Exxon was under way, documents from the US embassy in Venezuela, published by WikiLeaks, reveal a secret offensive by foreign oil companies.

It began on 18 January, when 'an urbane man, who looks like he just stepped out of a Brooks Brothers catalogue [an exclusive American clothing brand]' arrived at the heavily fortified American embassy complex in the millionaire district of Valle Arriba, outside the centre of Caracas. The description was by US ambassador William R Brownfield, who reported back to the State Department, the Department of Energy, military and security institutions such as

The United States Southern Command and the National Security Council, as well as other US diplomatic posts in Latin America and the world. The sophisticated 'Brooks Brothers' man was Thore E Kristiansen, president of Statoil's Venezuelan division.

Kristiansen appeared visibly distressed as he peppered the embassy staff with questions about Chávez and his economic reforms. Several times he referred to the president's oil policies as 'communist.' One of the issues the Statoil boss was responding to was a new tax on profits.

Statoil was not the only company to approach US representatives for advice on how to tackle the government oil offensive. 'We have noted during the past two months that private sector petroleum contacts have been more forthcoming with us [...] Some contacts clearly approach meetings with us as if they were going to a counselling session or visiting a priest,' the WikiLeaks document stated. However Statoil was not satisfied with merely seeking advice and comfort from the Americans. According to the documents, the Norwegian state company secretly attempted to organise an international boycott ahead of the next round of tendering of Venezuelan oil fields to foreign firms. Furthermore, the embassy document detail meetings with the vice-president of Statoil's Venezuelan subsidiary, Anders Hattestad. In January 2008, Hattestad described how Chávez had 'bit off more than he can chew' when a few months earlier he nationalised the oil fields in the Orinoco region. Venezuela was about to put new oil fields up for tender. According to the US ambassador, Hattestad believed that Chávez could be brought to his knees and forced to accept agreements that left the state with a smaller share of the profits, if the oil companies organised a secret boycott.

What motivated Statoil, a legitimate child of Norway's own oil nationalisation,* to shout about communism and propose an illegal boycott when the Venezuelans were, at least to a certain extent, following in the footsteps of Norwegian nationalisation? It was certainly a risky strategy. It was a breach of the laws regulating the sector and would mean a significantly diminished opportunity to obtain future licenses in a country with the world's largest proven oil reserves. In addition, Statoil's chief strategy for gaining entry into other oil markets was to profile itself as a state-friendly company. The many millions spent on marketing the 'kinder' Statoil brand abroad, went up in smoke on the day the WikiLeaks documents were released. Statoil would now have to compete exclusively on technology and price, just like all the other despised, but often indispensable multinational companies.

And what motivated Exxon? The company was still making enormous profits, even after Chávez' reforms. Why had the company gambled its future in Venezuela by going to war against PDVSA and Chávez?

Oil: The Blood of the Global Economy

As far as *The Economist* was concerned, a news magazine that has never disguised its disdain for Chávez, it was obvious what was happening. In the article 'Exxon's Wrathful Tiger Takes on Hugo Chávez,' the magazine wrote that the oil firm wanted to 'set an example.'

The article described how a wounded tiger (Exxon uses a tiger as its mascot) fought back against a greedy state. To understand the high-risk and punitive strategy used to fight back the Venezuelan oil offensive, one must look beyond the story of Hugo Chávez and delve into the larger narrative about black gold.

---

* Statoil grew under the protective care of the state, with privileged access to the best oil fields and the government's strategic restrictions on foreign companies.

That requires going back in time.

The conversion of hydrocarbons into water vapour and carbon dioxide releases enormous quantities of explosive energy. This energy has unleashed the equally explosive technological and financial forces responsible for the powerful changes in society that we call the Age of Oil. This is a global model of society where oil is undisputedly the single most important substance to the world economy. In 2006 it accounted for approximately one seventh of the world's combined gross domestic product. Neither people nor the goods they produce go anywhere without oil. Thanks to a revolution in the petrochemical industry, oil is now used in the production of textiles, plastic components for houses, cars, machines and a growing range of electronic gadgets we have come to rely on. The Oil Age has transformed the viscous underground liquid into an omnipresent companion, following us from cradle to grave – or more precisely, from the moment oil-based gloves pull us from our mother's womb until we bid our earthly existence a final farewell in fuel-fired cremation ovens.

It seems the metaphor 'black gold' is somewhat of an understatement.

This is a substance that has become as vital to the world economy as blood is to the human body.

Oil's fantastic qualities as a fuel means it has an enormous utility value, and it is this which is reflected in the price people pay at the pumps. The prices of petrol have risen by fits and starts, sometimes increasing by several hundred per cent in a matter of weeks. Still the customers keep coming, proving that even with prices at historic highs, private motorists and the transport industry would rather top up their tanks at exorbitant prices than go without. At the same time, the workforce, investment and operating costs required by the oil industry are reasonably low. So low that the term 'oil production' does not make a lot of sense. Simply stick a pipe in the ground, pump out the oil, and watch as it yields profits greater than anything else in the world. The Norwegian oil philosopher Helge Ryggvik defines the percentage of the profit made from oil extraction above the normal return invested in the economy, as ground rent.[85] In his book detailing the political economy of oil, *Til Siste Dråpe* (To the Last Drop), he imagines the world's oil deposits as gigantic caskets of gold hidden beneath the surface of the Earth. And whenever there is easy money and ambiguous ownership involved, a competition ensues. The competition for oil rent has been fierce, even brutal at times. A kind of early bird gets the worm. With lots of filthy waste.

Oil did not take off in the beginning, even after the invention of the internal combustion engine. The car was ridiculed as an inefficient piece of junk. War got things moving though. In 1916, the USA launched its first motorised military expedition, an unsuccessful excursion into Mexico to capture or kill the revolutionary leader Pancho Villa. By the end of the First World War, the British foreign secretary Lord Curzon of Kedleston was able to conclude that 'the Allies floated to victory on a sea of oil.' By the time the Second World War broke out, the oil-powered war machines were everywhere, on both sides, in the air, on land and sea.

Venezuela was the world's largest oil exporter at the time.

The Venezuelan oil was of such strategic importance that the war's real western front moved from the western shores of Europe all the way to the Caribbean, a few kilometres from Maracaibo Sea where the oil was pumped up. Hitler sent U-boats over the Atlantic Sea to carry execute 'Operation Drumbeat,' with the goal of sinking oil tankers and cutting off the fuel supplies of the Allies. To counter that, the USA established the Fourth Fleet in 1942, one of the world's largest floating war machines, equipped with bombers, helicopters, tanks and with the capacity to transport thousands of troops. Hundreds of vessels were sunk in this lesser known yet decisive phase of the Second World War. In theory, the war could have ended with a victory for Hitler's Germany if the powerful American Navy had not defeated the German U-boat offensive and secured Venezuelan oil for the war machinery of the western powers.

Until the end of the Second World War, oil was seen as a production factor – a means, more than an end in warfare. That changed. Excerpts from a historic conversation between President Roosevelt and the British ambassador in 1944, referenced by the USA's foremost oil historian, Daniel Yergin, shows that oil, even before the end of the war, had become a sought-after spoil of war: 'Persian oil,' [Roosevelt] said to the ambassador, 'is yours.' We split the oil from Iraq and Kuwait. When it comes to Saudi Arabia, it's ours.'[86]

After the war, the USA and Western Europe controlled most of the steadily increasing flow of oil from the Middle East, the new oil El Dorado. This kept the price of oil low and with even more new oil fields opening up, oil exporting countries held a bad hand in their negotiations with oil companies. The companies could threaten to move to another country if the governments didn't accept their demands for a bigger piece of the pie.

The first backlash came from the Iranian Prime Minister Mohammad Mossadegh. He nationalised Iran's oil industry on 1 May 1951, International Workers' Day, under a motto of 'democracy and social justice.'[*] However in 1953, Mossadegh was overthrown and imprisoned during a CIA and British-led coup. During and after Operation Ajax, the CIA codename for the coup, many of Mossadegh's allies were executed. Nationalisation was revoked. The Brits seized control of the oil fields which had been promised to them by Roosevelt.[87] But that did not solve the problem. Exporting countries had got a taste for oil money. In 1956, Egypt's progressive nationalist president, General Gamal Abdel Nasser, closed the Suez canal, through which two thirds of Europe's oil was transported, in protest over 'the great capitalistic monopolies in the developed countries' who are stealing the profits from the colonies' natural resources.

---

[*] Until then, the Anglo-Iranian Oil Company, later known as British Petroleum (BP) had secured itself seventy-four percent of the profits from the sale of Iran's oil, while the Iranian state was fobbed off with twenty-six percent.

But it was not just monopolistic capitalists preventing the poor oil exporters from retaining a larger portion of the oil's true worth. During the post-war period, many of the oil importing nations had begun charging citizens high taxes and royalties on oil and petrol. In fact import taxes and petrol royalties in the West made up a larger portion of the oil rent – that is the difference between the price consumers pay and the cost of pumping up and further refining the oil – with more ending up in the state coffers of the rich oil importing countries than that of the far poorer oil exporting countries. Confronted by both oil companies and Western governments, politicians from several Third World oil exporting countries quietly set in motion a visionary plan to coordinate their interests in the battle for the oil rent.

One of them was the Venezuelan oil minister Juan Pablo Pérez Alfonso.

Alfonso believed there had to be something wrong with the oil *prices* if the importing countries, primarily the USA and Western Europe, could afford to consume increasing quantities of oil – in fact the rapidly increasing prosperity in their societies was entirely based on cheap oil, while the producing countries saw their reserves disappearing at an increasingly greater rate without sharing in the prosperity. He argued vehemently for an 'instrument to defend [oil] prices in order to avoid the waste of money cause by oil which runs out and is not renewable.' In 1960, the Organisation of the Petroleum Exporting Countries (OPEC) was founded in Bagdad. The founding countries were Iraq, Iran, Kuwait, Saudi Arabia, and Venezuela. In the years that followed, Qatar, Indonesia, Libya, Algeria, Ecuador, Nigeria and the United Arab Emirates joined them. Soon western oil companies were kicked out of one OPEC country after the other, with national oil companies assuming control.

What must have been the greatest show of strength by Third World countries in history, was not well received by all parties. To the western oil companies, it was viewed as a coordinated raid to deprive them of the exclusive rights to half of all the world's oil.[88]

The large oil importing countries, the US and Western Europe, reacted with concern. But at a time when scepticism towards *big oil* extended far into the political establishment and mass media in the West, the national takeovers were not enough to provoke an extreme reaction. Not as long as the oil continued to flow and at the same low price. And it did. Right up until 1973. That was when OPEC turned off the taps in protest at US support for Israel in its war against Syria and Egypt. Only then did the world understand what had actually taken place in Bagdad thirteen years earlier.

The result of OPECs oil blockade was a fourfold increase in world oil prices, from three dollars a barrel to twelve, something which affected the expenses of the world's increasingly more oil-fired companies. As petrol prices in the West rose sky-high and beyond, OPEC, until then an obscure abbreviation that only made sense to oil industry insiders, was now on the tip of every motorist's tongue. The four letters became a part of people's daily life, news and vocabulary. OPECs quota system – whereby each country was allocated an export quota dependent on the size of the country's reserves – became an effective mechanism to raise or lower prices. Across the globe, people followed the OPEC meetings with great interest. They knew the outcome of the talks would be reflected at the petrol pumps later.

OPEC's harsh reminder that the supply and price of oil was not necessarily controlled by the people using it, came at the worst possible moment.

Around that same time, another important characteristic of black gold began to sink in with the world's oil executives. While river water renews itself in a self-sustaining cycle, and gold continues to shine for centuries regardless of how many times it changes hands, the ending of the spectacular oil story has already been written.

One day, we risk going empty.

At our current advanced stage of oil dependency – led by petroholic number one, the USA – the amount of oil we burn in one year takes 100 000 years for nature to produce. Drop by drop, barrel by barrel, tanker by tanker, we are nearing the bottom of the treasure chests.

In OPEC countries, higher oil prices led to a considerable growth in prosperity and modernisation. A new upper class and a flourishing middle class appeared in capital cities from Caracas to Bagdad. But to people in the West, it felt like they were being held hostage. The BBC described OPEC as a 'greedy and untrustworthy cartel.' Most OPEC countries were former colonies, many of them had been ruled from Paris and London until recently. The idea that these countries should have the right to govern themselves and their resources was a relatively new one, and by no means generally accepted. And with seventy-five per cent of the world's remaining proven oil reserves, they did not only govern themselves. They governed the flow of blood to the West's economic growth model. Pessimism grew in the USA. 'America's shaking hand curled into a clenched fist,' the author Sonia Shah wrote of Washington's response to this new threat. In 1979, Carter announced what came to be known as the Carter Doctrine. From then on, the policy of the US would be to 'smother any hostile act that might curb the flow of the [Persian] Gulf's oil by "any means necessary."'[89]

'Any means necessary' has ranged from exerting diplomatic and economic pressure to attempts by the US congress to implement global laws banning OPEC, as well as military interventions.

Nearly twenty years later, the respected *BusinessWeek* magazine was finally able to declare in 1998 that the key to eliminating OPEC, the greatest threat to the West's oil-fired economic system, was located in Venezuela. More precisely, in the Caracas district of Chuao, nestled between mango trees and villas, inside the ultra-modern headquarters of the world's largest state oil company, PDVSA.

'If you want a good reason or two why OPEC is on its last legs, talk to Luís Giusti. Few executives have done more to change the global oil industry outlook than the 54-year-old president of *Petróleos de*

Venezuela (PDVSA),' *BusinessWeek* wrote of the PDVSA president on 26 October 1998 after winning the magazine's manager of the year award.

Known as *el catire*, 'the blonde one,' for his fair hair and light complexion, Giusti was born on a Venezuelan oil field, educated in Texas and 'graduated' as a high-level technocrat after rising through the ranks of Shell, making him *the* prototype of an international oil executive. During Giusti's time as president of PDVSA in the nineties, Venezuela was known as 'Pinocchio' by the other OPEC members because of the large quantities of oil sold to the USA under the table. The BBC described the mechanism through which Venezuela did this, triggering a downward spiral: Some countries were not sticking to their quotas, leading to lower oil prices which other OPEC countries had to compensate for by increasing production, leading to even lower prices, with OPEC's power 'fading away.'

The low commodity prices 'squeezed' Venezuela and other Latin American countries, *BusinessWeek* wrote. But even at a pitiful ten dollars per barrel, the PDVSA president had no intention of cutting back production, or even attempting to meet OPEC quotas as a means of increasing the price of oil. On the contrary, *BusinessWeek* praised Giusti for 'his aim: to double production over the next ten years [from three million] to around six million barrels daily.' That would presumably be the nail in the coffin for OPEC. However Giusti's ambitions did not stop there. 'Since 1990, Giusti has spearheaded an ambitious policy to open the state-owned monopoly [the PDVSA monopoly on Venezuelan oil] to private companies ... '

The privatisation of PDVSA that Giusti fronted would give foreign firms access to the company's technology, competence, and an annual turnover of nearly thirty billion dollars. A figure higher than the state budget of many Third World countries. In addition to the enormous profits, there was something far more important at stake: control over the world's largest proven oil reserves. The PDVSA president had been so successful, *BusinessWeek* predicted that his efforts to liberalise the Venezuelan oil industry would be 'a crucial example for other Latin American reformers.' In particular, they had their sights set on the privatisation of the oil industry in Brazil, which was being profiled as one of the next oil giants. As the de facto leader of Venezuelan oil policy, not only did Giusti want to remove OPEC's influence on oil prices, he wanted the oil reserves of OPEC countries, calculated as having approximately eighty per cent of the world's remaining proven oil reserves, to be opened to foreign oil companies. *BusinessWeek* acknowledged that there was a problem with poverty and increasing economic problems in Venezuela in recent years – the period in which Giusti forced through his much lauded oil liberalisation package – without the article connecting the two developments.

There was however, someone who did.

Only months before the 1998 presidential election, and with a strange lieutenant colonel leading the opinion polls, conducting an election campaign full of fiery speeches about national control of the country's oil, *BusinessWeek* predicted rocky waters ahead for Giusti's grand project: 'Populist former coup leader, Hugo Chávez, the front-runner in Venezuela's presidential election campaign, promises to fire Giusti and to review the deal with foreign companies,' they explained in a slightly scornful tone, a tone echoed by other US financial news outlets. They also stressed what was at stake for the global oil market. However *BusinessWeek* did attempt to offer some reassurance: 'With or without Giusti, it is unlikely that Chávez or any president could roll back Giusti's oil policy [...] Giusti fundamentally changed the way Venezuelans think about how their society can benefit from their rich natural endowment [...] But inside or outside public life, Giusti seems likely to continue to influence Venezuelan energy and industrial policy. And his basic reforms seem certain to endure.' *BusinessWeek* also suggested Giusti as a future presidential candidate.

As we now know, that did not happen.

Only weeks after the *BusinessWeek* prediction, the Lieutenant Colonel was in Miraflores. As late as October 2002, *The Economist* wrote 'the famously wacky Chávez' had 'vowed to tear up contracts signed by the old government with foreign [oil] investors,' but that he 'did not dare to revoke them' when he first became president. When nationalisation began in 2007, Chávez made sure that not only was Giusti's plan for further privatisation stopped. He also rolled back the liberalisation thereby disproving the claim by the American business press that Giusti's oil policies were irreversible. PDVSA's death blow to OPEC, which would mean cheaper oil on the world market, was also averted. Less than two years after *BusinessWeek* described the Giusti's vision for how he would change the world, *el catire* was shown the door and Chávez was touring the OPEC countries attempting to resurrect the organisation.* Soon the nickname Pinocchio, as Venezuela had been referred to by OPEC, was replaced with one of the most dangerous terms a foreign leader could have in Washington and Texas: 'resource nationalist' and a 'price hawk.' That is, someone who meets force with force and manages to reduce production and increase prices on the world market.

Instead of 'spearheading' the privatisation of Latin America's energy resources, Venezuela took on the exact opposite role under Chávez. Soon Bolivia, Ecuador and Argentina presented initiatives for increased national control over their own energy sectors.

Here, in light of the decades-long conflict for control of the world's most strategic and profitable economic sector, is where the economic warfare against Chávez can best be understood: in the gap

---

* When Chávez was crossing the turbulent border region between Iran and Iraq in a jeep, Giusti was already headed for Washington. There he continued the war against OPEC as an energy advisor for the Bush administration. Giusti helped shape the report which formed the basis for the US invasion of Iraq, a country with the world's second largest proven oil reserves at that time. After Saddam Hussein was executed, the US-appointed regime announced its goal was to quadruple oil production.

between expectations for the leading role Venezuela would play in the USA's battle for control of global oil supplies – and the astounding desire and ability of Chávez to do the exact opposite.

A PHONE CALL FROM CHÁVEZ

Meeting in Santa Elena de Uairén

The Balkan Gypsy music, driven on by a screeching trumpet and the pounding rhythm of orchestra drums, should have seemed foreign in tropical Venezuela. But surrounded by the alternative youths with their fringes, Converse trainers and ripped trousers, set against a backdrop of tall broadleaves in a recently revamped and – for Caracas – far too well-kept park, it almost felt like being at a music festival in Europe.

In these surroundings, the Gypsy rock of No Smoking Orchestra, led by the famous filmmaker from the former Yugoslavia, Emir Kusturica, fit in perfectly. Kusturica had presumably come to meet his idol Chávez and to witness the Bolivarian revolution for himself. The audience was a growing group of young students who had discovered that the world offered more than Venezuela's mainstream youth culture of slick reggaeton, hair gel, muscles and make-up. I spotted a familiar face in the crowd. I had seen that face countless times on TV when Chávez was abroad or had foreign delegations visiting. I recognised him by the three-day stubble, the white, slightly wrinkled shirt, the glasses and the observant poker face. It was one of Chávez' main international advisors.

I walked over and tapped him on the shoulder.

'Hey, aren't you the guy who normally accompanies the president on his trips?'

'Yes,' he replied, getting the conversation started.

'Great concert, *pana* [mate],' I said.

'*Excelente*, brother,' he replied.

'By the way, I'm Eirik Vold from Norway. I've been trying to get an interview with the president.'

'Ah, *el noruego*,' he said straight-faced. 'We've been talking about you.'

Two months later, I received a phone call from the president's office. I was going to get my interview with Chávez.

27 June 2008 was going to be a big day for Venezuela and Brazil.

A meeting between the presidents of the two countries was scheduled with a goal of extending their collaborations. The meeting was set to take place in Santa Elena de Uairén, a remote Venezuelan town surrounded by dense rainforest and vast river systems near the Brazilian border. Hugo Chávez and Lula da Silva were now established as the two leaders in Latin America. As the larger country by far in terms of population, geographical area and GDP, Lula's Brazil still carried the most weight. But Lula did not have the same political manoeuvring space as Chávez, holding only a minority in congress and doing his best to avoid conflict with a conservative military, bureaucracy and business sector. Militarily consolidated, oil money flowing and with a much freer hand politically at home, Chávez could act as a more aggressive driving force for change in the region. His strong position within Venezuela meant that he could take greater risks in international politics, where forging new alliances independent of the USA singled him out as an enemy of Washington. Brazil moved significantly to the left in the wake of Chávez and simultaneously worked behind the scenes to increase its influence in the world, again at the expense of US dominance. Chávez and Lula met often over that period, always greeting each other with a powerful embrace. They boasted unrestrainedly about the other's political achievements, their friendship and their country's close economic and political connections. They called the Caracas-Brasília alliance a 'motor' in the process of creating a 'just, united and independent Latin America.' However, some wondered whether the two had different projects in mind, whether the two were actually in a rock-hard competition behind the scenes for leadership of the continent.

The international press had already shown an intense interest in the meeting. The two governments stated the meetings were to discuss vital Venezuelan-Brazilian energy projects and other bilateral matters. But everyone suspected that something more important was in the works. For days before, during and after the meeting, the two men dominated the news across the continent.

27 June 2008 was going to be a big day for me. My interview with the president was going to take place in Santa Elena de Uairén over the course of the meeting with Chávez and Lula.

The news had been unexpected and I only had a few days to prepare.

The location chosen was an isolated village, deep inside the rainforest. Getting there on my own steam would have been near impossible, meaning that I would likely be travelling with the president. The venue was small, so I would be near both the Chávez and the Lula delegations over the course of the trip – a unique opportunity to see the dynamic duo in action.

I was nervous. Chávez was charming most of the time and had a rare ability to make people feel comfortable in his company. I had seen him talking to poor people. Some would get nervous and would not utter a single word. Often the president resolved the situation by giving the person a big hug. With people who were unused to discussing complex political themes, or stammered due to their lack of vocabulary or the unfamiliar situation, he showed patience, his eyes and body language making it clear there was no rush. Chávez would happily listen to a cleaning lady with the same respect and interest as his staff listened to him.

However, there was no guarantee I could expect the same goodwill.

With Chávez, it was an entirely different matter when it came to politicians, journalists and experts. It was clear that he had different expectations of people in positions of power. Whether they were his own allies or as was often the case with journalists, people he considered opponents, the president had no scruples about expressing his displeasure with questions he considered irrelevant, stupid or unfair. A number of interviews I had seen developed into outright battles over the questions – even experienced journalists from the BBC and CNN had seen their time run out without eliciting anything of interest from the president. My interview could turn out to be a disaster. Just thinking about the people I had seen, confident and well-spoken people shrinking from the powerful and disgruntled gaze of Hugo Chávez without completing their sentences, it was enough to make me dizzy. I kept imagining a scenario where everything went wrong.

At the same time, Chávez was used to facing the opposition. Having followed him for years on Venezuelan media, it was easy to conclude that he had been subjected to many more critical questions than many western heads of state might expect from local journalists. In Norway, for example, then Prime Minister Jens Stoltenberg (current Secretary General of NATO) for example, was never faced with anything remotely close to the barrages of hostile questions often heard in Caracas. At times, Chavez' comments had been twisted beyond recognition. *The New York Times* once wrote that Chávez had claimed that the American dissident and linguist Noam Chomsky was dead. News of the blunder, intended to reveal his ignorance, spread round the world, from newspapers in Latin American to the *Taipei Times* in Taiwan.[90] But Chávez had never said anything like that. The *New York Times* apologised for the error and published a retraction. However, the majority of the papers around the world that had printed the ridiculous falsehood, including Venezuelan newspapers like *El Nacional* and *El Universal*, never printed a retraction.

But it was an entirely different matter that messed up my planned interview. The day before my big interview, I was told the meeting with Lula had been moved. The meeting would no longer take place in the Amazon, but in Caracas, at the presidential palace.

I was informed that my interview was off the agenda, with no explanation as to why. '*Tranquilo* (Easy) mate, you'll get another chance soon. We'll call you,' the voice on the phone said in a typical Venezuelan way. Obviously the news was discouraging. Assurances like *"tranquilo we'll sort it out for you soon"* were not often worth much in Venezuela. On the other hand – there were plenty of indications that I had one foot in the door now, and even though there were no guarantees, I saw no reason to give up. As long as my money did not run out, something which I was only able to accomplish through stricter and stricter rationing.

The next phone call was not long in coming. Only a few days after the meeting was cancelled, I was offered a new opportunity. This time it would be in Argentina.

A Hotel Room in Tucumán and the Battle for the Americas

29 June 2008, San Miguel de Tucumán, Argentina:

At one of the best hotels in the provincial capital, employees were putting the finishing touches on the hotel rooms where the large Venezuelan delegation would spend the night.

The occasion: a meeting of the South American trading block, Mercosur, set to begin in two days. The location for the summit was not selected by chance. San Miguel de Tucumán is the cradle of the Argentinian independence movement, the place where the southernmost of the Latin American colonies declared its independence in July 1816. Migration agreements, energy and the international food crisis were on the agenda, with the finance ministers of the member countries, Argentina, Brazil, Uruguay and Paraguay, finalising the documents that would form the basis for the July 1 summit. As well as the full members of Mercosur, Bolivia, Chile, Colombia, Ecuador, Mexico, Peru and Venezuela – the so-called associate members – were also taking part. It promised to be a decisive meeting. For that reason, the majority of the countries present had sent their respective presidents. One of the hotel rooms being prepared – likely by a female employee, perhaps from the impoverished neighbouring country of Paraguay – was reserved for Venezuela's president, Hugo Chávez.

Another room was reserved for Eirik Vold, *periodista/escritor noruego*, 'Norwegian journalist/author.'

I had not been told how long we were going to be in Argentina, but I expected to stay there last at least a day or two. You never really knew how long when Chávez went on a presidential trip. Sometimes it was dependent on the president's safety. He was also very impulsive. If an opportunity arose to do business, to spread the Bolivarian message to a sufficiently important arena or to forge new friendships and alliances, Chávez would not let a simple thing like a timetable stop him. Over the next twenty-four to forty-eight hours, I would be mingling with the Venezuelan delegation of ministers, advisors and bodyguards Chávez had brought with him. I was going to be on the inside, moving between state leaders from various political camps from all of Latin America, observing disputes, negotiations and handshakes between the region's most powerful men and women.

The official topics of discussion for the summit were interesting in themselves. Energy is largely synonymous with petroleum: oil and gas, an area where Venezuela was the continent's undisputed lead actor. In line with Chávez' vision for a more closely linked continent, Mercosur[*] had drawn up plans to allow passport-free travel between both member and associate member countries, that is all of South America (with the exception of the small nations of Suriname and Guyana). Reading between the lines though, the most contentious question at Tucumán was:

---

[*] In the beginning, Mercosur was nothing more than an agreement for free trade between member states. During the heydays of neoliberalism in the 1990s, Mercosur functioned as a gateway for American capital (by investing in one member state, they gained access to the other member countries). But the winds of change were blowing across Latin America. Chávez had barely got his foot in the door with Venezuela as an associate member, a purely symbolic status, when he declared his intentions: 'We need a new Mercosur. A Mercosur with a social agenda, a Mercosur that serves the people. If Mercosur does not strive to be something more than a pure free trade agreement, the organisation has no future.'

Should Venezuela be accepted as a full member of Mercosur?

With Chávez in power, Latin America was again one of the hottest conflict zones in the world, politically at least. Ecuadorian president Rafael Correa stated that Latin American summits used to be occasions where 'the presidents of the continent came together to enjoy good food in luxurious surroundings; approve whatever the IMF, the World Bank and the US government told them to; smile for the cameras and return home.' But – according to the Ecuadorian president – that was before Chávez shook things up: When he arrived at the summit, he made them see the harsh social reality of Latin America: the continued plundering of the continent's resources by foreign companies and the USA's undemocratic dominance. Before the meeting, Chávez had stated: 'We [Latin America] are heading towards full independence, but until we break with the external dependence and the internal exclusions in each country, we will not be truly independent.' He believed it was an absolute necessity to break US dominance in Latin America in order to achieve the deep social and political changes which the Latin American left were determined to achieve. The left was now in government across large parts of the continent.

Venezuela had applied for admission to Mercosur in 2006. The country received immediate support from President Lula in Brazil, Tabaré Vásquez in Uruguay and Néstor Kirchner in Argentina. In Argentina and Uruguay, the centre-left had secured the necessary majority in parliament to bring Venezuela in from the cold and into the Mercosur heat. In Brazil, President Lula did everything he could to win over a divided parliament, but the conservative opposition and the right wing of his own ruling coalition opposed the idea. The president of Paraguay, Nicanor Duarte, gave mixed signals. He avoided confronting Chávez, directly but members of parliament from Duarte's ultra-conservative Colorado party expressed their clear hostility.*

This was a matter of high-level politics. Everywhere, from the slums of Caracas where the walls were painted with 'Venezuela is Mercosur,' to Washington, Miami and the Argentinian newspaper columns, the struggle was interpreted as another battle in the great struggle for the future of the Americas.

US President George W Bush and Hugo Chávez stepped into the ring as the two leading contenders for that fight.

The Venezuelan president's plan to unite Latin America had been widely discussed. In Venezuela, the opposition and the press fluctuated between diagnosing the president with 'delusions of grandeur'[91] and describing Chávez as a puppet, a pawn in the fifty-year-old attempt by Fidel Castro to further the Cuban revolution. In Miami, the unquestioned capital of the Latin American upper class and the headquarters of the international Spanish-language media, some described the cooperation between Chávez and Castro as a conspiracy to subject all of Latin America to a communist dictatorship. At least that was the editorial line in papers like El Nuevo Herald and on USA's most important Spanish-language channel, Univisión.† The majority of the Spanish-language press in

---

* The Colorado party had governed Paraguay since 1947, most of the time with one-party rule, including during the extremely brutal Stroessner dictatorship. All the same, the party's parliamentarians stated that their opposition to letting Venezuela in was due to the democratic deficiencies of the Chávez government.

† In addition, different messages were aimed at the people of the two countries: The Cubans were told that Chávez was cynically exploiting Cuba to achieve his own political goals, that Venezuela was draining Cuba of medical personnel, teachers and other resources. In Venezuela on the contrary, the mouthpieces of Miami like El *Nuevo Herald* and Univisión claimed that the Castro regime was using the Venezuelans to drain the country of resources. On an almost daily basis, the Venezuelans were told that while they still lived in shanties, the PDVSA sponsored homebuilding projects in Cuba. And every time the power went out in Venezuela, the media rehashed the news about electricity

Miami (and Atlanta if we include CNN Español) delivered the same principal message: Chávez is dangerous to Latin America. The popular talk show host Jaime Bayly used his programme to suggest that Chávez should be killed before he could achieve his goal. His guests agreed.

In Venezuela and the rest of Latin America they used the term *megalomania* to describe Chávez' plans to create one vast Latin American kingdom.

Many believed that the economic, cultural and political differences between the countries were too great. Key countries like Chile, Colombia and Mexico were more similar ideologically and were political allies of Washington, and despite a number of left-wing governments, the USA was still the most important trading partner for many countries.* It was neither expedient nor possible to unite them into one political project, particularly under the leadership of a controversial figure like Hugo Chávez. That was the recurring tone from analysts – ranging from the Latin American section at the Royal Norwegian Ministry of Foreign Affairs (where I interviewed two of its experts in 2005) to Michael Shifter, Professor of Latin American Studies at Georgetown University, a member of the *Council on Foreign Relations*, a writer for the journal, *Foreign Affairs* and probably the USA's most quoted expert on the region. Discussing the topic of Latin America, *Time Magazine* wrote that 'the region is larger than Africa with national interests that are just as Balkanised.' They used the satirical term 'quixotic' to describe Chávez' goal of Latin American integration, referring to the famous Cervantes novel where the mentally deranged main character Don Quixote fights a futile, yet romantic battle for unachievable goals, and tilting at windmills – imagined enemies.[92]

An enormous gas pipeline project to connect Bolivia, Brazil, Venezuela and Argentina, one that Chávez announced with pomp

---

generators that at one time, many years ago, had been installed in Cuba using PDVSA money.
* China, Mercosur and Europe have gradually become more important trading partners for the larger Latin American countries.

and ceremony in 2006 but which was never realised, was often used as an example to show the vapidity behind grand ideas like *la patria grande* and Bolívar's sword. 'Four allied countries could not agree on a gas pipeline project but now Chávez is going to get thirty-two Latin American and Caribbean states to join one great Bolivarian republic,' the host for the programme *Entre periodistas* commented dryly.

Perhaps uniting Latin America was a quixotic plan. The idea has been around for nearly two hundred years without anyone making any significant progress in reaching that goal. Apart from the political obstacles and divide and rule great power politics, the Amazon and the Andes, the world's longest mountain range and biggest jungle area respectively, have for centuries constituted unsurmountable impediments for transport of humans and trade of the sort needed to knit a region more closely together. But where experts saw obstacles, Chávez saw dizzying potential. In addition to its enormous natural resources, Latin America has nearly six hundred million inhabitants, of which around ninety-four per cent speak Spanish or Portuguese, two languages that are very close to each other. Latin America has similar ethnic origins – indigenous peoples, European immigrants and African slaves: with each nation having a mixture of two or three of the aforementioned groups. From Mexico in the north (or USA if you include the country's fifty-two million *hispanos*) to Patagonia in the south, the people share a common identity as *Latinos*. Their shared history as former colonies gives the people a shared sense of both the past and the present. The distance between Chile and Mexico is the same as from UK to the Congo, but a Chilean and a Mexican both consider themselves *Latinos*. Most Latin Americans are Catholic and there are no significant religious conflicts on the continent. The Muslim Arabs – mostly Lebanese and Syrians – and the Jews who have immigrated to Latin America have not changed that. In the centre of Caracas, there is a synagogue, the city's largest mosque and a church only a stone's throw away from each other – but no stone has ever been thrown between them.

Comparing it to other regions in the world puts the potential for Latin American unification in perspective: In the Middle East, the people are divided along religious and ethnic lines, with Shia Muslims, Sunni Muslims, Christians, secularists, Arabs, Persians, Turks, Kurds and Berbers, just to mention a few. Ethnic divisions dominate Africa – and religious conflicts have led to war – while Southeast Asia is marked by national antagonisms forged over millennia, with competing superpower ambitions on top of the religious and ethnic divisions. Neither in Africa nor in Asia have supranational or international organisations managed to prevent these regions being weakened by constant war. Moderating the antagonisms to a level where the countries can act in unison and achieve a breakthrough in international politics, remains a remote prospect.

The few wars between Latin American nations have been brief. The rivalry displayed by the occasional border conflict is superficial. In modern times, the one international integration project of similar dimensions, one which had equally good historic, linguistic and cultural bases for unification as Latin America, were the territories which became the United States of America. Both the EU and the Soviet Union achieved unification, despite far greater cultural and linguistic differences and many more wars and conflicts than Latin America has ever had.

For Chávez, a man who thought globally and along overarching historic lines, there was nothing strange in the idea of unifying Latin America. The riddle for him was how their former colonial masters had managed to divide the continent, and how that division persisted for two hundred years, despite exceptionally favourable conditions for a union.

In Washington and in the offices of many of the world's largest multinational companies, a united Latin America was nothing less than a nightmare scenario. For them, having weak Latin American governments reliant on financial gifts and military support to stay in power was an ideal starting point to force through their demands for cheap access to the region's natural resources. Foreign companies and superpowers with an appetite for Latin America would have their negotiating positions weakened if they had to face governments acting as a block, no matter which political party was dominant. A Latin American power block influenced by Chávez' resource nationalism was the worst thing imaginable.

And that was exactly what Washington feared would come closer if Venezuela was admitted into Mercosur.

The Bush administration was determined to avoid such a catastrophe.

So in 2005, US ambassador John Danilovich, behind closed doors, arranged a series of meetings with members of the Brazilian government, leading politicians and military personnel. Danilovich discussed a variety of themes during these meetings but one name that always came up was Hugo Chávez.

By this point, the strategists in Washington had realised that Bush was so unpopular in Latin America that being attacked by him actually led to increased popularity. So instead they looked for a new strategy to block the Latin American independence agenda. Jorge Castañeda, Mexico's former Secretary of Foreign Affairs during the conservative government of Vicente Fox, wrote in an article that Latin America's up-and-coming left wing was divided into two camps. On the one side were 'the populists' who had turned away from the neoliberal Washington Consensus, adhered to the 'anti-Americanism' of the Castro government and had authoritarian traits. Chávez was the best example of this, according to Castañeda. On the other side was a modernised left-wing that had embraced neoliberalism and democracy, and where the 'old-school anti-Americanism has been tempered by years in exile, realism and resignation.' Brazil's president Lula was the most important example of this, along with Chile's centre-left coalition and the government of Uruguay.[93]

Castañeda called them the 'right left' and the 'wrong left'. This supplied the Bush administration with a kind of roadmap to follow in its aims to divide the continent, as well as setting the tone for the western media's coverage of Latin America in the years to follow.

When US Ambassador Danilovich sat down with Brazil's foreign minister in 2005, he was well aware that the supposed tension between Lula and Chávez was only wishful thinking. However the Bush administration had decided to make it a reality. An increasing number of America's leading politicians were sent to capital cities across Latin America in 2005. The USA Today wrote: 'Rice and President Bush have sharpened the rhetoric against Chávez, while at the same time praising Colombia and other Latin American allies.'[94] The criticism shifted from Chávez being a threat to US interests to him thwarting the ambitions of the rest of Latin America's leftist governments.

In his confidential report detailing the meeting with Brazil's foreign minister, sent to the State Department in Washington and revealed by WikiLeaks, Ambassador Danilovich described Chávez as 'a growing threat' to all of South America. The ambassador described a clear response from the Brazilian representative. 'We do not regard Chávez as a threat,' he said: 'We do not want to do anything that would damage our relationship with him.' A disappointed Danilovich concluded his report by stating that the foreign minister 'was not buying into' the American idea.[95] Danilovich continued writing to Washington, describing what he called 'poisonous anti-Americanism,' 'nationalists,' (in a negative sense), 'radical left-wing academics' (also not meant as a compliment by the US Republican) and general 'anti-American tendencies' from Lula's government. All the while, Condoleezza Rice kept smiling and continued her flattery of Lula's government. The Bush administration had not given up. They knew that making Lula, Kirchner and the other centre-left leaders stab Chávez in the back would come at a price. Bush expressed his open admiration for Brazil. Rice and Rumsfeld bragged about the centre-left governments in these countries, ones which were not as radical as the Chávez government, but which nonetheless were leading Latin America in the wrong direction, from Washington's point of view.

The Bush administration had every US ambassador in Latin America participating in the battle against Chávez. It became more difficult as the number of progressive left-wing governments in power increased in Latin America. In Bolivia, American aid workers were instructed by embassy staff to spy on Venezuelans living in the country.[96] In a classified document from the US embassy in Chile – published by WikiLeaks – in countries where the people had elected governments on friendly terms with Chávez, a recommendation was made to attempt to influence the military.

It was an old strategy. Throughout the 1900s, exerting influence on Latin America's armed forces was the USA's primary method of gaining political control over the region. Since 1961, twenty-three of Latin America's thirty-three countries have sent a significant number of military officers to be trained at the so-called School of the Americas (SOA)[*] at Fort Benning in the US.[†] The *New York Times* called it the 'School of the Dictators.' The school's list of graduates is a hall of fame for the best of Latin America's coup generals and military dictators. In 1996, the US Defence Department was forced to release the teaching manuals used for the Latin American officers at SOA. They include sections on extrajudicial execution, torture, illegal imprisonment, assassination and extortion. Not to mention ultra-conservative indoctrination, as

---

[*] From 2001, it has been called the Western Hemisphere Institute for Security Cooperation.(WHINSEC)

[†] One of the instructors, Major Joseph Blair, describes the training he gave to the Latin American officers as such: 'The doctrine that was taught was that if you want information you use physical power, you use false [illegal] imprisonment, you use threats to family members, you use virtually any method necessary to get what you want ... [including torture] and killing. If you can't get the information you want, if you don't get that person to shut up or stop what they're doing, you simply assassinate 'em and you assassinate 'em with one of your death squads.' Pilger, John (2007): War on democracy - School of Americas (documentary).

anyone who diverged from pure neoliberalism was considered an enemy.

For a Latin American president, leading a country where the military were trained and indoctrinated at the SOA meant you had to be constantly looking over your shoulder. For moderate reformers with no desire to follow Allende into martyrdom, it also entailed abandoning any ambitions of doing anything that diverged from what Washington deemed acceptable.

In 2005, an optimistic Ambassador Danilovich met the Brazilian minister of defence, General Jorge Armando Felix. The US were not certain where Felix stood on Chávez. But the Brazilian army was infamous for having utilised all of the methods taught at Fort Benning: from discrete persuasion, to extortion and threats of a military coup, grotesque torture and murder. The fact that Felix forged his army career during the US-supported military dictatorship was a positive indication.

In a classified report, also made public by WikiLeaks, the American ambassador described his meeting with the Brazilian minister of internal security. 'Chávez was disrupting Brazil's efforts to play a leading role politically and economically in South America,' Danilovich told Felix. The American ambassador noted his response: 'General Felix nodded his head and appeared to be very carefully measuring his response. He then said that he had his own personal opinions about Chávez (which he did not share) that were different from the Brazilian government's position.' Felix' presence in the government 'bodes well for US interests,' Danilovich concluded in the report. If he was correct, it did not bode well for Chávez.

Danilovich also spoke to Jose Dirceu, one of Lula's most trusted advisors. The Americans had managed to make world news out of Chávez' decision to exchange the army's ancient automatic weapons with new Russian Kalashnikovs. The ambassador said that the US was worried about the weapons purchase. Dirceu dismissed the idea that the sale of automatic weapons to Venezuela posed a threat to US security. But according to Danilovich, Dirceu nonetheless agreed to pass on a message to the Venezuelan president: 'You are playing with fire.'

Less than a year before the meeting in Mercosur, all of the US ambassadors of the Southern Cone (the southern part of South America comprised of Argentina, Bolivia, Brazil, Chile, Paraguay and Uruguay) held a secret conference in Rio de Janeiro. The subject: how to defeat Chávez on the international scene. Or as the title of the document indicated, written on 18 June 2007 for the conference by the six embassies: 'A Southern Cone Perspective on Countering Chávez and Reasserting US Leadership.' The document was classified by the US ambassador in Chile, Craig Kelly, as 'secret,' the highest level of secrecy of the US diplomatic cables published by WikiLeaks, and among the very few cables also sent to the CIA and the White House, as well as typical recipients like the State Department and US embassies in other countries in the region. The title clearly shows that defeating Chávez was not just a goal to defend US economic interests in Venezuela, but a strategy to weaken the leftist tide in the whole of Latin America and regain US dominance over its traditional 'backyard.' Some of the strategic advice and considerations mentioned in the document are: 'Know the enemy: We have to better understand how Chavez thinks and what he intends [...] Notwithstanding his tirades and antics, it would be a mistake to dismiss Hugo Chavez as just a clown or old school caudillo. He has a vision, however distorted, and he is taking calculated measures to advance it. To effectively counter the threat he represents, we need to know better his objectives and how he intends to pursue them. This requires better intelligence in all of our countries. [...] We should neither underestimate Chavez nor lose sight of his vulnerabilities.' One recommendation is to act cautiously 'when it's clear that Chavez's mouth has opened before his brain has engaged.' During my years in Venezuela I noticed exactly that happening quite a few times. However the document also recognized that when Chávez did engage his brain in strategic matters, he 'present[ed] a formidable foe' to the US ambitions for hegemony in South America. A foe equipped with effective rhetoric, historic momentum, personal charm and significant amounts of oil money that were generously handed out, often 'clandestinely' to increase his political clout in the region. The document, written after the conference in Rio de Janeiro and sent from the US embassy in Brasilia to the US State Department, the President and the CIA, concludes that 'it is clear we need more (and more flexible) resources and tools to counter Chavez' efforts to assume greater dominion over Latin America at the expense of US leadership and interests.'[97]

Latin American politics continued to gravitate around Chávez. Venezuela's potential admission to Mercosur in 2008 had risen to the top of the region's political agenda, in part because the result would give an indication of who had the upper hand in the struggle for power in Latin America.

In Tucumán, the two sides met with their respective presidents, foreign ministers, advisors and diplomats. The political games I saw playing out in the streets, meeting rooms and corridors would decide who was going to dominate the future of the world's most resource-rich continent. If Venezuela gained full membership to Mercosur, it would mean that the USA was in serious danger of losing the battle, and that Chávez would join an alliance that America no longer dared to attack openly. The attempt to isolate Venezuela, 'the socialist tumour,' had failed. If US allies in Paraguay and Brazil were able to keep Venezuela on the outside, Chávez would continue to live dangerously. Every handshake, every word, seating arrangement and hug; a discrete smile, a gesture or a joke with an intentional or intentional sting – the tiniest little thing could indicate which way the balance tipped.

Tucumán was going to be my opportunity to see Chávez utilising the full spectrum of skills that had turned him into a global political star. Chávez would presumably use them in combination: passionate rhetoric involving Bolívar, Martí and other independence heroes; street diplomacy with unrestrained pandering to the public as he did in Mar del Plata three years earlier; corridor diplomacy – for that he had a young French-Venezuelan international advisor whom he had he plucked up from the elite French Sorbonne University* – and not to mention, his famous oil diplomacy.

Perhaps Mercosur was Chávez' ulterior motive when he turned to Brazilian companies to develop Venezuela's infrastructure using the oil money that was pouring into the treasury. Offering billion dollar contracts for enormous bridge and roadbuilding projects, homebuilding and petrochemical industrial production to Brazil's largest private business conglomerate, Odebrecht, was likely to soften the resistance to Brazilian-Venezuelan cooperation where it was strongest: amongst the upper class.

Though not part of the official agenda, I was also hoping to get a glimpse of Chávez' famous *chequera petrolera*, his so-called oil chequebook, one which the Latin American media and right-wing always brought up when the Venezuelan government did business abroad. Chávez surprised many people, when in 2005 he offered to provide Paraguay's conservative Duarte government oil at favourable repayment conditions. It was classic Chávez pragmatism to offer energy security across the ideological divide. The agreement was similar to what Duarte's party and his allies in Paraguay's mass media had consistently described as malevolent oil imperialism and part of Chávez' attempt to enslave Latin America.† In light of this, a correspondingly pragmatic Duarte – the president of a small, impoverished country with no oil – accepted his offer. But would Chávez get anything in return?

---

* The man I had met at the Balkan Gypsy concert.
† Some years later, the US embassy in the Paraguayan capital of Asunción wrote to Washington delighted at the Paraguayan media's extreme anti-Chavism, detailing how this would prevent the two countries from becoming closer.

In 2008, when Chávez packed his bags to travel to the summit in Argentina with yours truly in tow, the status of the geopolitical power struggle was as such:

ALBA, the radical organisation that began as a thin north-south axis between Caracas and Havana, had now become a belt, spreading to the east and the west and stretching further north and south. The alliance had expanded north into Central America with Nicaragua and Honduras becoming members. To the west ALBA reached South America's Pacific coast with Ecuador, a country possessing considerable oil reserves. The southernmost outpost was Bolivia, South America's largest exporter of natural gas. And in the Caribbean the island nations of the Dominican Republic, Antigua and Barbuda, and Saint Vincent and the Grenadines had graduated from PetroCaribe to ALBA. In El Salvador, the socialist party FMLN had come to power led by the more moderate president Mauricio Funes.* Funes did not sign up to ALBA, but several municipalities run by FMLN joined and received Venezuelan aid to finance health programmes for the poor. A similar programme was launched in Peru, where voluntary activists constructed the so-called ALBA house. In several other Latin American countries, poor people with curable blindness were flown to Cuba to have their sight restored, paid for by Venezuela's *Misión Milagro*, the miracle mission.

Chávez and his allies had further strengthened the links between the countries. President Correa had taken the initiative for a common currency, the *sucre* – with a common development bank in the making. There have been a few attempts to replace American dollars as the currency of international trade, and they have all failed: At the beginning of the noughties, Saddam Hussein abandoned the dollar as a currency for oil trade, but following US intervention, he ended in the gallows. Gaddafi launched the gold dinar as a common African currency, but was killed soon after during an internal

---

* The USA spent considerable military and economic resources to wipe out the FMLN (Farabundo Martí para la Liberación Nacional or the Farabundo Martí National Liberation Front) in the eighties and nineties, back when the party was a guerrilla movement fighting a brutal US-allied regime.

rebellion by democracy advocates, Islamists movements, al-Qaeda and tribal leaders with military support from NATO. Despite past failures, Correa, Chávez and the other ALBA leaders decided to take a chance.

At international forums such as the UN, the OAS and USAN (Union of South American Nations), the ALBA countries voted as a bloc. One bloc of nine nations with nearly seventy million inhabitants, with a collective GDP of almost 600 billion dollars, with the world's largest oil reserves at their disposal and led by Hugo Chávez, a man who knew how to make the alliance's viewpoints heard.

That alone made it the greatest geopolitical and regional challenge to the USA since the Cuban revolution in 1959.

And then there was PetroCaribe. The Venezuelan oil alliance did not trigger any immediate Bolivarian revolutionary tsunami in the Caribbean. USSOUTHCOM (United States Southern Command) still had complete military control with eight military bases stationed in the region, including Guantánamo Bay in Cuba and Aruba which were only a few kilometres north of Venezuela. But a number of smaller nations, which previously had little room to manoeuvre to the left because of The White House, now had a direct line to Chávez and visited Caracas more frequently than Washington. Like the pirates who for centuries stole from the world's largest and most powerful ocean fleets in the archipelago of these waters, Chávez had managed to transform the Caribbean into navigable waters right under the nose of a hostile superpower.

Chávez' success in Central America and the Caribbean was surprising to many. Now he wanted to tighten his grip in the south. For that, he needed Mercosur.

In the meantime, US strategy to stop Chávez had shifted again.

The first few years after the failed military coup in 2002, Washington worked primarily behind the scenes.[98] Direct attacks against Chávez were less frequent and less vocal, usually coming from government officials and politicians at a lower level. But in

2006, US Secretary of Defence Donald Rumsfeld turned the temperature back up by comparing Chávez to Hitler. That same year, the CIA placed Venezuela on a list of the world's so-called top five 'hot spots.' US intelligence services officially established a special unit to 'transition' Venezuela and Cuba. In plain English, that meant regime change.

The US imposed an arms embargo on Venezuela and to legitimise that decision, they placed Venezuela on a list of countries that 'do not cooperate in the war on terror.' Chávez was accused of sympathising with FARC rebels in Colombia. The US media slowly became more brutal in their attacks on the Venezuelan president. A local politician from New York was called a 'son of a bitch' by a reporter from Fox News for trying to present a more nuanced picture of the Venezuelan president. Neither in the West nor in Venezuela did the media question that a country involved in two ongoing wars of aggression and exporting arms to innumerable war zones, had decided to deny weapons to a country that had *never* – in its two-hundred-year history – started a war. Chávez publicly stated several times that he believed the Bush administration was thinking about killing him. Chávez referred to the Monroe Doctrine, where US authorities gave themselves the authority to intervene anywhere in Latin America to ensure their strategic interests.[*]

Chávez' claims that the Americans wanted to assassinate him were simultaneously ridiculed and ignored by the international media. That is until the popular US televangelist Pat Robertson[†], one of Bush's most important supporters on the religious right, said the

---

[*] In the US, many were critical of how the Monroe Doctrine was used to topple Latin American governments, arm militia groups, organise military coups and assassinate politicians. Many believed the so-called 'murder doctrine' could backfire against the security of the USA's own citizens. In 1981, political assassination had become such a normal foreign policy tool for US intelligence organisations that Congress felt compelled to pressure President Reagan into passing a special ban on assassinating foreign leaders, the so-called assassination ban.

[†] An influential Christian conservative media mogul in the USA

following: 'If he [Chávez] thinks we're trying to assassinate him, I think that we really ought to go ahead and do it.'

Until then Chávez' best strategy to avoid war with the militarily dominant USA was to make it too expensive for them. The USA still imported nearly fifteen per cent of its oil from Venezuela. Chávez had eagerly displayed the voluntary militias guarding the country's oil industry, who had been trained to blow up the oil installations to prevent them from falling into the hands of the enemy in the event of war. Robertson said that assassinating Chávez would be 'a whole lot cheaper than starting a war and I don't think any oil shipments will stop [...] We have the ability to take him out and I think the time has come that we exercise that ability. We don't need another 200-billion-dollar war,' he said in reference to Iraq. 'It's a whole lot easier to have some of the covert operatives do the job and then get it over with.' Robertson also warned that Chávez was going to make the Venezuelan oil reserves 'a launching pad for communist infiltration and Muslim extremism all over the continent.' According to Robertson, assassinating Chávez would be in accordance with the Monroe doctrine.[99]

The Bush administration denied that it had plans to follow Robertson recommendation. All the same, Venezuela considered it a menacing threat: Forces close to the US president speaking of assassinating Chávez at the same time as the US imposed an arms embargo on Venezuela and accused the government of not cooperating in the 'war on terror.' USA's internal political dynamics did not bode well for Chávez. Bush's popularity was dropping like a lead balloon and there were strong indications that the next presidential election in 2008 would bring a Democrat to the White House. Historically the Republicans have launched more wars and interventions against progressive and nationalist movements and governments in Latin America than the Democrats. So for those wanting the US to take more drastic actions against Chávez, they would have to hurry.

A book published in 2006 paints a picture of how far the idea of going to war against Venezuela went in the foreign affairs establishment. The book is called *War Footing: 10 Steps America Must Take To Prevail in the Free World*. The basis for the book is that the USA – 'the greatest of all these freedom-loving countries' – is at war with totalitarian forces. First and foremost, with Islamist movements in the Middle East. And with Hugo Chávez, who is approaching America's soft underbelly, with his plan to attack the USA with the backing of the fanatic Sunni movement Al-Qaida and Shia-Muslim Iran. The main argument of the book is that the USA must be more willing to start wars. 'We know that the United States – and the world – paid a higher price because we waited until after Pearl Harbour to put the nation on a true war footing ... There are new totalitarians today,' the author argued, but they are 'every bit as determined as their predecessors to destroy the Free World.'[100] Latin America, according to the book has become 'a magnet for Islamist terrorists' and a 'breeding ground for hostile political movements with most of the landmass now under the control of anti-US politicians who are fuelled – like Saddam Hussein, Muammar Gadhafi and the Iranian mullahs before them – by seemingly endless streams of oil revenues. In this case, the key leader is Hugo Chávez, 'the billionaire dictator of Venezuela,' who had declared a *'Latino jihad* against the United States.' According to the author, Chávez planned 'total war against the USA.'*

The author, Frank J Gaffney, a heavyweight in America's neoconservative foreign policy milieu, formerly worked in the US Department of Defence under Reagan. Key people on the US military intelligence scene embraced the ideas espoused in his book, such as former CIA chief James Woolsey, former defence minister

---

* The chapter on Chávez includes a contribution by Thor Halvorssen Mendoza, a Norwegian-Venezuelan cousin of radical opposition leader Leopoldo López Mendoza (his second surname Mendoza is rarely used in the media). He moved to the USA at a young where he joined a mainly neocon environment and founded his own supposed human rights organization and currently heads a controversial yearly Human Rights Conference in Norway.

and CIA director, James Schlesinger. In the book, Bush is criticised for not leading a sufficiently aggressive line against Venezuela.

This was well into Bush's second term as President, and the American people had little appetite for engaging in new conflicts and setting off on new war adventures. And for those who wanted the USA to take military action against Venezuela, they knew that the chances for gaining approval for such a strategy with a Democrat in The White House were slim. Paradoxically, these factors contributed to increasing the fear of direct US intervention amongst the Chávez government. There is a trend in US political history whereby presidents approaching the end of their second term, meaning they are ineligible to stand for re-election, sometimes make unpopular decisions they would have been prevented from doing in their first term due to calculations about political costs. Hence the period leading up to the US presidential election was a window for the most extreme anti-Chávez camp: Now was the time to convince Bush to take direct action against Chávez.

Given this context, the battle to gain admission to Mercosur was also a survival strategy for Chávez. He had no idea how long his allies Lula and Kirchner, who openly defended him against attacks from the USA, would remain in power. However, it was logical to assume that the more integrated the Brazilian and Argentinian economies became with the Venezuelan economy, the stronger their opposition to American intervention against Chávez would be.

As I observed the political games play out ahead of the Tucumán summit, I realised that Venezuelan admission to Mercosur could be the difference between life and death. For the Bolivarian project, maybe even for Hugo Chávez in a literal sense.

As it turns out, the pressure was even greater than it appeared.

More factors were at play than the goodwill of Brazil and Argentina. Venezuela's path to Mercosur and my path to an interview with Chávez were about to collide with an entirely different storyline.

Death in Angostura: The Bombs That Killed Raul Reyes (and My Chávez Interview)

This story could have started somewhere between three thousand and eight thousand years ago, when the indigenous peoples of the eastern Andes region, as far as we know, chewed their first coco leaves.

Or it could have begun in the mid-1800s, when a scientific article by the Italian neurologist, physiologist and anthropologist Paolo Mantegazza made Europe aware of the sensational properties of the tough green leaves of the coca plant. In its chemically treated form, cocaine was bottled, first in wine, then in Coca-Cola, becoming an important ingredient in what may be the USA's greatest contribution to world gastronomy.

But it was not until the 1980s in the Colombian city of Medellín that Álvaro Uribe, Chávez' soon-to-be nemesis, took his first steps towards taking up a position of power as South America's most powerful outpost against the Bolivarian offensive, brought to power on a wave of anger against guerrilla activities, his own cunning and lots of money stemming from a derivate of the green leaves.

Some time ago, foreign chemists and scientists transformed coca leaves into cocaine, and the man who turned the drug into a billion-dollar international business, was the most notorious drug baron in the world, Pablo Escobar.

From Medellín, he ran the world's most powerful drug network, which at its peak is estimated to have generated revenues of up to eighteen billion dollars a year, more than most Latin American countries combined have in their currency reserves.[101] The money primarily came from the USA where the yuppie motto of 'work hard, play hard,' as well as a steady flow of cash, made a perfect market for the new drug. Wall Street brokers voraciously consumed the stimulating wonder drug in order to cope with stressful days at the stock exchange, before easing into breathless nights on the town.* To keep up with the explosive demand, Escobar and the Medellín cartel acquired a fleet of three hundred aeroplanes, two purpose-built submarines and an unknown number of trailers, trams, boats and helicopters, all operating from secret airports, harbours, entire Caribbean islands and large property complexes and distribution centres in Miami and New York.

Back in Medellín, Escobar was known as *el patrón*, the boss.

Nobody did anything without his permission. And why should they? Escobar was ruthless with his enemies, but generous with his friends. Thousands of people forged their financial, political, academic and even sporting careers by joining forces with *el patrón*. The young lawyer, Álvaro Uribe, emerged from anonymity in that way, catching the attention of the US Department of Defence, among others.

Between 1980 and 1982, when the Medellín cartel accumulated its air fleet and accelerated its cocaine exports to the USA and Europe, Uribe was the director of civil aeronautics in Colombia. Next he became the mayor of Medellín. There he established a financial power base that would help him continue up the system, and in 2002, he achieved his goal of becoming president. In 1991, when Uribe's political career had gained serious momentum, the US Defence Department gave the following description of him in a classified report: Álvaro Uribe Vélez – a Colombian politician dedicated to collaboration with the Medellín cartel at high government levels. Uribe was linked to businesses

---

* Even in Hollywood films, cocaine avoided any critical limelight, like in Crocodile Dundee, where cocaine users were portrayed as naive jesters in comical scenes – clownish and hyperactive or with their moustaches covered in white powder as they emerged from the toilet.

involved in narcotics activities in the US [...] Uribe has worked for the Medellín cartel and is a close personal friend of Pablo Escobar.'*

It was not until Uribe became president in 2002 that he entered the story about Chávez' Bolivarian crusade in Latin America.

In Washington, any worries about Uribe's past as a drug collaborator and go-between for the Medellín cartel and Colombia's economic and political elite, soon disappeared. In Uribe, the US would gain its most important ally in a continent spinning out of their control. Uribe and the Bush administration had at least one enemy in common: the radical left-wing FARC guerrillas. And Hugo Chávez.

The war against the guerrillas was personal for Uribe. His father, a rich landowner also suspected of having drug connections, had been killed by FARC back when the radical left-wing guerrillas were at war with the drug cartels. Uribe had vowed to avenge his death. He was going to wipe out the guerrillas militarily. Plan Colombia, the third largest military aid programme in the world, would provide him with US support.

Chávez on the contrary, had believed that guerrilla warfare was a legitimate last resort for poor farmers who had been suppressed (and massacred) for decades, with the majority of their political leaders and presidential candidates assassinated in a state controlled by the oligarchy and the USA. Chávez believed the Colombian state should open itself to peace and democracy by letting the Left participate in politics, and negotiate with the guerrillas. For that reason, some people in Venezuela feared that Uribe would wage political, economic, and in the worst case, military war against Chávez. After forty years at war with FARC, the most powerful and

---

* When the US government publicly accuses political opponents of being connected to the drug trade, it requires some degree of scepticism. However in this case, the man in question was a politician who would become the USA's most important ally in Latin America. The information connecting him to Escobar and the Medellín cartel was classified by his allies in the Pentagon.

best-equipped guerrilla force in the world, Colombia had Latin America's best trained government army.

Uribe had political support from the USA and a steady stream of dollars earmarked for the military, military technology and military advisors from the north, something which made him a formidable foe.

However Chávez quickly showed his pragmatic side by inviting Uribe to Caracas, declaring him as *mi nuevo mejor amigo*, my new best friend, in front of the Venezuelan, international and Colombian press.

Scenes of Chávez publicly embracing Uribe surprised many. Perfectly normal for your average Venezuelan, but against standard convention for leading political figures – he usually began conversations by asking how the wife and kids were doing. Chávez had several cards to play. One of them was steadily increasing buying power of the people, particularly after 2004. The strategic move for Chávez was to open the Venezuelan market up to Colombian exports. He did not view the neoliberal ideology of the Colombian government and the political and economic ties with the USA as reasons to prevent closer ties with Colombia. On the contrary. To overcome their political differences, Chávez' strategy was to create a personal relationship with Uribe, as well as increasing cultural and economic ties between the countries. Chávez also allowed several hundred thousand undocumented Colombian refugees who had been living and working in Venezuela without economic, social and political rights, to claim Venezuelan citizenship. He packaged agreements fostering economic cooperation with a declaration of love for 'the Colombian sister republic,' a vision whereby the two nations could be reunited.

That was exactly what the Colombian oligarchy feared most, Chávez and the knock-on effect of his social reforms. This was exactly where Venezuela expected pressure for a more belligerent policy to come from. By making the case for economic benefits to Colombian exporters, Chávez hoped to mitigate the opposition where it was strongest.

During this period, bilateral trade between Venezuela and Colombia doubled. Encouraged by the fruits of their good relationship, even with Latin America's most US-friendly president, Chávez embarked on a risky political adventure.

An adventure that would bring Colombia, ravaged by decades of civil war, several steps closer to peace, but would also lead to the deadly bomb attack in Angostura in the Sucumbíos province of the Ecuadorian jungle; threaten to unleash a full-scale regional war; derail the entire Latin American unification project, including the meeting in Tucumán, Argentina.

In August 2007 Chávez took the task of securing the release of the French-Colombian politician, Ingrid Betancourt, along with other FARC prisoners who had been abducted over the years.

When Betancourt was kidnapped in 2002, she became the most famous hostage in the world. There was a lot of international pressure on Colombian authorities to negotiate her release with the guerrillas. But Betancourt was soon forgotten, with some even believing her dead. This suited Uribe well, since his project was to wipe out the guerrilla militarily, not through negotiations. For that very reason, it seemed strange that Uribe gave Chávez permission to arrange the release of FARC hostages. Such a high-profile release would in all likelihood contribute to increased national and international support for FARC's requests to begin prisoner exchanges and peace negotiations, two things Uribe wanted to avoid at any price.

Perhaps Uribe had no other choice.

Chávez announced that in September 2007, he had received a letter from Manuel Marulanda, the FARC commander, that Betancourt was alive. 'I am prepared to travel into the depths of the jungle to talk to Marulanda about the release of Betancourt,' Chávez said at an international press conference. Chávez was still a president that the international media loved to hate. All the same, the media-friendly narrative was too good to be ignored – a revolutionary president willing to strap on his army boots, cross the front line of the world's oldest and bloodiest civil war, speak face to face with a guerrilla leader deep within the largest jungle in the world in order to secure the release of a French-Colombian daughter of a plutocrat. Suddenly everyone, in Colombia and across large parts of the world, was talking about Betancourt again. In France, her release was a matter of prestige. Even the country's conservative president, Nicolas Sarkozy, was forced to seize the opportunity and show support. He praised Chávez' initiative and immediately invited him to Paris. Latin America, Betancourt's family and the French president with the support of the EU, asked Uribe to refrain from any military offensive that could endanger the lives of the hostages, laying the groundwork for Chávez to succeed.

On one and the same day, Chávez managed to bring the relatives of American soldiers taken as prisoners of war by FARC, Colombian church leaders, Ingrid Betancourt's mother and someone representing Colombia's leftist political prisoners to the presidential palace. By including relatives of American POWs, even the Bush administration had to remain silent as he undermined the purpose of Plan Colombia, the USA's third largest military aid project in the world.

Supporters of the Colombian peace process, whom Uribe had previously described as guerrilla collaborators, were given a breath of fresh air. They launched a powerful offensive in their demands for peace, now safeguarded due to the international attention. Chávez had forced through a brand new agenda of peace and negotiations. This was the exact opposite of Uribe's goal of a rapid eradication of the guerrillas.

But the Colombian president secretly made preparations for his countermove.

On 21 November 2007, the Colombian government declared that Chávez no longer had permission to coordinate further prisoner releases. Uribe accused the Venezuelan president of having directly contacted members of Colombia's military high command to coordinate security, something he claimed was a breach of the conditions. Chávez, tantalisingly close to getting Betancourt freed, reacted furiously. According to him, Uribe was lying.

'I do not believe the Colombian government wants peace. They kick the table [a popular expression describing a bad loser sabotaging a game] to avoid a path to peace, and I have obviously lost all faith in the Colombian president.' A confidential document from 2008 written by the US ambassador in Colombia, James Brownfield, released by WikiLeaks, indicates that Chávez was probably right. Brownfield describes a meeting with the acting minister of foreign affairs in the Uribe government, Adriana Mejía, in which 'Mejia requested USG help to squash a French proposal to create a "group of friends" on the hostage issue.' According to Brownfield the French government was 'proposing the creation of a "Group of Friends" in exchange for a FARC commitment to free its "civilian" hostages. The group could then help achieve an exchange of the remaining hostages, as well as support a final peace process with the FARC.' A proposal very much in lines with Chávez' strategy of exploiting FARC's unilateral hostage releases to build international pressure on Uribe and weaken his argument that FARC was a terrorist organization with which no negotiation was possible. Brownfield writes that he 'assured her [Uribe's acting minister of foreign affairs] we would consult with our mission in Brussels to see what we could do to help' and addressed the document to US diplomatic missions in Europe, the State department's Bureau of Western Hemisphere Affairs as well as the Secretary of Defence and the CIA.

Chávez believed the USA and the Colombian oligarchy were behind the decision to break off what until then, had been successful negotiations. 'The war in Colombia is the pretence the imperialists needs to be close to Venezuela. I hope that Uribe will not allow himself to be used by the empire to go against Venezuela.'[102]

Nonetheless, Chávez did not break ties with Colombia, and on 10 January 2008, FARC released two hostages. The guerrillas, the released prisoners and their family thanked Chávez and asked Uribe to allow continued Venezuelan mediation to achieve more releases. This ensured that the process Chávez had begun, continued to attract international attention and kept Uribe against the wall, as families of other FARC hostages entered the international media spotlight with their pleas that Chávez be allowed to continue working towards more hostage releases. In the meantime however, enemies of the peace process did not sit idly by.

In the USA, Connie Mack, the new Republican chair of the House Subcommittee on the Western Hemisphere, stated that he wanted to have Venezuela placed on the 'State Sponsors of Terrorism' list.
    In Colombia, Uribe and his defence minister, presumably in collaboration with US military representatives, prepared an attack on FARC's interim base in Ecuador.
    In March 2008, aeroplanes and helicopters left their bases in Colombia and set course for the Ecuadorian border.
    FARC's 'secretary of state' Raul Reyes, had exposed himself during the negotiations to release Betancourt in exchange for imprisoned FARC members. Some believed a GPS chip had been installed in his Panamanian army boots, though more likely is that his on satellite phone conversations were traced. Whatever the case, Colombia's military knew his exact location. They bombed the temporary jungle camp in Sucumbíos in Ecuador, while Reyes and twenty-one other guerrilla warriors slept. All the guerrillas were killed, including Reyes and four Mexican students who were also present.
    There was also a deep irony to the attack. In Latin America, the name Angostura is mostly known in Latin America in reference to the Congress of Angostura (a Venezuelan town later named Ciudad Bolívar), in which delegates from Colombia and Venezuela legislated for what they intended to be a united republic called *la Gran Colombia*, which would also include part of what is now

Ecuador, once they were completely liberated from Spanish colonial rule. For several months after the bomb attack on the jungle area in northern Ecuador with the same name, Angostura became synonymous with the opposite, a violent campaign driving the three states closer to war than ever before.

Ecuador's president, Rafael Correa, reacted furiously to the bombing and immediately broke all ties with Colombia.

Uribe stated that Colombia had the right to attack FARC across its borders, hinting at both Ecuador and Venezuela. Chávez, who for years had been accused by American and Colombian media of actively supporting FARC in Venezuela, sent ten tank battalions to the Colombian border. He warned Uribe that a Colombian attack on Venezuelan soil would be considered an act of war and would be responded to accordingly. In the blink of an eye, Uribe's attack on Ecuador and open threat of war against Venezuela, had turned Latin America's political agenda on its head. The bombing in Angostura eliminated the opportunity for a Chávez-negotiated peace solution to Latin America's last civil war. Instead there was a danger that Colombia, backed by the US, would attack Venezuela. Worst case scenario, it could be the start of a bloody all-out regional war.

The international and Venezuelan media misrepresented Chávez' orders to defend Venezuela from potential Colombian incursions. They portrayed it as a threat. The BBC consulted 'analysts' who called the Venezuelan position 'madness' and claimed that Chávez 'threatened' Colombia because he was 'upset with the murder of Reyes.' The BBC did not offer anyone a chance to counter this, even though Chávez had been clear that it was a defensive move to defend the border against a possible incursion.[103] It was not until 2012, four years later, that Álvaro Uribe admitted that he had wanted 'a military operation in Venezuela,' but that he 'lacked the time' to plan the attack.[*] Until that point, the media from

---

[*] This despite a Colombian defence budget twice that of Venezuela, with Uribe backed by the USA. The military expenditures are documented by the Stockholm International Peace Research Institute, analysed on the blog Oilwars.blogspot.org:

Colombia, the USA and Venezuela, and as far afield as Spain and Norway, advanced the undocumented theory that Chávez had planned to instigate a war with Colombia, while simultaneously ridiculing the warning by Chávez that Uribe was planning an attack on Venezuela.[104]

In the days that followed, diplomatic attempts via several regional forums were made to ward off the threat of war that came about after Uribe's bombing attack. At meetings for the Organisation of American States (OAS), the USA was the only country to support Colombia's actions. All of Latin America and the Caribbean were in favour of a condemnation of Colombia. Ecuador and Venezuela considered the condemnation an insufficient guarantee that no further bombing attacks would take place, and staked everything on achieving an even clearer resolution at a summit in The Dominican Republic due to take place one week after the bombing. The meeting was a diplomatic show of power by the Latin American left, with Chávez centre stage.

It resulted in a complete condemnation of Uribe, who was forced to eat humble pie and pledge never to carry out similar attacks in the future.

US support for the Colombian bombing attack was frowned upon and only served to pave the way for the next historic step Chávez had planned to break US dominance of South America.

However the diplomatic defeat did not prevent Uribe from continuing preparations for an attack on Venezuela. When Uribe announced at the last moment that he would attend the Mercosur summit in Tucumán, Argentina, alarm bells went off in Caracas.

Chávez had to change his strategy.

---

http://oilwars.blogspot.no/2007/06/venezuelan-military-spending-busting.html
El Colombiano, 13.08.2012.
Accessible on the website:
http://www.elcolombiano.com/BancoConocimiento/A/alvaro_uribe_me_falto_tiempo_para_realizar_un_operativo_militar_en_venezuela/alvaro_uribe_me_falto_tiempo_para_realizar_un_operativo_militar_en_venezuela.asp

With Uribe in attendance, discussions about the bombing in Sucumbíos and the risk of the cold war between Colombia and Venezuela heating up would push other topics to the back of the agenda.

One item dropped from Chávez' agenda was an interview with a certain Norwegian journalist.

Missed Call from Miraflores

Me rio para no llorar, literally 'I am laughing to avoid crying.'
Al mal tiempo buena cara, 'Meet bad weather with a good face.'

It is easy to be happy in Venezuela – so easy in fact, that many global surveys have put Venezuela on the top ten list of the world's happiest people. But rules for what you have to do when the world opposes you offer few alternatives. You have to laugh, smile, joke or sing.

The repercussions of Uribe's bombing raid in the Ecuadorian jungle had caught up with me. My interview was cancelled, I was out of money, out of time and realised that I had spent an entire six months of my life waiting in vain. A few heavy days ensued in my eight-square-metre room. But as they say in Venezuela: *al mal tiempo, buena cara*. It was barely noon when I got on the Metro and headed west. My ex-girlfriend, who since the last time we met, had got her driving license, a car and a small flat across the street from her parents, picked me up at the station. The fact that Digitel, my mobile network, did not provide stable coverage to that *barrio* yet, suited me perfectly. I had no interest in anyone phoning me and disturbing me that day, and anyway, I was not expecting any important calls now that I had given up on my interview with Chávez – the entire purpose of my stay in Venezuela.

For that reason, I was surprised to hear the sudden beeping of text messages ticking in when I got coverage later that night on my way to grab some street food. The text messages notified me that I had messages on my voicemail. The first one had been left around noon: 'Hi, it's Maximilien, President Chávez' advisor. You have been granted an interview with the president. It will be at Miraflores at four o'clock this afternoon.' It was now nine o'clock. The next message: 'Eirik, are you there? Call me as soon as you can.' I nearly passed out. 'What's going on? The president is expecting you, we need confirmation. Now!' Message number four. 'What are you doing? You have an interview with the president. Pick up the phone.' I imagined the kind of insults I was going to get when I called back. For a moment I considered not returning his call to avoid the embarrassment, but then decided that no amount of humiliation could make up for the crazy blunder I had just made. 'Oh hi, it's you, what happened?' The voice was surprisingly calm. I explained the situation, excluding certain unnecessary details, and received an unexpected reply. '*Tranquilo*, Eirik. The president is going to Ecuador on 15 July. You're going to interview him on the trip. So you had better change your return ticket to a later date.'

The plans were explained to me as such: Chávez is going to Ecuador to break ground on a new oil refinery that was being built and operated by the state-owned oil companies of each country. Ecuador's president Rafael Correa was hosting the meeting. The location was Manta, a seaport on the Pacific, best known for amazing seafood and the USA's most important military base in South America. A number of Venezuelan ministers, military officials and PDVSA executives would be taking part. The flight would depart at seven o'clock in the morning from Simón Bolívar de Maiquetía, the international airport just outside the capital. We would return the same evening.

    I attempted to mentally prepare myself that this opportunity, like the previous three, would be cancelled. For days before the trip to Ecuador I sat in front of the TV flipping through the anti-Chávez channels on the lookout for any event that could lead to yet another cancellation. Perhaps the catastrophic result of the court case between Exxon and PDVSA, one which would lead to the immediate collapse of the country's economy. Or the Republicans in

Florida, with the help of an obliging US media, would finally manage to place Venezuela on the list of countries that 'sponsor terrorism' and impose new sanctions on the country. Or another Colombian bombing attack. The last possibility was the most likely, I thought, because immediately after the attack on Ecuador, Uribe had threatened military action against any country protecting FARC fighters. And not entirely unexpected, the private media in Venezuela had quickly sensed an opportunity and reported that leading guerrilla members were in Venezuela. Including claims by Globovisión and Televen that the FARC commander Joaquín Gómez was being protected by the Venezuelan national guard.[105] The claim was almost a direct invitation for Uribe to attack Venezuela.

But none of these things happened. Colombia's military – which had never hesitated to blame Chávez for anything – dismissed the Globovisión story of FARC commanders in Venezuela, calling it a lie. Apart from that, the news was exactly as I had grown accustomed to over the past six years: Journalists, NGOs, business leaders and politicians, to varying degrees of factual basis, accusing the Chávez government of corruption, incompetency, Castro-communism, food shortages, dictatorship and crime. All the while, claiming that Chávez had stifled freedom of expression. But those kinds of recycled accusations had been repeated for years on end, and they always bounced right off Chávez. There was no change to the agenda. So on 15 July 2008, wearing jeans and a wrinkled shirt, holding my passport, a notebook, a pen and a tape recorder, I waited by the nearest main road for the president's advisor to pick me up. At around five thirty in the morning, my mobile rang. 'We're in a black car. Just around the corner.' Moments later the car was there. The day started quietly. For a Venezuelan, Chávez' international advisor was a quiet man. We discussed the practical details of the journey until we arrived at the international airport, entering via a rear entrance.

Exit Uncle Sam, Enter Chávez

There was a relaxed atmosphere in the departure lounge. A few dozen people had already arrived. Most were dressed in red shirts and belonged to the president's entourage. Then the oil people arrived. Some of them were in suits, while others had clothes and symbols that clearly identified them as PDVSA staff. One person arrived in a red baseball jacket. It was Rafael Ramírez – president of PDVSA and Oil Minister, considered by many to be one of the world's most powerful men. While everyone waited for Chávez, a third group entered the room. The military. They were from the various branches of the armed forces and of various ranks. Some were from the presidential honour guard, wearing olive green uniforms and red berets. Some may have even participated in the historic counter-coup on 13 April 2002, when the soldiers turned their weapons away from the sea of people and pointed them at the military coup leaders. The large military turnout hinted that the trip was about more than just trade and diplomacy. Then Chávez arrived. I only saw him from a distance, when I was queueing up at passport control.

On my way out to the plane, I stood watching the rest of the delegation boarding. One of the president's entourage clearly noticed my amazement at all the military personnel present. He must have known that I was a journalist when he walked up to me and commented: 'This is how we do it. This is no game. We are challenging the imperialists, and we are going to fight until we have achieved total freedom for Latin America. They have the most powerful foreign policy machinery in the world. Now they [Colombia with American assistance] have bombed Ecuador and are trying to frighten President Correa into succumbing to the pressure. So we must show our Ecuadorian brothers that we stand with them one hundred per cent, and that we will do everything we can to support them.'

Surrounded by military vehicles, vigilant bodyguards and uniformed officers, the message was amplified. The people I was boarding the plane with, they meant business.

For a moment I thought about security. How safe was it to be on a plane with Hugo Chávez? All things considered, there were a lot of people openly calling for his assassination or declaring him 'a military target.' I remember one of the first big news stories I heard about Venezuela, it was about an assassination attempt made against the aeroplane Chávez was on board. The president was on his way back from a state visit in Norway where he had met King Harald and Prime Minister Bondevik. The plot was uncovered and the plane was able to change course and land at another airport. The terrorists managed to get away, leaving behind rocket launchers and other advanced weaponry, according to the newspaper, Últimas Noticias.

Had the assassination been successful, Chávez would not have been the first progressive Latin American president to end up in the burnt-out wreck of a plane. In 1981, Panamanian leader Omar Torrijos and Ecuadorian president Jaime Roldós were both killed in aeroplane accidents. The two leaders had both been declared enemies of US economic and geopolitical interests. The accidents occurred a few months apart, just after Ronald Reagan came to power, at a time when the USA was heavily involved in warfare in Central America. Neither of the accidents were ever explained, but in the book, *Confessions of an Economic Hitman*, John Perkins, formerly a prominent member of the US banking sector, presents strong evidence that the CIA planted explosives aboard the two planes. In recent years, the Cuban-Venezuelan terrorist Luis Posada Carriles had also become an important topic in Venezuela. In 1975, Posada helped plant explosives on a Cuban plane that killed seventy-three people, among them a number of promising young athletes. According to the *New York Times*, Posada, dubbed 'Latin America's bin Laden,' worked for the Venezuelan security services and the CIA. He was sentenced and imprisoned in Venezuela, but was helped to escape.[106] He currently resided in Miami, where he made frequent appearances with Bush's Republican friends.

But how likely was it that an assassination attempt would be made against Chávez' plane at that exact moment? Not very likely at all, I reasoned. Apparently Chávez had once been reproached by Fidel Castro for not taking his personal security seriously enough. Castro believed he exposed himself by continuing to act like a normal man after becoming president. One example was how Chávez never hesitated to sample the food and drink people offered him on his countless trips to the slums and villages. It did not matter to him if the tin cup or plastic plate was clean, or how many people had eaten from the same cutlery. Chávez did exactly what other poor Venezuelans do when they are offered something – he accepted it with gratitude and emptied his plate.* Lately though the president had reluctantly taken on Castro's advice and tightened up his security routine. This included what he ate, how many bodyguards he took with him, where he went, when he travelled and in what kind of vehicle.

At the airport I recognised two bodyguards who were almost always seen with the president. One of them was a young man with indigenous features. The other was a blonde woman. And then there were the Cubans. That is, people I assumed to be Cubans. They moved with confidence, scanning from side to side. Usually at a distance of between ten and one hundred metres from the president. Most were dark-skinned, powerfully built men of above-average height dressed in dark suits. There are few physical characteristics that set Cubans apart from Venezuelans, but there

---

* A well-known example is when Chávez stopped in the middle of a public appearance and asked his bodyguards to allow a small boy to come forward who had crawled to the edge of the stage to meet the president. Chávez asked the boy what he was eating, whereupon the two-year-old stuck his fingers in his mouth and pulled out a half-eaten biscuit and offered it to the president. Without hesitating, Chávez ate the mushy mess straight from the boy's fingers, like any normal Venezuelan family man from a poor background would have done with his own child.

was something about their expressions, their posture and their bearing. Something I could not quite place convinced me that they were highly-trained Cuban security officers. A few hours later I heard one of them speak in a distinctive Cuban accent, revealing that they were in fact Castro's men. The opposition and the media often accused Chávez of favouring Cuban security, even using it as an argument to urge Venezuelan officers to once again take up arms against him. Seeing these men up close, it was easy to understand why Chávez allowed Cubans into the heart of his security set-up.

My wandering thoughts about potential security threats were quickly interrupted when I was directed to my seat. The atmosphere was cheerful and relaxed. Like me, most of the people must have been up before five a.m. I was surrounded by high-ranking government officials, advisors and military personnel yawning loudly. Many made the most of the three-hour flight to get a little extra sleep. Some snored, others chatted. An hour before landing, I noticed a familiar head poking out of the door in front of me, from the room where the president's key ministers and generals were sitting.

'Why is everyone moping around?' It was the Minister of Foreign Affairs, Nicolás Maduro. A wide grin revealed itself beneath his moustache, and with his cheeky comment, the rest of the delegation was on alert. People pulled out their computers, books and briefcases. They were serious and focussed. Conversations went from the mundane to intense geopolitical debates. The advisor next to me was writing frenetically, presumably analyses, tips and observations Chávez could make use of during his meetings that day. People around me prepared for landing. Back to business.

For the time being, the trip to Ecuador was the last stop on an itinerary, which by all accounts was a race around the Americas between Bush and Chávez. When Bush went to Uruguay, Chávez showed up on the other side of the Rio de la Plata border river in Argentina. We don't need to be ruled by the imperialists, he had shouted, again in front of tens of thousands of crazy Argentinian at a football stadium. When Bush travelled to Colombia, Chávez landed on the other side of the Amazon jungle in Bolivia, joined by his ally, the socialist president and indigenous leader Evo Morales. Chávez' message was the same, plus fifteen million dollars for flood victims in the east of the country – once again in front of large crowds, where Chávez was seen as South America's leader in the battle for independence from US dominance. From there both competitors travelled north. Bush to Guatemala and Chávez to Nicaragua. The two enemies ended the race on their own side of the Caribbean, with Bush in Mexico and Chávez in Jamaica and Haiti, where he attacked the USA's proposed mega-projects for the production of biodiesel in Latin America. 'Bush wants to grow sugar cane and corn across large swathes of land to create energy for cars, while three hundred million people in Latin America and the Caribbean do not have enough food,' Chávez said to the Haitians, the poorest nation in the region. The USA 'urgently needs to break the growing alliance of the left-wing regimes [...] The increase of radical redistribution policies must be stopped,' NRK wrote about the Bush administration's battle with Chávez.[107]

When we landed in Manta, I had a clear indication of who was on the offensive in the race. The first thing I noticed when the pilot made his approach, was the planes with 'US Army' written on them. Part of Manta served as an American military base, USA's most important base on the South American mainland. But President Correa had already given notice to the Americans that they had to leave. Nevertheless in an interview with a conservative Miami-based TV channel with close ties to the Republicans, Correa had opened up the possibility of delaying the eviction, despite him viewing the US military base as a serious threat to the country's independence. 'If the USA gives Ecuador a military base in Florida, then they can keep their base in Manta,' he said with obvious sarcasm, knowing full well that the US authorities would never allow such a thing.

The plane came to a stop. As Chávez, dressed in an army-green top with a red T-shirt visible underneath, walked down the stairs of the plane, I saw American soldiers behind barbed-wire fencing on the other side of the runway, preparing for the imminent dismantling of the military base. The symbolism was telling: US Army out, Chávez in.

Surrounded by soldiers and officers from the Ecuadorian Air Force, President Rafael Correa hurried across the runway to greet Chávez. You did not get the sense that these were two normal political allies, as they met with a firm embrace and powerful thumps on the shoulders, but rather that they were brothers and comrades-in-arms.

In general, Chávez had quite a knack with people, particularly soldiers. It may have even saved his life during the coup six years earlier. When he turned to speak to the Ecuadorian soldiers, he looked them straight in the eyes and told them that they were the soldiers of the future, that they needed to be patriotic like the independence generals Bolívar and Sucre, working in the service of the people and the great fatherland – Latin America. Never again would soldiers have to degrade themselves by bowing to the imperialists or the oligarchy. The young men were left standing with a familiar expression, one I had seen many times before. Visibly moved, as though they had just met a rock star, and convinced they were part of something big.

While Chávez dished out firm handshakes and pats on the back, another figure emerged from a small plane a short distance away. At first the haze of heat rising from the scorching asphalt made it difficult to see, even though the man was not far away. He was jogging casually towards us now, wearing jeans, a white shirt with rolled-up sleeves and aviator glasses.

The aviator glasses gave him away, it was the former Nicaraguan guerrilla, Daniel Ortega.

As leader of the Sandinista guerrillas, FSLN,[*] Ortega managed to topple the Somoza dictatorship in 1979, which thanks

---

[*] The Sandinista guerrillas were named after Augusto César Sandino, a farmer who became a guerrilla leader and fought against US military intervention in

to US support, had ruled the country with an iron fist for forty-three years.* Ortega redistributed wealth, wiped out illiteracy with Cuban assistance and instituted a democratic multi-party system. Reagan declared him an enemy. The CIA trained, financed and ordered the Contras, a feared terrorist militia, to launch a bloody civil war in the country. Some of the favoured methods of the Contras, including rape, torture and murder, were so beastly that in the end, US Congress banned further financing of the militia, though the CIA continued to do in secret.[108] The Contras' reign of terror took the lives of between thirty thousand and one hundred thousand people, destroying the economy, leading to food shortages and inflation of seventeen hundred per cent. Before the presidential election in 1990, the US financed candidate Violeta Chamorro based her entire election campaign on the threat that the Contras would only end the terror if Ortega resigned. That was enough for a considerable number of war-weary socialists to turn their back on Ortega, and he lost the election.

No one had mentioned that Daniel Ortega was going to be at the airport in Manta that day, and most seemed as surprised as I was. But Ortega was a surprising man. He resigned after the election defeat in 1990 and had to look on as the subsequent right-wing government introduced neoliberalism and revoked the welfare services of the poor. But the military was still filled with Ortega's former brothers in arms. In contrast to the military in Nicaragua's neighbouring countries, which in the nineties indiscriminately slaughtered the left wing, the Nicaraguan army refused to be used as a tool to crush Ortega and his movement. In 2006 he was re-elected.

Nicaragua. Sandino achieved his goal of ousting the US military in 1933. With that the war was over and Sandino became an important leader in the peaceful battle for the redistribution of land, organising poor farmers into cooperatives and trade unions. The oligarchy and the conservative regime continued to view him as a threat, and had him imprisoned and executed in 1934.
* Some in the US political elite considered Somoza a 'Frankenstein dictator', but a necessary evil in the battle against communism:
Paterson, Thomas et al (2009): *American Foreign Relations: A History*, Volume 2: Since 1895, 7th Edition, Wadsworth, pp. 162–168.

A bit older, a bit of horse trading leaving the enemy richer and his socialist principles poorer, but still positioned to bring the country out of the conservative, US backed fold.

At the airport in Manta, with the soon-to-be dismantled military base in the background and Correa and Chávez at his side, Ortega solemnly pledged to do everything in his power to help the Bolivarian crusade. A military orchestra played the three national anthems and then Ortega made a brief speech. 'We belong to the same fatherland, *la patria grande*, from the Rio Grande [the border between Mexico and the US] to Patagonia [the southern tip of South America]. In this imperialistic and neocolonial world, we can only survive and triumph if we stand together.' Then Ortega turned towards Chávez and announced that only a few days earlier, two of Nicaragua's Central American neighbours, Honduras and Guatemala, had joined ALBA and PetroCaribe.

Hugo Chávez, Rafael Correa, Daniel Ortega – the three musketeers, it was impossible to miss the association – walked off a little, put their heads together for a few minutes before bidding farewell to Ortega as he turned and walked back to the small plane. I never found out what they discussed.

'Chávez, Ecuador Is Also Your Fatherland'

Chávez had a busy schedule in Ecuador. The first stop was to officially launch the building work on the oil refinery, a few miles away. From there they would travel to Manta's city centre to meet with international oil executive from the private and the public sector. A helicopter was waiting for the president and his closest advisors, while I ended up in a black SUV, squished together on the backseat with Deputy Foreign Minister Francisco Arias Cardenas and two others. The conversation was informal with jokes and friendly jabs, as Venezuelans often do amongst friends. Defying the Caribbean Bachata music blasting from the car stereo, they analysed their plans for the trip, shaking with every bump we hit on the dusty road leading to the future oil refinery.

The area was large, flat and remote. With almost no buildings in the vicinity. Nonetheless, several hundred poor Ecuadorians from the surrounding villages had come to hear Chávez and Correa speak. Chávez was undoubtedly the main attraction. In front of a euphoric audience he talked in favour of inter-state companies as opposed to transnational companies. He was referring to an alliance of state-owned companies from allied countries. One of the biggest economic curses of Latin America and the Third World has long been the lack of capital available for heavy investment in strategic economic and industrial sectors. That was why countries were forced to hand over their natural resources and industries to foreign companies. The oil refinery Correa and Chávez were going to construct was a pioneering project towards the new solution. With inter-state companies, the countries of Latin America would gradually gain control over their own economies. 'What we do today at this location, [to take control of our resources] will determine what our children are able to do in fifty years,' Chávez said.

People listened with interest, but it was only when he mentioned the battle against imperialism that the cheering reached the clear blue sky. 'All empires grow, achieve their glory, then decline in the end. We will make the empire fall,' he shouted. The applause was interspersed with chanting from the audience. 'Out with the gringo base in Manta,' 'Bolívar's sword is sweeping across Latin America.'

In his speech, Rafael Correa explained that his impression of the Venezuelan president had been less than positive for a long time, and described how he got to know the real Chávez: 'I was at an international summit in Asunción [Paraguay] and was impressed. Chávez was the only one who said something coherent and sensible.' This was during a chaotic period when Correa was finance minister in one of the many short-lived Ecuadorian governments before he became president, back when Chávez was the only left-wing president in South America. 'The media cheat us with all their lies,' he said and called Venezuela's president a 'pioneer for the historic process of change in Latin America.' Chávez called the process 'the second independence,' following up on the work that Bolívar began but was unable to complete. Correa talked about a great 'era of change.'

Correa said that he endorsed Chávez' idea of socialism for the twenty-first century, though he insisted that the Ecuadorian variant must take its own national context into consideration, just as the Venezuelan variant did. 'Ecuador is also your fatherland, Chávez,' he said, revealing what would become the most important issue for the two presidents over the coming years: to create a new regional organisation for all of Latin America and the Caribbean, without the USA. The organisation would replace the US dominated OAS as the most important international organ in the region. It would deprive Washington of its most important formal agency for political control over Latin America. 'We must unite into one fist,' Correa said.

After the speech, the usual Chávez hysteria ensued. Hundreds of people flocked around him to shake his hand, give him a hug or offer him a present. I am not quite sure how it happened, but soon afterwards, Chávez was sitting in a rusted-out pick-up someone had lent him. He told Correa to jump in. With their bodyguards desperately running after them, Chávez floored it and left a cloud of dust on the road. He had wanted to talk to more farmers in the region, he later explained. I was running as well, to reach the car that would take us to our next stop. Chávez was scheduled to have lunch with representatives of the Ecuadorian and international oil industry and have a private meeting with the Ecuadorian government. Together with a breathless deputy foreign minister, who had mud and sand all over his dark suit trousers, we managed to hop into the car just as the driver started the engine. We had to hurry, because rumours that Chávez was in the area had spread amongst the locals and the road was soon blocked off by swarms of people.

Chávez was in many ways an atypical president, though a typical Latin American. For example, he was convinced that physical meetings, face to face, always had a greater chance of success than indirect communication via letters, phone calls or diplomats. For that reason, he had seven government ministers with him, one of his most key military advisors, as well as the PDVSA executives, all there to forge a personal link with Correa's minsters and generals.

No European leader travelled as much or with as many ministers as Chávez. Correa had provided an important explanation for that earlier that day: The Latin American oligarchy uses the mass media for negative campaigning against Chávez, presenting him as a threat to their respective homelands and sowing discord between him and his allies. An explanation perhaps surprisingly confirmed by the US ambassador to Ecuador, Linda Jewell, who a few months later wrote that 'there is more than a grain of truth to Correa's observation that the Ecuadorian media play a political role, in this case the role of the opposition. Many media outlet owners come from the elite business class that feels threatened by Correa's reform agenda, and defend their own economic interests via their outlets. In addition, Ecuador's weak political parties have left a political vacuum, which has been filled in part by criticism of Correa by some of the large Ecuadorian TV stations and newspapers.' Of course, the ambassador's analysis was sent as a confidential document to the government in Washington, not meant for the public, as the US government continued to publicly push the narrative of 'authoritarian governments versus the independent private media' through NGOs and the media. Nevertheless that precise description would fit most Latin American countries, where the press at times went to extreme lengths in demonizing Chávez, making the entire project for regional cooperation more difficult. A need to bypass the media, with its obvious bias, was also the reason Chávez and Lula had made an agreement to meet in person at least three times a year.[109]

I had not been told when my interview with Chávez was going to take place. And following the private meeting between the two presidents and their ministers, and the lunch with the oil people, doubt began creeping in again. It was getting late. Apart from the short helicopter ride and the private meeting, Chávez had only been out of my sight once: to get five minutes of rest in his hotel room.

A Political Animal

Towards the end of the day, a few friendly journalists from the president's press corps and a private TV station tried to convince me to continue on to Bolivia where Chávez would be making an appearance the following day. The three-hour flight back to Caracas was Chávez' only possibility to get some badly needed sleep during the twenty hour trip, and the journalists who had experience covering the presidents travels doubted he would sacrifice that possibility for me. After a lot of toing and froing, I decided to stick with the original plan and hop inside the last car before it headed back to the airport so I could take the presidential plane back to Caracas together with Chávez.

  It was a gamble. Obviously I was aware of the rumour that the president only slept four hours a day, but still I assumed there was a high probability that he would postpone the interview in order to get some rest. The offer to stay in Ecuador with the other journalists had been quite tempting. I could have travelled directly to Bolivia the following day and try to get my interview then, where hopefully it would be less hectic. But after my previous blunder with my mobile phone, I dared not risk it.

  It turned out to be a good decision. During an emotional parting between Chávez and Correa on the runway outside the presidential plane, one of Chávez' men grabbed me and led me over to the two presidents. Chávez held out his hand: 'Ah, you're the Swedish guy who talks like a *malandro* from the *barrio*. The boys told me about you.' The president laughed loudly and gave me a firm thump on the back. 'Noruego, señor presidente', I replied slightly puzzled.

A few months earlier, I had ended up at a party in a middle-class neighbourhood where for once, I met some Chavistas. During a friendly bit of banter with a new friend, I had stuck out my middle finger and said 'sit on this and dance the *joropo*. [a Venezuelan folk dance]' Though I did not realise it at the time, one of the people who burst out laughing when I said this was in Chávez' inner circle. It struck me then that the president may have been referring to that event when he greeted me, which would also explain his unusually cheerful laughter, even for Chávez. Without loosening his grip on my shoulders, Chávez shouted to Correa and introduced me. 'I believe we have an honest boy here. From the far north, from Norway, can you believe it,' Chávez said. 'No, Hugo, he is from Venezuela,' Correa said after exchanging a few words with me, intended as a compliment to my Spanish.

Someone started shouting and waving a flag. We hurried up the stairs and boarded the plane.

Soon the president's daughter came to my seat. She showed me into Chávez' office aboard the plane. He was wearing glasses and reading some papers when I came in.

'Hi Eirik. Welcome to my office, how are you doing?'

He looked up from the page he was reading, which turned out to be the day's international news.

The president started reading out loud. An AFP[*] story about how Venezuela, through Citgo, a PDVSA subsidiary, was developing energy-saving initiatives for poor Americans. For several years, Chávez had been collaborating with Joseph Kennedy from the Democratic Party together with grass roots organisations in poorer parts of the northern states to deliver subsidised heating oil. The president continued reading until he was interrupted by the phone. The moment it rang, I was asked to turn off my recorder. I got the sense that it was General Alberto Müller Rojas calling, one of Chávez' most prominent advisors on military and political matters.

---

[*] Agence France Presse - an international news agency based in Paris.

General Müller had taken part in the rebellion against the military dictator Pérez Jiménez in 1958, and instructed Chávez at the military academy in the seventies, where the two became close friends. Müller was presumed to be the brain behind Chávez' military defence doctrine for asymmetrical warfare: decentralised popular militias, guerrilla tactics and special focus on protecting or destroying the country's oil installations in the event of an invasion. There had been a few public spats between the two, but the free-speaking general was now back in the ranks. It was a good day, the president said on the phone. 'Extremely productive.' He hung up, read a few more articles, yawned loudly and put down his papers.

Chávez looked at me for a moment.

'You must be exhausted, you look more tired now than you did this morning,' he said. 'We can chat for a while, and then we can try to get a bit of rest later. What did you think of today? Have you been to Ecuador before?'

The droning of the engines picked up, and while I fiddled with my seat belt and thought about how to start, Chávez declared in a serious tone: 'The two of you, you and Maria [the president's daughter was still next to me] are witness to a birth, a new era.'

He wanted to talk about the international offensive this journey was a part of.

I wanted to know about Chávez the person and the thinker.

Following his election in 1998, the Venezuelan president had forced his way onto a geopolitical and ideological landscape that had not moved since the Cold War, unleashing a series of chain reactions that sent ripple effects around the world. But still there was something chaotic and unpredictable about how the consequences of Chávez' ideas, words and decisions toppled old ideological and political structures and built up new ones.

'I want to know everything,' I said, 'about your own political development, from your childhood until today. About what you did and thought when you pursued the guerrillas in the jungle in the eighties, during the Caracas uprising and massacre, during your own attempted coup, everything that has influenced your political career.'

'We could talk about that for five days non-stop,' he said with a laugh.

'When did you first become interested in politics?'

'To answer that I have to use what I believe is a very old concept. Eduardo Galeano uses it a lot.'

Suddenly he was awake and gesticulating in his particular energetic way.

'I was a roaming child. I sold fresh and dried fruit in small villages. On squares, at schools, on public transport, at the circus, at festivals. And already on that country road, I was confronted by a reality. I remember the feeling of unease when faced with poverty, deprivation and injustice. I remember arriving at a small shanty in a tiny village. There I began to understand deprivation. My interest in politics, what I believe is politics, stems from that. Politics is precisely that, to allow yourself to be moved by an ethical and spiritual impulse, to identify yourself with the lives of others, to care about prosperity and deprivation in society in general. When I had that first impulse, that desire to help someone, when I felt the pain of seeing someone suffering, I was already involved in politics. Not to say that I had any thoughts of joining a political party or anything like that. Since that time, this feeling of unease has matured inside me; it motivated me as I passed through the stages that have led me here, and then I ended up in this battle [batalla] for life, for the people, for society and for the country. Aristotle speaks of the political animal. I believe I was born a political animal.'

'What was it like going to war against the guerrillas? What have you taken from that time? Do you think that you are fighting for the same ideals now that the guerrillas you pursued were fighting for back then?'*

---

* Chávez, who had elbowed his way to the limelight of the global political stage over these past years, was normally dressed in red and was always talking about socialism. Therefore it might seem paradoxical that for years during his military

'Ever since the 1960s, my life has had moments of contact with the guerrilla war. Indirect contact, but still a form of contact, ever since my childhood. The village where I was born was on the frontline of the guerrilla war at the time. This was a guerrilla war inspired by the Cuban Revolution. And after the Punto Fijo Pact,* the pact of the elite that locked the people out of politics, an era of terrible repression launched by the state. Ever since my childhood I heard about the guerrillas and their fight. I remember the soldiers who came. Sometimes they took over the school and made it an anti-guerrilla unit. On one occasion, my father was imprisoned in one of these anti-guerrilla camps when I was a child. He was imprisoned, but not because he was a guerrilla fighter. He had been with a group of friends, and was arrested because they did not obey the soldiers when told to stop. He was imprisoned for a day or two, and I remember going to see him with my mother, near my village. Later in my youth, in Barinas, the capital of the state where I was born, I got to know some former guerrillas. I got to know families where the father was from the left and he told me about the guerrillas, about a certain Fidel Castro, about a certain Che Guevara. I remember clearly the day they killed Che Guevara. It was written about in the newspapers, and you heard the rumours. Like the child I was, I had a kind of cinematic hope. Even though the papers wrote that Che's guerrilla division was surrounded, that more and more of his comrades fell in battle, and that it was only a matter of time before it was Che's turn, I believed to the very end that they could not kill him. I believed Fidel Castro would send helicopters to save him. My first personal encounter with the guerrilla war occurred near the Colombian border in 1976 and in 1977, and later in the east of the country. At one point, as a young officer, I was actually on the verge of joining the guerrillas. Luckily I did not. What is certain, is that by then, I had already plotted a political course, I had a much

---

career he was charged with wiping out *the* symbol of the Latin American left-wing: the guerrilla fighters.
* The pact was signed in 1958 between the two ruling parties AD and COPEI – who took turns governing Venezuela until Chávez rose to power.

more precise understanding of politics. At the age of twenty, I decided to found a revolutionary movement.'

It was in 1977 that Chávez and a group of closely aligned officers founded the secretive MBR-200 movement, with the objective of carrying out a revolution in Venezuela. But the event that really accelerated the conspiratorial movement would only take place twelve years later, in 1989. Chávez was not on duty when the army was ordered to suppress the protests over the IMF package. But many soldiers who were ordered to carry loaded weapons, refused to obey. The indignation grew.

'If I had been called out to participate in that massacre, I do not know what I would have done, but I can assure you that I would never have obeyed.* I would never have done as so many other soldiers did, massacring people who asked for nothing more than justice. This was in 1989, and the social deprivation had spread across all of Venezuela. And as if the deprivation was not enough – President Carlos Andrés Pérez took it one step further by implementing the IMF shock policies. That was what made the country explode. I felt a deep pang of guilt, as a member of an army sent out by a corrupt, oppressive, and murderous government. Naturally this only fuelled the revolutionary movement and contributed to the rebellion three years later on 4 February 1992. All of these are connected. An impulse since childhood, an awakening provoked by the poverty around me.'

Chávez took a brief, almost imperceptible pause, just enough to draw in enough air so that the tone of his next sentence would match its content.

'I come from the catacombs of poverty. I was a poor child, a working child, a village child. And later a soldier, by then already aware of the problematics of poverty. Then I began to study politics,

---

* That may be the reason Chávez did not have his command taken from him back then and was assigned miscellaneous administrative tasks at the presidential palace. If we believe the rumours, Chávez had already been singled out as a potential troublemaker by the government appointed military authorities.

the political practice, the military practice. Theory and practice all the way, can you imagine, the experience of being in anti-guerrilla units – whilst reading the theories the guerrillas are founded on.'

He was interrupted by one of the flight attendants. She brought in some smoked pork chops with rice and salad. Chávez was not tempted by the fruit juice the stewardess offered him, instead asking for a glass of *colita*, a red mineral water, supposedly fruit flavoured. *Colita* is probably the most artificial drink on the Venezuelan soft drinks market, a favourite amongst the kids of the *barrio*. He indicated to the hostess that there were two hungry men, not just one, waited for my plate to arrive and then told me to dig in. I was not surprised that Chávez was hungry. Since we disembarked the plane in Ecuador around ten o'clock in the morning, more than fourteen hours earlier, the president had eaten just once. But the lavish seafood served at the lunch for the international oil executives had not been to his liking. I was sat a couple of tables away from Chávez and curiously observed him picking at the shellfish soup. I did not leave a drop.

'Correa insisted that the shellfish symphony was very good, but I didn't care for it,' Chávez said. But the smoked pork chops, he set upon them mercilessly. As he did, he continued telling me about the long lines of his own political development. By the time the president was gnawing at the bones – Venezuelans usually prefer meat where you can eat straight from the bone – the story about his early years as president was complete.

'In the beginning, the relationship between the Bolivarian government and the Venezuelan bourgeoisie was a kind of honeymoon. Even big business in the US wanted to team up with me. It was an attempt by the imperialists and the bourgeoisie to co-opt the government from within. They wanted to 'tame the beast'. 'The beast' being me. That was what they called me, those who thought I was a threat to their privileges. 'We were unable to slay the beast [in the election]. So we will have to tame him.' Then a coordinated attempt was made to get me to renege on my promise to change society. The bourgeoisie, the oligarchy, attempted to influence friends and family members, attempted to get them to influence me in the hope that my government would continue protecting their privileges. And even though they could not influence me directly, they used their leverage at important ministries. They had key people in the Defence Department, the Justice Department, the Finance Department, the Central Bank. Not to mention full control of PDVSA. The USA was also part of my honeymoon period with the bourgeoisie. I went to the White House, I went to the IMF, I threw the opening pitch at Yankee Stadium and opened the New York Stock Exchange. I had meetings with the biggest capitalists and bankers in the empire, and they came to visit me in Venezuela. But over time I realised that if I continued down the path of naivety they were leading me along, I would end up a traitor ... '

'Do you mean like *Gutierrez* ...?' I asked, one of Correa's predecessors in Ecuador, who had promised radical redistribution to the poor, but who quickly allowed himself to be bought, frightened or persuaded into abandoning his promises of reform.

'Yes, like him, and like so many others. I would have become one of them. So I began to isolate myself. I began to seek solitude, to think, to reflect. I began to read old speeches, to remind myself of where I came from, the entire journey we had taken to arrive here. To remember the dead who were left along the way, who had sacrificed their lives for believing in me.'

At a little past one a.m. Venezuelan time, around 10 000 feet about sea level with Colombia below us, Chávez talked about his dramatic break with the economic elite.

'Then we began to pass laws that had a more revolutionary character. Like the Agriculture Act and the Banking Act, which reduced the power of the banking sector, the bourgeoisie and the landowners, the Catholic Church – that is the uppermost hierarchy of the Catholic Church – the monopolies, and above all the oligarchy, both the national and the transnational. This radicalised the revolution. The elites decided to press for a coup d'état when they understood that their attempts to 'tame the beast' had failed.

Why did they fail? It was the knowledge of my duty towards the people. Think of the old expression 'crossing the Rubicon.' I crossed my Rubicon, there is no way back. Every day it becomes clearer to me that my task is to deepen the revolution. Even though it is peaceful, and even though it has been infiltrated, precisely because of the distinctive nature of the process, even though you are often forced to "sleep with the enemy," every day it slowly becomes a more authentic socialist revolution.'

'Many were surprised that you declared socialism as the political goal of the Bolivarian revolution. Was that a turnabout? And is it realistic to resurrect socialism in the twenty-first century?'

'After all these years, I don't think there can be talk of a turnabout. I have never been on the right, so working towards socialism cannot be seen as a reversal. I have always been revolutionary and belonged to the left. At a very young age I was reading Karl Marx, Mao Zedong, Che Guevara, Bolívar. When we founded the Bolivarian movement in the army, we talked about a movement to make a break. I had contact with former guerrilla leaders and revolutionary trade unionists. But remember what the world was like in 1992 when we first took up arms. The fall of the Berlin Wall in 1989, the fall of Ortega's Sandinista government in Nicaragua in 1990, the collapse of the Soviet Union and socialism in Eastern Europe. Look at the pressure we had to withstand. The political storm we went through. The lights went out for socialism as we knew it. The only light still burning was in revolutionary Cuba; Fidel was still carrying the torch. At the time people stopped discussing socialism and imperialism entirely, as a result of the massive global ideological pressure from the right. After the confusion of the nineties, after the unbridled display of power from the oligarchy and the imperialists, it took time. But through my personal confrontation with these powers, I was convinced that the time was ripe to dust off and fly the flag of socialism. As Trotsky

said, "every revolution needs the whip of the counter-revolution."*
The time was ripe to launch a new anti-imperialistic and socialist offensive. And mark my words, we challenged the world to participate in the debate about socialism for the twenty-first century, and I now have no fewer than forty or fifty books about the new socialism which have been recently published in a number of languages. Quite simply, socialism has been resurrected. And people are talking about anti-imperialism again. I don't know if you were at the PetroCaribe meeting on Isla Margarita earlier today. But there was a president there, who five or ten years ago talked about nothing but neoliberalism. Now he is talking about anti-imperialism.'

'You're referring to Fernández, the president of the Dominican Republic?'

'Yes. And Colon [Guatemala's newly-elected centre-left president] and Zelaya [Honduras' new president from the centrist party, Partido Liberal]. Not to mention Ortega, who has always been anti-imperialist.'

'But how far will you go with your economic policies? How much is the state going to own in Venezuelan socialism? Obviously there was a reason it collapsed in the east.'

Chávez thought for a long time before answering.

'Socialisation of the means of production, whether government or social property, is instrumental. The fact that for the first time, the Venezuelan state has control of the petroleum industry, the petroleum reserves, the downstream operations, the revenue, it is a means to achieve something, not a goal in itself. The goal cannot be for the state to own the means of production. What is the goal? The goal is to hand over the power that owning the means of production gives to the people and the local communities. And now we are back to our starting point. Democracy means that

---

* Leon Trotsky was a Russian revolutionary who led the Red Army, but later fell out with Stalin. What Chávez meant by the Trotsky quote was that it was the oligarchy's use of economic power, lockout, sabotage and speculation (read: counter-revolution) that made him realise it was impossible to govern without taking greater control over the economy.

people govern and have real power in society, it cannot simply be the right to vote and the right to express opinions. No, we must have economic democracy, social democracy, and political democracy. For example, over the last few years we have transferred thirty-six billion dollars of oil revenue into the National Development Fund. Money that used to vanish from the country. If you examine the accounts of the Venezuelan National Bank, you will find that between 1980 and 2000, more than 150 billion dollars left the country. Who took the money? The Venezuelan financial oligarchy and their international partners. All the while the state is saddled with even more debt. So the fact that we, with the help of the oil revenues, are launching a plan for agricultural revolution, that we are financing *Misión Robinson*, *Misión Sucre* and *Misión Rivas* [large-scale programmes for illiteracy, primary and university education for previously excluded poor people], *Misión Cultura*, *Madres del barrio* [Mothers of the barrios, which supports poor single mothers], *Mercal*, which offers subsidised food to around twelve or thirteen million Venezuelans [nearly half the population], all this from the billions of dollars that used to simply vanish. This is giving real power to the people. This is making Venezuela a true democracy. An economic democracy. Control of CANTV [the national phone company which was privatised in the nineties and re-nationalised in 2006] means that the country has communications resources. This has allowed us to increase coverage and reduce prices. The poor now have access to phones, not to mention the Internet. Venezuela is investing massively in the Internet, something which offers people enormous opportunities, which previously were reserved for the upper class. And in addition, we have the revenues the nationalised CANTV generates for the state. We can now reinvest this money in society to implement social development.'

'Previous attempts to achieve socialism have most often ended up as dictatorships. Your government has been criticised for authoritarian tendencies. Is there room for democracy in socialism for the twenty-first century?'

'Democracy must be one of the cornerstones of socialism for the twenty-first century. One of the missteps in earlier attempts to achieve socialism was to limit democracy. I believe we must do the opposite. That is what we are attempting in Venezuela. Because what is democracy actually? The farce of arranging elections every five or six years and excluding people the rest of the time, that is not good enough. That is bourgeoisie democracy. I'm talking about genuine democracy which – in addition to regular elections – functions at a deeper level. It is about giving power to the people. Teaching 1.5 million illiterate people to read, this is power. Millions of people were previously excluded from primary, secondary and higher education. Courses, popular culture in the *barrios*. Transferral of organisational power to the people. Financial power through the communal banks. We provide resources for the local councils, *consejos comunales*. [Local grass roots organisations that operate in every Venezuelan municipality.] They make proposals, make demands, criticise us, and I have instructed the mayors, state governors, ministers and everyone to listen to them and to include them in the decision-making process and the implementation of these decisions. All of it, democracy. Elections at grass-roots level, candidates for local elections, for the regional leadership and for the national leadership in the socialist party PSUV.* Massive participation in all internal processes. Democracy must be a fundamental component of the new socialism.'

'The big question for people on the political left, at least in the West, is whether the Bolivarian revolution will be the first socialist project not to be crushed by coup, invasion, civil war or other forms of intervention from the North – and at the same time avoid ending up as a one-party-state?'

'That is a good question. A good question which history alone can answer. The answer is dependent on many factors that go beyond the borders of Venezuela. Until a few years ago, Venezuela

---

* PSUV, the United Socialist Party of Venezuela, the party Chávez founded in 2007

was alone on this path. There was only Cuba, but that is a country that does not quite match your definition of democracy, of the multi-party system and broad freedoms. In Venezuela we have many freedoms. Some would say that the opposition and the oligarchy have too many freedoms. They have the freedom to work for foreign agents against their own country and people, the freedom to attack democratic institutions, commit economic sabotage, call for a military coup against elected authorities. To wage an information war. The war waged by the elite is a great challenge. But we have managed to awaken the masses and in doing so, consolidate the changes. At the same time, new progressive governments have joined us, Rafael Correa in Ecuador, Evo Morales in Bolivia, who has a socialist movement supporting him. Fernando Lugo, Paraguay's newly elected president, he talks about socialism with no shame at all. Daniel Ortega won the election in Nicaragua. So the development whereby progressive forces are expanding and being strengthened in the Caribbean, Central America and South America means that the Venezuelan project has an even greater chance of success. And while we wait for less antagonistic governments in the North, we bolster our alliances with countries like Russia and China, so internationally, we have many strings to our bow.'

'You are often criticised of attacking freedom of expression. Aftenposten, a Norwegian paper, wrote a few years ago that you had banned any political debate before 11 o'clock in the evening.' Chávez sat quietly for a long while. He did not say anything but his expression suggested he was wondering whether I was a complete idiot.

'Well, you should investigate who owns that paper, or what kind of interests are behind that paper. What makes someone write something so ridiculous? We debate twenty-four hours a day here, and most of the media are waging an information war against the revolution and against our democracy.'

Chávez stopped again, took a breath, and continued in a steady voice.

'They call me a tyrant, a dictator, someone who infringes on people's human rights, they compare me to Hitler. They attempt to ridicule me as though I were mad, power-hungry. But I am exactly as you see me now. So why all this mudslinging, why all these lies? This is about the fear of the elite. And I believe that the demonising, the mudslinging in Europe that is directed at us and at me in particular, and at our Bolivarian revolution, it does not come free of charge. The European elite are terrified of what they call the knock-on effect. They are implementing cuts and neoliberal policies, they are taking away the rights of the workers, the pensioners and the students, they cut people's wages only to enrich themselves. And they manage to do all this, not because the people asked for these policies, but because they have managed to make people to give up, to believe that there is no alternative to the cuts that only serve the rich. If Europeans, if the people of Europe, actually knew what was happening in Venezuela, what we are achieving in Venezuela – obviously with all of our flaws and deficiencies – by reducing the wealth of the financial assets and giving power to the people. If they knew how much we have reduced poverty, and how we have increased pension payments, student grants, founded new universities, offered new public services. If they knew that we are putting it into practice, it would make the ground shake under the feet of the European elite. That is why they do not want the people to see what is happening. That is the reason for the fierce disinformation campaign by the European media, trying to tarnish what we are attempting to achieve.'

'The Nordic social democracies are at the top of the world in social equality. Is that a possible route for Venezuela?'

'To my knowledge, what I have seen on my journeys to Europe, welfare states have been a success in a number of countries. It would be interesting to study the particulars in these countries, how it was possible to establish a successful welfare state there in particular? Under which preconditions? For example, I am certain that these countries never allowed the kind of neoliberal policies which are now reducing more and more societies to rubble. They were strongly influenced by Keynesianism* so in some instances, they have had success, yes. But [Chávez considers for a moment] capitalism, which they never abandoned completely, entered a new phase at the end of the last century, the so-called neoliberal globalisation phase, which I would call the phase of madness, many of the European welfare states have been shaken. I hope I am mistaken, but I believe many are in decline or are being weakened, while the rest are threatened by the global crisis now engulfing capitalism. But these are observations from afar. My knowledge of these countries is insufficient to be able to discuss their internal social conditions.'

'Would you recommend that Europe change course and reverse the economic liberalisation process?'

'First and foremost: I am not in a position to recommend what others should do. From such a distance and lacking the knowledge of what is taking place in Europe. No. I dedicate myself almost exclusively to what is happening in Venezuela and to the Latin American integration process. And even though we have good ties to several African, European and Asian countries, I do not feel that I should offer them too much advice. But I hope and I believe that what is happening in Latin America, in some way or other, will influence Europe.'

'If you believe you are unfairly portrayed by European media, do you have any plans to change the way you are perceived?'

'I can travel there, give talks, participate in conferences, which I have done in fact. Perhaps we could have spent money on publicity. But no matter how hard we try, the wall of disinformation that the media monopolies have raised around us is so predominant, we cannot surmount it. To be completely honest, I do not really care what they think about me and the Bolivarian revolution in Europe. Why? Because one day, Europe too will awaken, one day the USA too will awaken. I do not spend a lot of time wondering what they

---

* Keynesianism, among other things, is about stimulating the economy through public investment.

think of me in the North. Besides, although there are some nations where the principle of equality is strong, I believe that to some extent, the societies in the North are living in a surreal world. As [the French-Spanish journalist] Ignacio Ramonet describes it, there is a media dictatorship. The odd journalist comes to Venezuela, sees what we are doing, investigates and reports objectively about what we have accomplished, how everyone is better off, without embellishment of course. But there are too few of them. Most journalists print unbalanced negative propaganda. And many, like the newspaper you quoted about banning political debate, print lie upon lie in order to tarnish us. Perhaps you are one of the few who will tell the truth about what is happening here.' Chávez could not conceal his hope and expectation for that to happen.

'On the other hand, the propaganda storm against us sometimes has a boomerang effect. I was in Spain on one occasion, after the coup, and when I left the hotel, I saw a group of young people, around a hundred perhaps, with banners and placards expressing their support for Venezuela. And I asked a woman: "What are you doing in Madrid? Why are you supporting Venezuela?" She replied: "I don't know very much about what is happening in Venezuela, but I thought that if the USA is attacking you, you must be doing something right. So I began to dig deeper." Sean Penn said the same thing after seeing [Pat] Robertson, Bush's friend, telling people I should be assassinated. It made him think that I must be doing something good, so he came to visit me. Naomi Campbell said the same, she was just here. Many others have said the same thing, artists, thinkers, philosophers. A network called *Hands Off Venezuela* has been founded. It is a network of solidarity that strives to get the truth out. And there are movements starting up many places in the world which support our revolution, a response to all the lies the media dictatorship of the world elite is forcing upon the people of the world.'

'How do you view the geopolitical situation in the world; do you see the development of a new cold war with the creation of two blocs?'

'I believe The Cold War has re-emerged in a way. A Cold War, yes, but not quite so cold everywhere. The war in Iraq, Afghanistan, the Middle East. That is a hot war. And at times, the temperature has risen here too. I believe we are seeing an attempt to create a new cold war scenario. But the circumstances have changed. We no longer have a unipolar world order. Cuba was completely isolated during the Cold War. The USA managed to completely isolate Cuba from the rest of the Caribbean and Latin America. For seven years, the imperialists have tried to isolate the Bolivarian revolution. But as a result, we have received even greater sympathy, we have seen more allied governments. That is why I believe that the current situation in the world does not indicate that we will end up in the same cold war pattern as during the twentieth century. We have world disorder! And from that, a new multipolar world order will grow. If that occurs, a cold war as we knew it will be impossible. That is why we have hastened our efforts to create a South American power bloc. Venezuela, Brazil, Argentina, Uruguay, Bolivia, Ecuador and now Paraguay as well. A bloc like PetroCaribe, which is not an ideological alliance but a strategic one. These make it impossible to isolate us. And that makes it incredibly difficult to invade us, as they did in Grenada, Panama, Nicaragua, Guatemala. Even though you should never underestimate the strength of your enemy, I believe a new world order is on its way. To a large extent, the success of our socialist project depends on it.'

'What is the greatest threat to the Bolivarian revolution?'

'There are many different threats. Putting them in order would be an interesting exercise, but the seriousness of these threats varies. A minor threat today can be a major threat tomorrow, and vice versa. Attempts by the imperialists to slow down and crush our revolution is undoubtedly one of the major threats. But there are also key internal powers threatening the revolution. It has been said that revolution carries counter-revolution with it. I believe that is true. Nothing forms out of nothing. Despite us having a revolutionary government and a revolutionary movement in society, many of the past evils of capitalism survive beneath the surface, in the culture, the economy, old sins, old approaches. The new society, the new model is born out of the old, it is born contaminated. Greed, corruption, crime. If the revolutionary process is not able to cure itself, the illness will spread like a cancer and destroy us from within. The Soviet Union collapsed, imploding after seventy years, the enemy was within and it collapsed. Primarily during the Stalin era. Fidel said recently, that even the Cuban revolution is not irreversible. So there are many internal enemies: a lack of revolutionary awareness, ideological weakness, corruption, old habits.'

'What about all those people driving around in expensive cars, the latest Hummers and all that, shouting slogans about socialism and dressed in red?'

'That is one of the greatest problems in the upper echelons of the revolution. Some people lose their direction. A revolutionary cannot and must not lapse into making the same mistakes which we are fighting against. Corruption is a terrible enemy. Waste, consumerism. It is an educational task beyond the capacity of one person. I try to do my part, with words, with examples, with ideas. But I have no chance on my own. For this task, we need a great collective. So what the socialist party is doing to raise awareness is vital to counteract our old habits. We must educate each other to a certain extent, not just with words, but through action. By developing the party and its members, education, information campaigns aimed at society to put a stop to people's greed of.'

'Where do you find all the energy to endure days like today, year after year?'

'Many thought it was impossible to change the world. Because of the oligarchy, American imperialism, their ideology and their individualistic disunited values, the passivity that they have forced on people through the media, the publicity, the political dominance. They thought we could not defeat their economic power. But the Venezuelan people have shown that it is possible and we are now attempting to lead the way in a process to liberate all of Latin America and the Caribbean from old structures, old chains, capitalism and imperialism. That is why I am here. That is why we are working to further this process, today in Ecuador, then back to Caracas, tomorrow to Bolivia with Evo and Lula, then back to Caracas for an event with PSUV, which is on the eve of its first regional elections later this year, then to Managua to celebrate the twenty-ninth anniversary of the Sandinista Revolution, from there back to Caracas and then off to Moscow. It is a question of being the driving force for our changes, wherever possible. It is a matter of consciousness. Without consciousness you lose your direction, your strengths are depleted quicker. Consciousness can provide inexhaustible strengths. But I have realised that the energy is not my own. Everyone who greets you, who shouts out to you, who embraces you. Correa with his energy. The people transmit their energy. I collect it and control it. They are not my own strengths. There are times when an entire day in bed is needed. To recover your strength, no longer for the soul but for the body, the muscles. But there is an inexhaustible supply of energy there, an endogenous energy which reproduces itself and an exogenic energy that comes from outside.'

During this last line of reasoning, the president's daughter moved discretely behind Chávez. She pointed at the clock and looked at me. María Gabriel clearly had no faith that her father would choose to use the remaining forty-five minutes of the flight to rest. At the earliest, he would be back at the presidential residence by four in the morning, twenty-three hours after leaving. His voice was still energetic, but his eyes looked narrower. I took the hint from his daughter and thanked Chávez for taking the time to speak to me.

'How long have we been talking? An hour?'

'No, an hour and a half. Ninety minutes.'

'Yes, I hope you have got something useful out of our conversation. You had better get some rest now, Eirik.'

On the Precipice?

One of the many election promises Chávez made in 1998 was to put a stop to the explosive increase in violent crime in the country, with the state holding a legal responsibility to protect its citizens. In Venezuela, there was a striking need for this. Crime was already so high that it affected almost every sphere of society. Education, business, public health, infrastructure, urban development, culture and transport were each in their own way negatively impacted by the rampant crime and the fear associated with it.

Chávez vowed to do something about it.

In the years following his rise to power, crime was not mentioned much. Neither by government officials nor on state TV. But there were regular reports of so-called *operativos de seguridad*, security campaigns, where the National Guard or the army were tasked with patrolling the streets to prevent assaults, robberies and other criminal activity, as well as operations by individual police forces against organized crime. One day state TV would report that an *operativo* in a western district of Caracas had reduced the murder rate by twenty or thirty per cent. The next week, the same thing happened in an unsafe district in Maracaibo or Valencia. In addition, the Chávez government began reporting new progress in the battle against poverty and idleness – evils of the unjust capitalist system which according to the president, were the root of crime. If you connected the uplifting figures announced after the government's *operativos* with the news of the social improvements shown by the state channel, you could easily get the impression that the problem would soon be solved.

The reality was far from that.

The indisputable truth was that thirteen years after Chávez came to power, the government had completely failed to ensure the safety of the people. The murder rate from 1999, a whopping twenty-five homicides per one hundred thousand inhabitants, had not been reduced. On the contrary it had risen. In 2011 there were forty-five murders per one hundred thousand inhabitants. This made Venezuela the fourth most violent country in an extremely violent Latin America.

Behind the cold statistics of the murder rate lay the fate of hundreds of thousands of people. People dying far too young, people losing their loved ones, children growing up without a father. I heard stories from friends on a regular basis. The latest victim was one of the police officers I got to know after my kidnapping in Caracas. A cheerful man in his late twenties, always joking and poking fun, he had been heading to his daughter's birthday party when he happened to glance at the wrong woman – and was shot and killed by her jealous boyfriend. More than ten shots to the head and chest meant that he was so disfigured, his body had to be covered and could not be viewed, as prescribed by Catholic rites.

The victims were not limited to those who were killed, traumatised or ruined and their loved ones. The increasingly pervasive fear had a paralysing effect on society. For example the drastic increase in the number of armed robberies on some bus routes on the outskirts of Caracas meant that people I knew refused to take the bus at night. If it was important enough and they could afford it, they took a taxi instead. But when taxis also started being attacked – or worse yet, the drivers themselves robbed or kidnapped their passengers – many stopped taking taxis at night as well. So-called red zones, places people avoided after dark, spread to most of the country's cities and urban areas. It was a vicious circle. The deserted areas gave criminals even more scope to act. Of all the major cities, Caracas was likely the only place where the trend moved in the opposite direction for some time, starting in 2010. In the capital, large-scale improvements to parks, pedestrian areas and plazas as well as associated cultural facilities, lighting and security measures had brought the crowds back to places which only a few years earlier had been largely abandoned and left to criminals and drug addicts after dark. Unfortunately this did not appear to be the case in other cities, both those run by Chavistas and those run by the opposition. It did not last long in Caracas either.

Why had it gone so wrong? According to the private media, which in contrast to the state channel dedicated plenty of columns and airtime to the issue, only one person was to blame: Hugo Chávez.

The president was accused of having stimulated the violence and of excusing the crime by pointing out that the perpetrators were poor and hungry. The media and the opposition politicians often referred to a speech Chávez once made, where he said that he too would have stolen if he could not afford to eat. Viewed in tandem with the merciless rhetoric Chávez used against the oligarchy, some interpreted this and other similar statements, as a call for the poor to steal from the rich. My friend Antonio did not believe Chávez was in league with the criminals, but he was convinced that the president wilfully neglected to secure rich neighbourhoods. The opposition usually blamed it on incompetence and a lack of prioritisation on the part of the government.

The true picture of causation however, was more complex. A few key factors stood out. Chávez inherited a severely deficient state apparatus to get the job done. There were too few judges, too few investigators, too few court officials, a police corps that was too small and poorly coordinated, and a prison service in complete decay. In addition all the aforementioned branches were ripe with corruption. A criminal with money, if he did not manage to pay off the police officer who arrested him, could keep trying all the way up the system, from the police chief to the prosecutor, the judges and the prison officers. Chances were that one of them would give in if there was enough money on the table. The police in Venezuela have a distinctive feature whereby each mayor and state governor administer their own police force. The federal government had no authority over the local police, who are perhaps the single most important tool to fight crime. In the first half of Chávez' time in government, and in the years before, during and after the military coup, the various branches of the police were as much a part of the political conflict as they were a tool for combatting crime. The central government had no way of coordinating the local police force's strategy to maintain law and order.

The same went for the judiciary. As president, Chávez had absolutely no authority to make replacements. The president's parliamentary majority allowed him to expand the high court, bringing in more judges to balance the judicial body politically, particularly important following the military coup when sitting high court judges decided that the coup had not been illegal. At any rate, the lower local courts was where violent crime was most often dealt with, not the high court. And though the opposition might be right in its claim that Chávez had gradually managed to stack the higher courts with politically loyal judges, it was the deadly combination of insufficient resources and corruption in the lower courts that continued to be the main obstacle in the fight against crime.

Then there was the drug-related crime. According to UN figures, Venezuela does not manufacture any of the world's cocaine, but during most of Chávez' tenure, cocaine exports from Colombia, the world's largest cocaine producer, were on the rise. Much of the smuggling took place via Venezuela. With the huge sums of money users in Europe and the US were paying for cocaine, the cartels could buy border guards, police officers, judges and politicians. Increased importation of cocaine and drugs similar to crack fostered criminal networks and contributed to the increased level of violence in the *barrios* where many of the addicts lived.

Over the course of Chávez' rule, the total number of Colombian refugees and migrant workers in Venezuela had reached between two and four million. That made Venezuela one of the world's largest recipients of refugees. Chávez offered them the right to Venezuelan citizenship. With the new social reforms, thousands of Colombians from the border area began crossing the border daily to access welfare services, which in Venezuela were free for everyone. With the enormous flow of welfare commuters and immigrants, inevitably there were also paramilitaries, drug smugglers and others hidden amongst them who brought weapons and criminal networks into the country.

It was one thing that the police did not do enough to tackle the crime. However in Chávez' Venezuela, just like in the past, law enforcement was also *a part of it*.

As early as 2002, I was robbed by a group of officers from the Caracas police force, Policía Metropolitana. Officers from the same police force were suspected of participating in the attack on me in 2008. When I asked the Justice Minister Tarek El Aissami about the violence problem, he admitted that a massive thirty-three per cent of officers in Policía Metropolitana have either had complaints filed against them or were under investigation. He also said that between fifteen and twenty per cent of all crimes in Venezuela were committed by police officers. This included murder and kidnapping.

Chávez was still not without a strategy to improve the country's police corps. In 2006 he introduced a new police training programme which was longer and had special obligatory courses in human rights. In 2008 and 2009, he founded a new university for police training, and a new national police force, *Policía Nacional Bolivariana* (PNB). Policía Metropolitana was gradually phased out, and only a minority was transferred to PNB after a thorough screening process. PNB is still not in place everywhere in Venezuela. But with every class of police graduates from the new university, more patrols hit the streets in even more cities.

In 2011, when the number of newly-trained officers from the new university was high enough for the PNB to patrol the majority of Caracas, the infamous Policía Metropolitana was finally dismantled.

Police officers I knew were still divided in their opinion on the new and more humanistic guidelines they were taught and subject to. The reforms introduced stricter rules for when weapons could be used and expanded the rights of suspected criminals. 'Before people were terrified when our police force went into the *barrio*. We were respected and could do our job,' a policeman told me. He believed the limits placed on the use of weapons introduced to secure the suspect's legal rights, had changed the balance of power in favour of the criminals. An officer from the security police DISIP had the opposite view. DISIP was a small force, part of the Justice Department, which was used to tackle crime considered 'a threat to the nation's security.' My friend remembered the time when it was called 'The political police' – back when they also hunted opposition politicians. He said he still had nightmares from the screaming in the cells where political prisoners and suspected criminals were regularly tortured.

'Our salary is still too low. And there are too few of us. But you don't know what a relief it is to work for a police force which, despite its flaws, no longer uses torture. Now we are a professional force. I thank Chávez for that.'

Under Chávez, the security police was no longer used to systematically terrorize political opponents. The president actively strove to break down the implicit acceptance of torture that prevailed in parts of the police corps. Perhaps the humanization and the attempted professionalization, along with the improved education of the Venezuelan police force would have helped if the crash in oil prices had not sent the real wages of police officers crashing along with it, taking away the will of many officers to risk their lives arresting violent *maladros*, who often times were arrested, only to bribe their way back to freedom and go after the police officers who arrested them.

Corruption was another one of the main themes of Chávez' election campaign.

The corrupt elite from AD and COPEI, who had taken money from the municipal, state, and national budgets and stuffed it straight into their pockets, had finally been replaced by honest people. The oil money could be used to benefit the people.

Traditionally the biggest source of corruption in Venezuela is with contractors: Private enterprises offer bribes to obtain grotesquely overpriced contracts on infrastructure work for the state or the municipality. Chávez had a long-term strategy to increase the state's capacity to undertake that kind of work. But it was a demanding process, and the drastic increase in the number and size of public works meant that the use of contractors continued. Often with the same result: enormous sums disappearing from the treasury into the hands of corrupt officials and private business owners. In addition, currency controls introduced in 2003 to stop the flight of capital following the military coup and the oil shutdown, had opened up a new form of corruption. Businesses applying for foreign currency through the state's foreign currency centre, CADIVI, sold their US dollars for twice the price on the black market instead of using the money to import vital goods and new technology as assumed. In 2013 the real value of the Venezuelan currency collapsed, with the black market value of the dollar up to ten times that of the CADIVI rate, a difference that would constitute a massive incentive for corruption. In some cases CADIVI was defrauded, in other cases CADIVI employees were accepting bribes from speculators. According to former government minister Hector Navarro, a jaw-dropping 300 billion USD was fraudulently skimmed off the top through the CADIVI mechanism between 2003, when Chávez implemented currency controls, and 2012. An apparent lack of will from the judiciary and the government to address this plundering of state money is striking. One theory is that Chávez somehow let a segment of Venezuelan business benefit from buying cheap dollars from the state, in an effort to divide the oligarchy and avoid civil war. And then the arrangement gradually spun out of control as the black market price of the dollar increased and the web of government officials and business people grew, developing into a powerful interest group, a true parasite with tentacles of influence that reached deep inside the judiciary, the media and even the opposition, enabling the orgy of corruption to continue practically unhindered.

  A key factor in the continued prevalence of corruption at all levels of Venezuelan society has a historical basis: Corruption was established as a system as far back as when emissaries of the Spanish crown discretely skimmed off the shipments of gold and natural resources being shipped to the empire on the far side of the Atlantic. One of the most significant features of the colonial system was the enormous physical distance separating the Latin American colonies where the assets were drawn from and the ruling centre in Seville, Spain. That distance proved to be a breeding ground for corruption from the get-go. Stealing was the only way slaves could get a few extra calories for themselves or their children in order to stave off an early death from malnutrition. And even after slavery was abolished, repression of the poor continued, making it impossible for the impoverished majority to fight for better wages through political and professional organisations.

For a long time, fighting for the redistribution of wealth has been more dangerous than stealing.

For generations, certain forms of corruption and nepotism have effectively been accepted into the collective conscience as a means of survival. Ending more than five hundred years of uninterrupted corruption, a culture of corruption that has latched on to the private sector, the state and civil society, that takes time.

Chávez considered himself a revolutionary. But he did not tear down the existing state structures as a revolution traditionally presupposes. He allowed 1.4 million civil servants to keep their jobs, even though they were all hired during an era when having contacts with the ruling parties AD and COPEI was the only way to secure a job with the state. Chávez ensured that key positions were taken by his people. But the gradual transition of including the poor majority in public administration did not mean the end of corruption. 'The new is polluted by the old as soon as it is born,' Chávez used to say of how bureaucracy and corruption continued to influence the state apparatus.

Naturally, there are opportunistic people with a thirst for money who will be drawn towards the segment of society where the flow of money is greatest. In an oil country like Venezuela, where enormous sums of money pass through the state apparatus, public institutions are inevitably attractive to these kind of corrupt opportunists. Paradoxically, the unstable political situation that came about in 2001 – when the government's economic reforms led to drastic responses by the oligarchy and the USA – provided breathing space for Chávez in the fight against corruption. With the attempted coup, the oil shutdown and attacks by the Bush administration, it was almost an established truth that the Chávez reform project would fail. This made the Chávez administration less attractive to corrupt opportunists, as they were expecting regime change to occur at any moment. In that way the stage was largely left to the idealists. By 2005 however, it was clear that the right wing no longer had enough support in the army to topple Chávez via a military coup. At the same time, his popular welfare reforms made the president even more difficult to defeat through democratic means.

The political stability that ensued was positive for Venezuela. But the side effect was that the state apparatus became more attractive for those seeking personal gain. Some of those who donned their red T-shirts, shouted *viva Chávez* and promised to work for the good of the revolution, were first and foremost motivated by a desire for power and money.

Antonio met many people like that when his firm worked with public institutions: 'A couple of times I was offered overpriced contracts in exchange for cash under the table. Other times, when I was part of construction projects, I saw what other contractors were charging and the kind of work they do. You put two and two together, and realise there has to be corruption.' Not all of Antonio's claims about the Chávez government were accurate, but I saw no reason to doubt him on this occasion. Or to doubt that what he described was widespread. He probably only saw the tip of the iceberg.

When I spoke to the president about corruption, he called it an evil, admitting that it was as much of a threat to the Bolivarian revolution as US imperialism. He was right. I often noticed that even those who criticised corruption most – whether Chavistas or anti-Chavistas – took it for granted that when a brother, friend or partner got a job in the public sector, they should also gain from it. Either by jumping the queue for some kind of welfare service, or getting a job. Corruption is deeply-rooted in Venezuelan society. As late as 2011, Omaira's daughter was passed over on the application list for *Misión Vivienda*, free flats for the poor, allegedly because someone had paid their way to jump the queue.

The nature of corruption makes it difficult to track and to quantify. Therefore, it was hard to know for certain whether corruption had increased, as the opposition and the media regularly claim, or if Chávez had made important strides, as the government claimed. One of the most famous corruption cases came about in 2007 when RCTV published images of a parking garage at the Fuerte Tiuna military base, filled with a colourful variety of American luxury Hummers. 'Is this what they call socialism for the twenty-first century,' the host asked with the photo of the cars filling the screen. However, it turned out that the picture was of a parking garage in the USA, clipped from an American website, cut and pasted to make it look like Fuerte Tiuna.

In its report from 2008, Transparency International (TI) slated PDVSA for its lack of transparency. The report later became the source of crass accusations made against Chávez, both in Venezuela and elsewhere in the world, a typical example of how even apparently independent and prestigious organisations like TI were unable to avoid politicising the corruption issue in Venezuela. An independent journalist writing an opinion piece for *The Guardian* uncovered so many gross and obvious errors, that his only conclusion was that the TI lacked transparency. The corruption report, it turned out, was written by known anti-Chavistas, some of whom worked for US-funded organisations, and some who had openly supported the military coup against Chávez.[110] However, there is no reason to doubt the existence of massive corruption in the Venezuelan oil industry.

In an ideal democracy, the political opposition, independent organisations and a critical media contribute to winning the battle against corruption. In Venezuela though, the political polarization also split most mass media into two camps, those who supported Chávez and those who opposed him, neither of whom had objective investigative journalism as a priority. While the state media saw it as their only task to defend Chávez and attack the opposition, the private media's role as a propaganda tool for the economic elite made it difficult to separate the many cases of true corruption from the constant stream of false and unsubstantiated accusations against the government. In those circumstances, it was easy for state and government officials who were genuinely corrupt, to refute the accusations as 'political propaganda' and get away with it without losing support from the voters. And what can you say about media owners who contributed to the military coup – by spreading a blatant lie that Chávez had 'voluntary resigned' – and supporting the installation of a business-friendly dictator? That too is corruption, many Chavistas believed. Some almost automatically rejected accusations of corruption coming from these media outlets, even when the accusations proved to be correct.

Statistics that revealed a reduction in poverty and increased social equalisation left no doubt that Chávez had achieved at least one historical victory over the overriding form of corruption: the near wholesale purchase of Venezuelan politics by the oligarchy. During the Fourth Republic, the rich elite had quite simply purchased political and administrative power in the country, at all levels, guaranteeing policies which meant that they could profit from the oil revenues. In bypassing this corrupt, cumbersome and ultra-conservative bureaucracy and channelling the oil money directly from PDVSA into social programmes, all of the opposition's predictions that poverty would only increase with Chávez in power were put to shame as he improved social conditions at record speed. But bypassing the normal state bureaucracy came at a high cost. The flow of oil money from PDVSA to the social programmes suffered from a severe lack of transparency and control mechanisms against corruption. And the consequences were disastrous.

Towards the end of 2006 and in early 2007, there was some discussion of inflation and shortages when Chávez began the process of drawing up a new socialist constitution. Despite the Venezuelan and the international media both depicting a reality seemingly from another planet, practically all of the important economic variables were pointing sky-high in 2007. That must have been decisive factor for Chávez, believing the time was ripe to take a big and risky step: to draw up a new socialist constitution and put it to a referendum. In politics, Chávez acted a bit like a boxer stepping into the ring: Try to maintain your balance before committing to a risky move – and when the opportunity appears, do not hesitate. You strike.

But 2007, the year he launched his socialist constitutional reforms, was also the year serious growing pains surfaced in the Venezuelan economy.

Increased buying power led to increased demand on almost all types of goods and services. Both imported and domestic. This led to a rise in inflation.

At the beginning of the year, Chávez had declared his goal of reducing inflation from seventeen per cent, the figure for 2006, to twelve per cent in 2007. Instead inflation increased to twenty-three per cent.

At the same time, Chávez introduced price controls so that the price of basic foodstuffs would not be squeezed by the growth in demand. That year, a number of the regulated goods began disappearing from supermarket shelves. Powdered milk would disappear one day, cornmeal the next, and toilet paper the day after. If a particular product was missing from one supermarket, you could usually find it at another one or in another district, and if not, it was usually back on the shelves after a day or two.

The food industry, where Venezuela's richest man, Lorenzo Mendoza, had made his fortune, blamed shortages on government price controls. He claimed it was no longer profitable to produce certain goods. The government said it was a lie. Chávez accused a number of supermarket owners and producers of cutting production or withholding foodstuffs in a move to force the state to remove price controls (or on a deeper level, to create disgruntlement which could lead to regime change.) But with the right wing using its significant power over the media to conjure up potential frights such as ration cards, starvation and constant shortages, the sight of empty shelves had a powerful effect on the population. Chávez asked people to compare: The supermarket shelves used to be packed but people could not afford to buy food; now there was the occasional shortage of some goods, but the poor were eating more food and better quality food. 'Where is the milk? In the stomachs of the poor,' Chávez and his supporters argued. But there was a high price to pay for the occasional lack of certain products.

Chávez lost the 2007 referendum by a margin of one per cent. He had to abandon his efforts to implement important socialist reforms and welfare services by constitutional means.

During the Chávez government, the problems never went as far as requiring ration cards. The shortage of products never exploded into something bigger. The Venezuelan people continued to consume even more and better quality food, while the figures for starvation and malnourishment fell. But prices continued to rise, at times steeply. Individual goods continued to disappear from the shelves, particularly before key elections. A similar situation was occurring on the domestic electricity market.

Very few people – including government economists and Chávez himself – had expected the significant rise in prosperity that occurred in Venezuela after the government took control of PDVSA in 2003 and oil prices began to rise. People in the slums and villages were able to buy fridges, freezers and computers. New restaurants, shops, factories and sports centres required ovens, lighting and machinery, and for the upper and middle class, people were installing air-conditioning units everywhere. But six years after overcoming the oil shutdown and setting out on an economic growth adventure, the negative side of growth caught up with

Venezuela. Venezuela's electricity usage per capita was among the highest in Latin America. Total electricity consumption increased by fifty per cent between 1999 and 2010, according to government figures.[111] In the years of rapid growth, electricity consumption quickly neared the maximum capacity of the country's nationalised hydroelectric power stations. In 2010, the weather phenomenon El Niño caused a drought which nearly led to complete power failure in half of the country. Chávez responded by implementing a strict electricity rationing programme. Large parts of the country had to manage without electricity once or twice a day or even several days a week. Chávez blamed the outages on overconsumption by the upper class, something he believed was the reason Venezuela used more electricity than any other country in Latin America. To remedy the problem he implemented a new, differential pricing system, where large consumers had to pay more per kilowatt hour than those who consumed very little, so that the poor were not disproportionately affected. In addition, the government distributed free Cuban energy-saving lightbulbs in every city.

But in that same year, 2010, the socialist party suffered its worst parliamentary elections and barely managed to win a majority.

Both the shortages and the blackouts frustrated people in their daily lives. During that time, production bottlenecks were encountered by small and large businesses lacking the supplies and electricity to keep production going. Not everyone was convinced by the government's argument that the problems were due to the weather and increased prosperity and consumption.

One of the key visions for the Bolivarian revolution was finding a way to solve the oil problem - a resource which Venezuela's most prominent oilman, Juan Pérez Alfonso, refers to as 'the devil's excrement.' This has led to a phenomenon researchers refer to as 'the resource curse': in the Venezuelan case an economy dependent on oil which is heavily reliant on imports and fails to make advancements in productivity or modernisation.

Chávez never managed to solve the oil problem. Certainly the total production of food and other goods and services increased under his rule. But at the same time, the buying power of the population increased such that the total import volume increased far more than domestic production. The state took control of key heavy industries, and in doing so, for a time managed to divert concrete, reinforced iron and petrochemical products into social enterprises like homebuilding, where a shortage of these products had long caused a construction bottleneck. But this did not contribute to industrial production as the share of GDP increased. The total private and public investments fluctuated from year to year, but on average they remained approximately the same.

In agriculture, Chávez' long-term ambition was to increase food production. This ambition was faced with the constant conflict of a need to have enough cheap food for the poor. The farmers and the agricultural cooperatives needed higher food prices in order to be able to increase the efficiency of production and utilise fallow land. The poor needed cheap food, as much as they could get and as quickly as possible, something which in the short term could only be solved through massive imports. Chávez tried to strike a pragmatic balance and ensured that domestic production increased at more or less the same rate as imports.

Statistics reveal that oil sales, which in the decade before Chávez came to power constituted on average eighty per cent of export revenues, in 2011 made up ninety-five per cent of export revenues. However two factors tone down the impression of a complete fiasco. Firstly, the sector of the economy unrelated to oil also increased exponentially over the same period, but a steady reduction in poverty meant that a larger portion of goods were consumed within Venezuela and thus not available for export. Secondly, the increase in oil sales as a proportion of export revenue was to a large extent due to the spike in oil prices.

Nevertheless, the conclusion must be that Chávez left an economy which – no matter how you calculate it – was at least as dependent on oil as when he came to power. And thus a society ill-prepared for the unexpected and drastic fall in oil prices that would come.

And then there was the Chavistan manner of implementing socialism. When I first got to know the general social and political outlook of the Venezuelan upper class in 2003, I was deeply surprised by their outright hatred for the poor. I did not expect the privileged to feel guilty about thriving in a country were the majority struggled to get enough to eat, but the extremely condescending attitudes towards the poor was shocking. Many said the poor were too ignorant and did not deserve the right to vote, while at the same expressing their anger at Chávez' literacy and educational programmes for the poor. My friend Antonio never expressed any such hatred, on the contrary he often asked me what my friends in the *barrio* thought about certain political issues and listened with an open mind. Still, like most opposition sympathisers from the upper and middle classes, not only did he consider the government's social programmes 'pure populism', but he also accused Chávez' poor followers who benefited from the programmes of being 'accustomed to receiving things from the state without working.' And then the usual 'Give a man a fish, and you feed him for a day. Teach a man to fish, and you feed him for a lifetime.' It was hard to take that argument seriously, coming from a social class that had never lifted a finger to teach the poor, yet was now frenetically mobilising efforts to topple the first government in decades that had actually made a large-scale effort to educate the poor. However dubious the motivation of many of those criticising the poor for expecting to receive resources and services from the state without making any effort themselves, and the government for handing out money for short-term electoral gains, slowly and imperceptibly I came to realize that there was certainly a grain of truth to the argument, although it was often rather exaggerated. It started with 'credits' to facilitate the creation of cooperatives and microenterprise, credits which many never paid back and thus became de facto subsidies. Still worse, some of the so-called productive entities never produced anything at all, and with no control mechanisms to cope with the exponentially increasing number of units receiving credits and subsidies, the money often went directly into members' pockets. Later, a professor at the Bolivarian University expressed his frustration at student organisations at the university that never once asked for a library, but demanded free tracksuits and shoes and organised protests against teachers for failing students who did not study. When Chávez said that the poor had just as much right to higher education as the rich, to many that meant they had just as much right to a university degree as anyone else, and that any professor who denied them a degree because of poor performance was a traitor or insensible to the difficulties posed by the social realities in the *barrios*. It was difficult to blame students who came from a social environment or families where there was no tradition or culture of accessing higher education and no knowledge of what was expected of them at university. However, teachers were frustrated by a politically appointed university leadership that preferred to freely hand out degrees, simultaneously satisfying student's expectations and the government's quantitative goals of increasing the number of graduates instead of trying to implement academic standards and face the initial discontent this would cause amongst disappointed students.

Apart from the exchange control, the biggest disaster of the Bolivarian revolution turned out to be the expropriated companies.
Any revolutionary process of change in a society like Venezuela, with limited traditions for grassroots organisation and independent cooperative production, must inevitably go through phases of trying and failing in the search for ways of organizing modes of production that ensure a sufficient level of productivity, satisfaction of social needs and political survival. This was not an easy task to undertake whilst simultaneously trying to seize the political initiative on the entire continent from the world's only superpower and fighting off attempted military coups and economic sabotage at home. No one can deny that Chávez hedged his bets on

the Venezuelan people's capacity for self-organization and that he took bold initiatives to make it the backbone of his political project. And it might be true that some of them stopped behaving like economically rational entities and attempted to use their economic and market power to sabotage or starve the people into submission and into abandoning the Chavista project. In some cases, expropriating companies made it possible to channel strategically vital products to social programmes, such as cement factories redirecting their goods to government housing projects instead of exporting them for profit. Another rare success was the national telecommunications company, CANTV, which managed to expand the poor's access to telephony and the internet at an impressive rate, an effort that earned Venezuela an award from the UN.

But there is no denying that the vast majority of companies taken from their owners and handed over to government bureaucrats, with varying levels of participation from local councils or other grassroots organisations, by and large failed to maintain any decent level of productivity. During fifteen years of Chávez government, the Bolivarian Revolution never found a satisfactory model of organising production. And many of the experiments turned out far worse than the capitalist enterprises they replaced.

During his time in power, Chávez repeated two central promises in almost every one of his speeches. The first was *no volverán*, 'they're not coming back.' The promise was in reference to the corrupt, ultra-conservative elite who had ruled Venezuela until 1998. The second was that 'Venezuela would never again be a colony,' either literally or in the sense of being dominated by the USA. Chávez guaranteed the people that as long as he could stand on his own two feet, the former political elite, who were financed by the USA and the Venezuelan oligarchy, would never again have the political power to subjugate the poor. He promised to tip the balance of power so far in the people's favour that the revolution would be irreversible. But the economic elite still controlled the means of influence that could enable it to defeat the Bolivarian process of change. The most important being the media: rich private investors, who had serious financial reasons to use their media power to defeat the reform process, controlled ninety per cent of the market. WikiLeaks documents reveal that the USA continued to channel millions of dollars to supposedly independent NGOs, journalists and politicians in Venezuela, with regime change as its goal. Despite this imbalance, Chávez with his exceptional charisma, rhetorical abilities and leadership qualities, managed to overcome the military coup, the oil production shutdown and to defeat the right-wing opposition in election after election. Chávez' successors will have no guarantee that without Chávez, the balance will not tip against them.

WHO WAS HUGO CHÁVEZ?

Chávez and Latin America's Cast of Characters

Latin America has it all: magnificent discoveries, adventures, golden treasures, awe-inspiring indigenous empires, wars and revolutions. The history of the region is so full of love, blood, betrayal, surrealistic events and sudden upheavals, that it can be just as easily understood through the magical realism of Gabriel García Márquez' novels as through academic essays.

Obviously there is no getting round history books, political economy and social analysis in trying to understand the century-long drama that continues to this day, and which has taken one of its most interesting plot twists in the past decade. Personally I thoroughly enjoyed ploughing through thousands of pages of Latin American reading material for my courses in social geography and history at the University of Oslo. But no amount of political or academic literature could prepare me for what I was going to experience as I observed Chávez' revolution from the inside. Being robbed by the police. Meeting nuclear physicist Fidel Castro Jr, grandson of the more famous Fidel Castro. Seeing a sixty-year-old blonde abandon her cigarette stall on Plaza Bolívar to launch an attack on Chávez' deputy minister of foreign affairs, Francisco Arias Cárdenas, apparently still furious at his betrayal of the president during the military coup eight years earlier. Chávez opening the casket of what an international research team believed to be the 180-year-old remains of Simón Bolívar, while tweeting to his three million followers that he sensed the presence of the independence hero. Standing inside a women's prison surrounded by drug smugglers, thieves and murderers and hearing Mozart's violin tones coming from the same varnished fingers that had used a knife to stab an unfaithful lover to death only a year earlier.[*] Not to mention

---

[*] Venezuela has developed the world's largest and most famous system of classical music training for poor young people. The system was started in the 1970s by the founder José Abreu, but only became world famous after Chávez

the remarkable sight of the filthy rich with clenched fists, painted faces, chanting political slogans and urging people to 'fight the power.' Studying sociology at a university headed by the priest charged with the essential task of blessing the abortive right-wing dictatorship of Pedro Carmona during the now infamous ceremony in Miraflores. Or the strangest thing of all: eating pork chops and drinking *Colita* with Hugo Chávez ten thousand feet above Colombia, as he described how he started the earthquake that shifted the balance of power in the Americas.

While the Bolivarian whirlwind swept across the region and created a new ideological landscape in Latin America, a global information war raged in an attempt to define the Chávez phenomenon. Was he a common military dictator? A revolutionary communist? A dangerous populist autocrat? Or the successor to Simón Bolívar? Who was he really? A brief look at some of the main characters of Latin America's history can provide some clues as to how the Bolivarian leader can be defined.

Hugo Chávez came into being through the crossing of genes and cultures of three continents: America, Africa and Europe. The thinking, the decisions that made him a historical phenomenon, came about as a result of leadership traditions, economic and political processes, and conflicts of interest and ideologies gleaned from five different centuries. So to understand Chávez you have to go back in time – far beyond his childhood years spent on the Venezuelan plains, as far back as Columbus' discovery of what he believed was India in 1492. The chapter of the Latin American story that begins with European colonisation is profoundly tragic. The so-called discovery launched the longest prolonged genocide and plundering of natural resources in history. Even two hundred years after independence and the abolition of slavery, the descendants of

---

multiplied the financing in the second half of the noughties. Then the number of members increased from a few thousand to over four hundred thousand, and special arrangements were made to bring in new groups of people, including people who were physically and mentally disabled as well as convicted prisoners.

Africans and indigenous peoples, those who were bound, whipped and killed, were still among the world's most humiliated people. But if the ending of Latin America's story of suppression appeared to be written long ago, the plot is still full of unpredictable twists and turns. The colourful characters in the story of Latin American get much of the credit for this. From them we can discover the many roots which would finally grow together to create the Hugo Chávez phenomenon.

In the years following the sixteenth century conquest of the continent, Europeans dominated the Latin American narrative. The so-called *conquistadors* were official military emissaries sent from Spain and Portugal. With them came explorers driven by a thirst for adventure, power, curiosity and not least, greed: a desire to find the mythical cities of gold. Often they had a combination of motives. Chávez would presumably turn in his grave if he was linked to these blood-spattered figures who enriched themselves through plundering, genocide and slavery. But the fact that Latin America's European contributions came through individuals who were willing to take extreme risks, has left traces that are still visible in the people of Latin American. It may be a cliché, but there is still some truth that Latin Americans seem less averse to risk than others. That fearlessness surfaces when a Latin American, regardless of the shame of rejection, declares their love to an unknown woman in the streets, or when he or she puffs out their chest and tells an armed robber to go to hell. When Chávez stepped onto the podium at the UN assembly in New York in 2006 and – instead of giving his planned speech – made the sign of the cross, said it 'smelt of sulphur' and called Bush 'the devil,' perhaps he could not have anticipated the consequences. Nor when he expropriated the oil reserves from the world's most powerful oil companies. Something tells me that it was not just the radical politician, but also the risk-taking adventurer in Chávez acting in these moments.

Amongst Latin America's reckless newcomers and their victims, the indigenous peoples and imported slaves, heroes were also found. In Venezuela, Chief Guaicaipuro formed a powerful alliance of indigenous tribes that kept the Spanish conquistadors out of the Caracas region for several years and inflicted great losses on the invaders. Guaicaipuro was killed by the Spaniards but survived as a symbol of indigenous pride. Perhaps the greatest indigenous resistance hero in Latin America was Túpac Katari of the Aymara people further south in the Andes region. He put together an army of forty thousand, defeated the Spaniards in an area which today roughly constitutes Bolivia and laid siege to La Paz. Never before had the Spanish colonial regime been exposed to such a well-organised attack in the South American interior. Colonial forces in La Paz had to get the assistance of entire army divisions from Lima (in what is now Peru) and Buenos Aires (Argentina) to break the siege. After being betrayed by one of his own, Tupac Katari was sentenced to death by dismemberment. The chief just managed to let out a warning in his mother tongue Quechua before the four horses tied to each of his limbs, tore him to pieces:

'You kill me now, but I will return as millions.'

Chávez was fond of this quote. He often used the story of Tupac Katari to evoke images of the historic injustice that his Bolivarian revolution was attempting to remedy.

When Chávez came to power, those who sentenced Tupac Katari to dismemberment and indiscriminately murdered the indigenous peoples were still referred to as 'explorers.' *Indio*, Indians, was still a term of abuse, even among people who had obvious indigenous features. Through the medium of TV, Venezuelans were taught to admire the white and the rich, and to look down on everyone else, like it was the most natural thing in the world. Chávez wanted to change how Venezuelans viewed themselves and their history. He renamed the so-called discovery of America, what is called 'Columbus Day' in the USA, to the 'Day of Indigenous Resistance.' Venezuelans should be proud of being the 'children of Guaicaipuro,' he said.

When Chávez began making the case for socialism, he sometimes referred to *el socialismo indígena,* socialism of the indigenous peoples, referring to the egalitarian society where there was no private property, which was practiced in a number of societies before colonisation.* In doing so, he changed how Venezuelans viewed both the legacy of the indigenous peoples and socialism. He made socialism appear less foreign by saying that it also had Latin American roots and at the same time showed that Latin America had not just been wild and barbaric before the conquerors arrived, but had organised societies with egalitarian features, which had continued relevance in society.

During the years I lived in Venezuela, I noticed gradual changes to how the indigenous population were viewed. Fewer people used the word *indio* in its meaning of ignorant, uncivilised and unintelligent. Chávez threw his weight behind improving the status of the indigenous people. The languages of Venezuela's indigenous populations were recognised as official Venezuelan mother tongues; the indigenous population had their own minister and for the first time in the country's history, they were visible in the educational system, state media and socialist party propaganda. The indigenous people's rights were also recognised in the constitution – which was also printed in their mother tongues. Starting in 1999, the government made determined efforts to reach out to the often extremely isolated rainforest regions where the indigenous peoples lived. This development was also noticed outside of Venezuela: from the Central American Mayans in the north to the Mapuche in Chile in the south, indigenous leaders took Chávez to their hearts. But even though he saw himself as a kind of successor to the indigenous resistance leaders, it was far from an indigenous revolution he was leading. The pure indigenous population in Venezuela is far too small for that, making up only one or two per cent of the population. Venezuela is one of the world's most

---

* Other pre-Columbian societies, like the Inca and Aztec kingdoms, were organised in a far more hierarchical manner.

thoroughly Mestizofied countries, with at least two thirds of the population having a mix of indigenous, African and European roots.

At the beginning of the nineteenth century, the colonial power was severely weakened. The idea of independence from Europe slowly took root in larger segments of Latin America's population. Enter *el libertador*, the liberator.

In Chile, Commander Bernardo O'Higgins* led the liberation movement. In Argentina and large swathes of the southern part of the continent, it was led by José de San Martín. The most famous *libertador*, Simón Bolívar, freed the rest of the continent, a territory larger than that controlled by people such as Alexander the Great, Caesar Augustus (founder of the Roman Empire) and Genghis Khan. On the Latin American mainland, white descendants of the European colonialists, so-called *criollos*, led the liberation movement. *El libertador* then, was born into the upper class and usually had a military education. But at some point, he abandoned the conservative ideas that usually followed with such a background, devoting himself instead to revolutionary thinking. Most often this change took place in Europe, where many of them were sent to learn how to handle the silverware according to the noble etiquette of the mother continent. Ironically, some ended up being inspired by the French Revolution and the ideas it espoused.

However the idea of extending European thinking on equality to apply to the indigenous people and the slaves was something *el libertador* Simón Bolívar had to learn the hard way. Only after the colonial generals, in a desperate yet effective bid to retain control, began freeing slaves to fight on the side of the Spanish Crown, did *los libertadores* realise that they would have to do the same in order to win the war. And so they did. The first time I met a girl with Bolívar as her surname, I liked to think that the blood of the

---

* *O'Higgins was described as a short and stocky blue-eyed man of Irish descent, but was meant to have had certain features to indicate that there were also indigenous roots in the family tree.

liberation hero himself pumped within her. Then I met another Bolívar. It was only shortly afterwards when I met a third Bolívar and wondered if half of the Venezuelan population had Bolívar as a surname, that I discovered the liberation hero had left his surname at the disposal of the slaves he freed, who usually did not have a surname.

O'Higgins, San Martín and Bolívar were all 'Latin Americanists.' They believed in a united Latin America without borders and several times led their armies across enormous distances to come to each other's aid during the war against the colonial powers. Venezuela's *libertadores* were also great geopolitical strategists who thought and acted far outside their own continental and own political sphere in order to achieve their goal of independence. Francisco de Miranda, who made the first moves towards independence in Venezuela, has his name carved into the Arc de Triomphe in Paris for his efforts as an officer in the revolutionary wars. He also had help from the British Empire in the battle against the Spanish Empire in Latin America. There are also rumours that Miranda seduced Russia's Tsarina Catherine the Great and in that way received economic and political support for his Latin American project. Bolívar, who took over after Miranda, had an Irish officer at his side most of the time, and carried a lock of George Washington's hair as one of his most precious items.

Nevertheless after achieving liberation, *los libertadores* were forced to watch on as their progressive social ideas and their vision of continental unification were sidelined by the new power elite.

Chávez styled himself as Bolívar's successor. There is undeniably a significant continuity in the Bolivarian project. Even the historical context has something in common. Both enter the story at the start of a new century, where the superpowers, Spain in the case of Bolívar and the USA for Chávez, are losing international influence. The decline of these two great powers contributed to instigating the liberation process in both cases.

Chávez was also inspired by Miranda and Bolívar's global sphere of action and their pragmatism in building an international alliance. When Chávez travelled to Iran, Belarus and China, some interpreted it as 'anti-Americanism' or an expression that he was particularly enthusiastic about countries with authoritarian governments. Perhaps Chávez' more idealistic fans had hoped he would be the first democratic president in history who did not forge ties with authoritarian regimes in other countries. But when it came to safeguarding the country against US attempts to isolate Venezuela economically and politically, Chávez was omnivorous, much like his prototypes. Any government who wanted to do business with Venezuela on favourable economic or political terms, was welcomed with open arms. This went for Berlusconi, Sarkozy and Bill Clinton as well as Assad and Gaddafi. And not least the heavyweights of Russia and China, who after being let in from the cold by Chávez, began to establish themselves in Latin America. Many of these regimes had as much in common with Chávez ideologically as the British Empire had with Miranda and Bolívar. The Russians and the Chinese did not travel to Latin America to run a charity, but to serve their own economic and strategic interests. But Chávez had learnt from his prototypes that the region could only progress towards greater independence by drawing in heavy foreign counterweights to the reigning superpower, the USA.

Questioned by a CNN reporter about how Simón Bolívar would rate him as his successor, Chávez answered surprisingly straightforward, that on a scale of zero to one hundred, he would get fifty-five. He was probably too modest. Because towards the end of his project, Chávez achieved formidable, historic victories in the battle for a united and independent Latin America, one which *los libertadores* had begun. His success can be best described by the American diplomats who were sent to stop him. In 2012 Venezuela finally became a member of Mercosur. But even more decisive was a meeting in Mexico in 2010, where Chávez was trying to found a new regional organisation for Latin America and the Caribbean, without the US and Canada. The US delegates present at the meeting described the confrontation between Chávez and Uribe by saying that they 'nearly came to blows' before Cuba's president, Raul Castro got between them. But despite all the derogatory language, US delegates admitted that the meeting had a clear victor. 'Calderon [Mexico's US allied president] had simply put a group of the worst types together in a room, expecting to outsmart them. Instead, Brazil outplayed him completely and Venezuela outplayed Brazil.'[112] On 3 December 2011, CELAC, the Community of Latin American and Caribbean States, was officially founded in Caracas. Thirty-two state leaders signed the declaration.

In CELAC, Latin America and the Caribbean had for the first time in history an international organisation that united all the nations in the region without a dominant superpower. Even conservative bastions like Chile and Colombia enthusiastically joined the organisation. The large turnout of state leaders in Caracas showed that CELAC had pushed OAS off the throne as the most important regional organisation. With ALBA, CELAC and USAN, organisations which Chávez had stepped into the breach for, Latin America finally had the adequate institutional means to resist economic dictates from multinational companies and financial institutes.

WikiLeaks documents reveal that Washington's fear of Chávez was so great that in 2009, when the Panamanian government asked the USA to bomb a suspected FARC camp, the Americans declined because 'it would be a propaganda victory for Hugo Chávez.' By setting a tough example with Uribe after his attack on Ecuador, Chávez had managed to prevent the US and Uribe from extending the Colombian civil war into its neighbouring countries. The following year Colombia had a new conservative president, Juan Manuel Santos. Chávez convinced him to reinstate the collaboration process that Uribe had brought to a brutal conclusion. With Uribe out of the way, the Chávez government was able to continue the mediation between the Colombian government and the FARC guerrillas. And in spite of the enormous amount of propaganda portraying Chávez' peace efforts in Colombia as aggressive meddling, even Colombia's conservative president Santos, a former defence minister of Uribe, has repeatedly acknowledged that Chávez' efforts were instrumental in the historic peace treaty that is due to be signed in 2016, ending the world's oldest civil war and the last armed political conflict in Latin America. Both the objective – a more independent Latin America – and the primary foes – external superpowers and the national oligarchies – of Chávez and the *libertadores* had many similarities. Still, Chávez operated in the political, historical and institutional context of the twenty-first century. As a national leader he operated with means and methods that were different from those of Simón Bolívar, for example, who for a period of time ruled with the almost unlimited political power of a dictator. For that reason, we must move forward in history to find a category to match Chávez' form of rule.

With the end of the colonial period, the colonialist, the slave and to some extent, the 'Indian' (he has been exterminated or marginalised in most of Latin America but endures in the Andes, in Guatemala and in southern Mexico) exit our story. That is, they go through a transformation. So-called *pardos*, browns, were the children of black slaves and white fathers. Often through rape.[*] In other cases illicit, but genuine affairs between whites and blacks came about with the same result: a growing number of *pardos*. A similar development took place with the indigenous peoples, who gradually began mixing with blacks and *pardos*. This unique process is called *el mestizaje*. So our new character, *el mestizo*, who would come to comprise the majority of the Latin American population, was originally the child of perhaps the most prolonged act of injustice in history.

El mestizo come in various forms, in a variety of colours and features. Some have inherited the narrow eyes of the indigenous peoples, others the rounder eyes of their African and European forefathers. With many, their African features, full lips, broad noses and curly hair match their dark skin tone, while those with fair skin

---

[*] For a time, raping black slaves was recommended to white men in the colonies to counteract certain health problems associated with ageing.

usually have more European features. But often the reverse was true. Venezuelan *bachacos* (*bachacas* for women) are those who have inherited African features but have pale skin. Some even have natural blonde Afros and blue eyes, while others with pitch-black skin have smooth hair and European features. However, what might be the most beautiful feature of the poor *mestizo* is on the inside: the almost complete absence of racism as we know it in the Western world and beyond. You can see it in the Venezuelan *barrios*, almost exclusively populated by *mestizos* of all shades between white and black, without it being the cause of any conflict between them. But unfortunately *el mestizo* has also inherited the lowest rung on the social ladder. In the villages he appeared as *campesino*, the landless or near landless farmhand, while in the cities he was the worker with no rights. During the two hundred years which followed, only a tiny minority were given the opportunity to emerge from the degradation. The average *mestizo* was completely excluded from political power.

In the case of Venezuela, all the way up until 1998.

However, throughout the twentieth century it became more common for *mestizos* to rise in society, and perhaps more common in Venezuela than in many other countries. Hugo Chávez' parents, for example, were teachers. Poor, yes, but their occupation carried a certain status with it. Gradually *Mestizos* were able to climb higher, both in politics and in business, but their skin colour, facial features and hair were things many would try to tone down to the best of their ability. Hence the enormous sums of money the middle class spend on hair-straightening products and rhinoplasty. When *El Nacional* wrote that a female minister 'danced the *tambor*' (the most African style of Venezuelan music and dance) and 'must have spent an entire day at the hairdressers straightening her hair,' it clearly sounded like an accusation.[113] Dancing the *tambor* was only for the jungles and the *barrios* – an African connection which the accused minister was expected to deny or be ashamed of. That was not the case with the Chávez government. Instead, Chávez hired a *tambor* orchestra to write campaign songs for him. During his many long speeches, he almost never missed an opportunity to speak proudly of his roots. An *indio* grandmother, a *negro* grandfather. He often highlighted the indigenous and African features of those around him, whether it was a construction worker at an infrastructure project he inspired or *la negra* Antonia, the former governor in the state of Portuguesa, Antonia Muñoz. It evoked a feeling of dignity. Omaira often called Chávez *mi negro*. The president and her had something in common, she believed.

As far as Africa, the president explained the relationship as such in an interview:

'When we were children, we were told that we had a mother country. And that mother country was Spain. However later in life we came to realise that we had several mother countries. And one of the greatest mother countries of all is without doubt Africa. We love Africa. And every day our African roots becomes more apparent.'

Over the last decade, there has hardly been a single African country where a Venezuelan diplomat has not knocked on the door with a proposal to improve diplomatic and economic ties, the opportunity to open a consulate or an embassy in Caracas, or to participate as an observer at a Latin American summit in Venezuela. The whole thing draped with ingratiating words about the mother continent's central role in Venezuelan society. And of the need to reunite Latin America and Africa, but on their terms, not on those of the former colonial powers. To this end, Chávez did not allow himself to be selective. Every African nation willing to approach Venezuela could expect to be welcomed with open arms by Chávez, whether they had a neoliberal government with a strong relationship with the USA, or so-called pariah countries, like Libya and Zimbabwe.

Hearing about the widespread racism amongst Latin America's white upper class, a person might be surprised at the friendly tone that marks the relationship between rich white people and poor people with dark skin in Venezuela. You would see pats on the shoulder, smiles and hear terms like *amigo*, *pana* and *hermano*, friend, mate and brother, when people like my friend Antonio went to the auto repair shop, bought a newspaper, or purchased oysters from a fisherman at the beach. In all my years in Venezuela, I have never seen anyone use someone's skin colour as a term of abuse, face to face.

But it is one thing to be pleasant to the poor dark-skinned person selling you an *empanada* or upgrading the internet in your building.

It is an entirely different matter when he becomes president.

At the beginning of Chávez' mandate, the elite had a strong reaction to seeing the *mestizos* reaching the highest position of power in the country (although *mestizos* were not entirely absent from previous governments). The country's major media outlets referred to Chávez as *mico, chimpancé* and other animals of the monkey genus. Caricatures rained down on then education minister, Aristóbulo Istúriz, who had an even darker complexion than Chávez – with monkey-like characteristics also the most common means of attack. Chavez explained that his ethnic background was one of the reasons behind his views on society and his motivation. As both *mestizo* and president, Chávez paved a rough and fierce path through the visible and invisible racism that still existed in Venezuela. In the villages founded by escaped slaves, like Birongo, where Omaira was born, Chávez always received more votes than the national average. Primarily due to class-related factors, but also because the president was the first to elevate the region's African cultural heritage and inspire people to be proud of their dark skin colour. In a way, every single election victory for Chávez was also a smack in the face of those who believed power belonged to the white and the rich.

Opposition candidates even dance the *tambor* now, although cynics and Chavistas might say their attempts to connect culturally with poor, dark-skinned voters are out of sheer necessity in order to get their votes. But Chávez really got the message through, across the political spectrum. By the end of his government, none of the newspapers owned by the economic elite called Chávez and his supporters 'brown monkeys' any more. Whereas before Chávez, racism could be used a powerful tool to exclude the poor majority from exerting political influence, racism now tended to exclude the person who expressed such views.

However the conscious fight against racism is only one of many aspects of the Chávez phenomenon.

With the formation of the new Latin American republics, a new character appears in the palaces which until then have been inhabited by the Spanish empire's viceroys: *el presidente*.

Through the 1800s, the plot was driven by so-called *caudillos*, an authoritarian and slightly primitive version of *el presidente*.

El caudillo rules without any clearly defined ideology, through military might and personal authority rather than law and justice. He often has a moustache, a holster across his chest, a *sombrero*, and usually rides into the capital surrounded by a cloud of dust and gunpowder, while he and the soldiers shout *muerte al tirano*, 'death to the tyrant.' In the case of Venezuela, speaking with a heavy Andean dialect, as most of the country's *caudillos* came from the Andes region in the western part of the country. After conquering the capital and declaring himself president, he rules until a new *caudillo* comes riding in, introducing the role of *el tirano*. The Venezuelan author Mariano Picón Salas elegantly summed up the *caudillos* anti-modernising role in Latin America with his observation that Venezuela only entered the twentieth century when the last great *caudillo*, Juan Vicente Gómez, died in 1936.

With the twentieth century, *el presidente* has his tailors prepare him a proper suit, and he leaves the uniform (temporarily, at least) of his predecessor, the *caudillo*, in the attic.

Latin America's new leaders are often elected by the people in more or less democratic elections. But despite having constitutions that allow for extensive presidential powers, impressive palaces, armed guards and a continued authoritative and masculine appearance (he keeps the moustache for most of the twentieth century) *el presidente* struggles to make any significant impact on our story. Constitutional limitations, the principle of the separation of power,* is not what has prevented *el presidente* from carrying out grand reforms and burning himself into the region's collective memory.

Of far more importance is the *oligarch*. The battle at Ayacucho in 1824, when the Spaniards lost to Bolívar, perhaps signified the end of the colonialist. But for his legitimate son, the Latin American oligarch, the party had just begun. He (the oligarch is a white man of pure Spanish or other European lineage) inherited the right to skim the cream off the flow of natural resources which continued to flow from Latin America to Europe and the USA; fortunes their ancestors had acquired through the utilisation of slavery and the fertile regions stolen from the indigenous peoples who had been forced out. The oligarch lost the right of his ancestors to keep slaves as household pets, but descendants of the slaves, *el mestizo*, were in abundance, available to be exploited as a virtually free labour force. With money came the ability to influence politics. Very few *presidentes* wanted to or dared to take any steps that would alter the social relations in a direction that would anger the continent's powerful oligarchy. From the 1900s, a new character entered the story, a character who made social reforms an even riskier venture:

Tío Sam, Uncle Sam.

US Major General Smedley Butler spent thirty-three years in the fastest and best international expeditionary force at the beginning of the 1900s. He became one of the country's most decorated fighters. The Major General began his international career in the East, where he crushed two anti-colonial rebellions in China and the Philippines. Then he tattooed his chest with a large eagle, an anchor, and a globe, and set sail for Latin America. It is difficult to find a better representative of the early *Tío Sam* than Major General Butler. He summed up his activity in Latin America as such: 'During that period I spent most of my time as a high-class muscleman for Big Business, for Wall Street and the bankers. In short, I was a racketeer, a gangster for capitalism. I helped make Mexico [...] safe for American oil interests in 1914.* I helped make Haiti and Cuba a decent place for the National City Bank boys to collect revenues [...] I helped purify Nicaragua for the International Banking House of Brown Brothers.'[114]

Ensuring revenues from Haiti for 'the boys of National City Bank', for example, meant that the US occupied the country for twenty years. During those years the Americans reintroduced segregation on islands where the black majority had previously carried out the first successful slave rebellions one hundred and fifty years earlier. An investigation from the US Senate concluded that the largest massacre carried out by the Major General's forces took the lives of 1,500 insubordinate plantation workers, who resisted the reinstatement of race segregation and slave-like working and living conditions.

Ever since Latin America's liberation from Spain, the USA has considered the continent as part of its backyard. Or 'sphere of influence,' as defined in the so-called Monroe Doctrine in 1823, summed up with the slogan 'America for the Americans.' Originally this slogan was intended as an anti-colonial statement. The USA, a liberated former colony itself, assured it would protect Latin America from rising European powers with an appetite for the region's abundant natural resources, at a time when recently liberated Latin American states still did not have the political or military strength to defend themselves. Some credited the USA with completing the task of Bolívar when around 1900, US naval forces destroyed the Spanish forces and seized their remaining colonies in the Caribbean, among them Cuba. But any notion that US policy towards Latin America was based on anti-colonial solidarity had already been rejected by Bolívar almost a century earlier when he famously predicted that the 'United States seems destined by Providence to plague America with torments in the name of freedom.'

---

* Mexico would have had the world's largest oil reserves, if the US had not invaded and annexed half the country, including Texas, where the largest deposits were hidden just below the surface.

Sure enough after Bolívar's death, the Monroe Doctrine was used to legitimise US intervention in independent Latin American republics. And Cuba, which the Americans conquered from the Spaniards in 1898, remained an American protectorate under complete US dominance until the revolution in 1959. The USA had obtained the northern half of Mexico's territory by 1850, coincidentally the half containing most of the territory's undiscovered onshore oil reserves. Puerto Rico, also conquered from the Spaniards the same year as Cuba, was simply annexed by the USA. The inhabitants, who are ruled from Washington, in good old-fashioned colonial spirit, still do not have the right to vote in US presidential elections.

Throughout the twentieth century, it was essential for the USA to keep Latin America's left wing out of power – initially to maintain access to the region's enormous natural resources; and following the Second World War, out of fear that Marxists would let the Soviet Union into their backyard. Common interests between the Latin American oligarchs and the USA manifested itself in several ways. In 1962 Commander General William Yarborough, leader of the Special Warfare Centre at Fort Bragg, USA, was sent to South America to find out how to prevent communism from spreading to the people. The recommendation he sent back to the US, after having studied the Colombian example, read like a death sentence:

'A concerted effort should be made to select civilian and military personnel for clandestine training in resistance operations [...] and as necessary execute paramilitary, sabotage – and/or terrorist activities against known Communist proponents.'[115]

And it was certainly deemed necessary on many occasions and over a long period of time. Yarborough died in 2005 after a lengthy and successful military career. He had essentially signed the death warrant of more than one hundred thousand Colombian farmers, agricultural workers and labourers – primarily *mestizos* – sending Marxists and non-Marxists alike to their anonymous mass graves. The paramilitary forces that he organised, financed and armed, continue to add to that tally, day after day. *As we speak.*

Paramilitary forces and death squads successfully contributed to keep the leftists out of power during most of the twentieth century. But the violent suppression, recommended and financed by Uncle Sam, also bred a powerful opponent:

El guerrillero, the guerrilla fighter.

Perhaps former US president John F Kennedy explained it best:

'Those who make peaceful revolution impossible, will make violent revolution inevitable.'

In every single country in Latin America, men and women, poor *mestizos*, indigenous people and a few white university-educated leaders from the middle class, with their ragged uniforms, Kalashnikovs and Marxist books, have at some point attempted to 'crush the oligarchy, imperialism and capitalism' through armed struggle. The guerrilla soldier has been the object of enormous hero worship and fascination both inside and outside Latin America. Che Guevara, for example is said to be the most depicted man since Jesus Christ, and has inspired both armed and peaceful political action across the planet. But many would say that *el guerrillero* has by and large endured a tragic fate. Often, he or she has fought for decades with no visible results other than rivers of blood and the tears of thousands of martyrs, most of them anonymous; a few world-famous, like Che Guevara while others still became infamous for their horrendous crimes, such as the radical left-wing guerrilla group in Peru, Shining Path. But despite the tragedy – the guerrillas at times managed to frighten the elites into making considerable concessions in the form of social improvements as well. The clearest example was President Kennedy's so-called Alliance for Progress, where the US essentially demanded that all allied governments in Latin America implement some redistributive policies in order to prevent deprivation from becoming a breeding ground for further revolutions, no small achievement in a region governed by wealthy elites who were extremely resistant to social change.

In Cuba and Nicaragua, *los guerrilleros* still managed to take power through armed revolution, in 1959 and 1979, respectively. The Nicaraguan Revolution had to surrender to the Contras ten years later, but the former guerrilla leader Ortega managed to implement a multi-party democracy that was never reversed and somehow survived both physically and politically, enabling him to take power again through the ballot box in 2006. In Cuba, Castro crushed the old machinery of power and implemented deep-reaching reforms that made the island a beacon for Latin America's left, from Social Democrats like Lula to the radical left-wing guerrillas, not to mention Hugo Chávez. Some guerrilla fighters who failed to carry out armed revolution, gained political experience and credibility, later enabling them to take power through democratic elections. The current president of El Salvador, Salvador Sánchez Cerén was a commander of the FML during the civil war. Both Uruguay's Pepe Mujica and the Brazilian president Dilma Rousseff carried out bold guerrilla operations against brutal US-supported dictatorships for which they were imprisoned and tortured for years.

Chávez however, was no guerrilla warrior. On the contrary, he commanded forces which had the task of crushing the remnants of the Venezuelan guerrilla rebellion. But it was at this time that Chávez came to realise the senselessness of poor soldiers doing the errands of the oligarchy. And as he revealed to me in the interview, his agony was so great that he considered joining the guerrillas at one point. During Chávez' presidency, Che Guevara gradually began to hold a bigger role in the Bolivarian cast of heroes. The guerrilla legend was frequently mentioned in Chávez' speeches as an example of anti-imperialistic analysis and idealistic self-sacrifice, as well as appearing on T-shirts, flags and murals. On the other hand, while Chávez sympathized with the original causes of FARC, he also stated that the days of guerrilla warfare were over, and both pressured FARC to lay down their arms, while pushing forward a peace process aimed to guarantee security and political participation for the guerrilla fighters and commanders once peace is achieved.

El presidente has his reasons for keeping a low profile in the story of Latin America. For if there was one thing that he learnt in the it was that if he infringed on the power of national elites and US interests, then the military, led by their coup officers in dark sunglasses, were never far away. Salvador Allende was carried from the presidential palace under a bloodstained sheet in 1973. Others had to run away or be escorted by uniformed officers: Árbenz in Guatemala in 1954; Bosch in The Dominican Republic in 1963; Goulart in Brazil in 1964; Aristide in Haiti in 2004 and Zelaya in Honduras in 2009. To name but a few.

Strictly speaking, Allende was the only elected Latin American president who was an openly declared Marxist. But for those with the desire and the aptitude to challenge the elite, it was not enough to espouse the ideas of social democracy; to state that you have never read Marx or, as in the case of Zelaya, were a member of Honduras' *Partido Liberal*. They were still labelled as dangerous communists, autocrats, anti-American populists or the like by US authorities and local media before they were forcibly removed from power and cast in the tragic role of martyrs.

Until the recent centre-left wave initiated by Chávez, most of the continent's progressive elected leaders have reversed course over time in order to avoid a fierce reaction from local elites and the USA; reneged on their election promises of nationalisation or redistribution of wealth; left the fundamental social structures as they were; governed without any opposition from the powerful elite and then disappeared from history without leaving any mentionable trace.

An important exception, though, was the populist.

Argentina's former president Juan Perón is the personification of *el populista*. He is probably the one elected president from the previous century remembered by most Latin Americans. Not for having been overthrown and killed, but for what he achieved during his time in government.

Perón and people like him, such as Brazil's former president Getúlio Vargas, Panama's Omar Torrijos and Peru's Juan Alvarado Velasco, implemented fundamental reforms in the periods they ruled in the 1930s, 40s, 50s, 60s and 70s. The so-called populists – a controversial term – deprived the oligarchs of political power, gave the state a leading role in industrialisation projects, nationalised natural resources, placed limits on the power and privilege of the financial sector and ensured wage increases and welfare arrangements that improved the living conditions of the poor. However these are by no means socialists we are talking about: Both Perón and Vargas have long been taboo subjects for the radical left. They were accused of buying support from the working class by offering limited reforms, and in that way stealing the political initiative from contemporary up-and-coming revolutionary movements – to then suppress these movements and allow capitalism to remain as it was. As for the general contribution of the Latin American populists, the jury is still out.

The coup officers could have remained an important, but faceless character in the story about Latin America. A character content to do the dirty work by crushing left-wing movements and deposing presidents, before handing over power to a representative from the civilian elite; someone nobody remembered after the dust from the military coup had settled. But some wanted more.

Meet *el dictador militar*, the military dictator.

Augusto Pinochet is perhaps the most famous example: He remained in the presidential palace after bombing and sinking Allende's socialist government, and appointed himself president instead of passing the task to a conservative representative from the political elite.

In the 1970s, military dictators dominated large parts of Latin America, from Patagonia in the south, to Central America in the north. Among the oligarchs, *el dictador militar* was usually the hero of the story. The man who saved them from the communist abyss. Also in Venezuela, which in contrast to the rest of the region did not have a *dictador militar* after 1958, Pinochet and his military coup were celebrated by the elites – at times even on mainstream channels like Globovisión, especially during the first half of Chávez' presidency. The brutal efficiency in suppressing leftist and social movements displayed by Pinochet, Jorge Videla (Argentina) and Hugo Banzer (Bolivia), made the military dictator a main character in the story of Latin America.

Caudillo, coup officers, *libertador*, populist, military dictator and communist.
All are terms, either on their own or in combination, which have been used to describe Hugo Chávez.
Chávez did not storm into Venezuelan politics on the back of a horse like the Andean *caudillos* before him. However, the parachutes and tanks that led him to the presidential palace under the cover of dark on 4 February 1992 may well be considered a modern upgrade. Chávez also shared the impatience of the *caudillos* as he strove to rise to power. And according to the opposition, also in its execution. He refused to be ruled by the old bureaucracy or to play by the old rules. Chávez judged individual institutions on the basis of their usefulness for the social and political goals of the Bolivarian revolution – beyond that the institutions per se were of limited importance to him. When Chávez appeared in uniform and spoke to the people in rustic terms with his simple, hard-hitting reasoning, many saw the ghost of the *caudillos*.[*] He was a coup officer, at least on that night in 1992. But the similarities ended there.
Still, it was difficult to see where Chávez would fit in amongst the other characters in the story. He had neither foreign superpowers nor the local oligarchy supporting him. And a populist? There is no doubt that some of Chávez' policies could be considered populistic. He knew how to tug on the heartstrings of the nation. He

---

[*] Including today's foremost philosopher on neoliberalism, Francis Fukuyama, USA's most famous expert on Latin America, Jorge Castañeda, and the former Venezuelan communist, Teodoro Petkoff.

used it for all it was worth to whip up engagement, as only Latin America's greatest political firebrands had done before him. As a young recruit, Chávez was sent to Peru for military training and was inspired by the rule of General Velasco Alvarado. Just like the Peruvian and other populists, Chávez attacked the oligarchy. After the introductory honeymoon period, as Chávez called it, one by one, the oligarchy's lobbyists were barred from the corridors of government departments. The president's rhetorical campaign also contributed strongly to weakening the political status of the oligarchy amongst the population.* But he proceeded much more carefully in taking away their economic power. Even after Chávez declared socialism as the guiding principle of the Bolivarian revolution, the private sector remained far larger than the public sector. Among Latin America's most radical revolutionaries, some of the same criticism that had previously been directed at Perón was also directed at Chávez.

Chávez was not a weathercock populist, that is, someone who seeks political power not by taking on the powerful elite, but by telling people what they want to hear and then clinging to power by taking the path of least resistance. On the contrary, Chávez gradually introduced new arguments and ideas which challenged deeply ingrained opinions in society, even amongst his own supporters. Chávez called himself a socialist and a feminist, defended the rights of homosexuals, adopted the cause of drug addicts and criminals, and increased taxes on alcohol and tobacco. These were all risky moves, which in Latin American politics tended to reduce the number of votes instead of increasing them, at least in the short term. But Chávez took a gamble that his own pedagogical abilities

---

* According to Chávez, in the eighties and nineties Fedecámaras usually appointed the country's industry, trade and finance ministers during the AD and COPEI governments, when both parties which were in a gradual decline. In 2002 when the right wing briefly returned to power, they appointed the leader of Fedecámaras, Pedro Carmona, as president. Today Fedecámaras has been completely sidelined in regards to government appointments in Venezuela.

and practical political initiatives would remove any scepticism and make these new ideas attractive to the majority. With great effectiveness, he broke down many of the ingrained patterns of thinking that came with the old-fashioned social divide. He left Venezuela with one of the world's largest socialist parties, with around six million members, a number of important women's organisations, a workplace that included support for the inclusion of people with physical and mental impairments, and led marches – which crossed the political divide – where the rainbow flag flew for the first time.

But as leader of a peaceful revolution, who on average held at least one election per year, he was also pragmatic and, in good populist tradition, chose not to fight all of his battles at one time. Chávez never campaigned for abortion rights. He abolished the Catholic Church's religious monopoly in society and called for religious equality, but he never spoke of removing Christianity from the schools. He never argued for the dissolution of the nuclear family, as the socialist Friedrich Engels called for. On the contrary. Chávez often referred to Jesus Christ as *el comandante* above all *comandantes*, 'the greatest revolutionary of all' or 'the very first socialist.' In line with Catholic tradition, Chávez made the family the foundation of his project; *la familia* was going to enjoy the social reforms of the Bolivarian revolution. So Chávez was radical in many ways but at the same time played on a number of traditional cultural features. Still, he was unique. The populists before him could feel secure in the economic, technological and military support of the Soviet Union. Chávez began his offensive in a world where the USA was the world's only superpower. Ideologically, he clearly moved further to the left and presumably left behind a larger and more politically defined group of supporters than most. And not least: Whereas populists had no desire to see more active participation in policymaking from their supporters, Chávez spent fourteen years systematically working for the opposite. Venezuelan grass roots organisations blossomed in impressive numbers under Chávez, and they were not content to simply vote for a president and celebrate at mass rallies – they made demands, formulated specific recommendations and directed criticism at the government. And where the people's demand for participation collided with the new red-clad political elite's desire for control, Chávez often sided with the people. At the expense of his own public servants, ministers and state governors.

Among Latin America's far-right elite in Miami and the Republican Party in the USA, it was not uncommon to refer to Chávez as a 'military dictator.' Chávez himself never tried to hide his military background.

The thing that frightened me most about the Venezuelan president when I saw him in 2002, was his appearance. Dressed in a military uniform, his posture and his voice revealed a lot about the president, even before I had learnt Spanish. Over the course of several weeks I began to understand the words – 'coup-mongers, turncoats, traitors, disgraceful, corrupt thugs' – and my initial impressions were reinforced. His voice thundered as he spoke to the ecstatic crowds. On the surface, Chávez shared a lot of the same features as well-known authoritarian rulers.

It turned out that the military aspect was not limited to rhetoric and appearance. It was also a central part of his political project. Many in his staff had a military background. Chávez gradually increased his control over the armed forces. He renamed them *Las Fuerzas Armadas Bolivarianas*, the Bolivarian Armed Forces, to formalise their loyalty to his Bolivarian nation-building project. In 2007 his close ally, Defence Minister Raúl Baduel introduced *patria socialismo o muerte*, 'fatherland, socialism or death,' as the military's official battle cry. In addition, a voluntary Bolivarian militia was founded, *La Milicia Bolivariana*. Even campaign activists who had no military background, organised themselves into groups according to military designations like 'battalions.'

For some, this was enough to write off Chávez as yet another *caudillo*.

The historian Rubén Peñalver, from my former university, Universidad Católica Andrés Bello, possibly the most important intellectual bastion of the opposition, labelled Chávez' militarisation as praetorian. The term refers to the Roman Emperor's so-called Praetorian Guard, an elite military force which at times had an important political role in the Roman Empire. Among intellectual Chávez opponents, one of the primary criticisms was that the military had assumed roles in society which in the forty years before Chávez came to power, belonged in the civilian sphere. International human rights organisations like Human Rights Watch (HRW) also criticised Chávez for his militarism.

Military personnel occupying senior positions in the political administration are usually associated with violent suppression. His critics also mention that he had 'politicised' both the army and the judicial system. The accusation rests on a premise that these institutions were politically neutral before Chávez came to power. Neither the army nor the judiciary shouted ideological battle cries during the Fourth Republic, during the forty years of AD and COPEI rule before Chávez. For a long time, military personnel were even deprived of the right to vote. But both institutions continued to function in their traditional roles as protectors of the privileges of the elite. Without any form of democratic debate, the Venezuelan military forged close links with the USA. Venezuelan officers received political indoctrination, military training and torture training at the so-called 'dictator school,' the School of the Americas in the USA. The US military also had special access to Venezuela's most important military base and an office at the Venezuelan Department of Defence.

However the conservative function of the judiciary and the army in the time before Chávez were most obvious when the privileges of the elite were under threat. The clearest examples of this were when the military smothered the dawning popular protest movement during the Caracas massacre in 1989, and when the officers removed Chávez in 2002. The Venezuelan legal system, which on paper was independent of the government, guaranteed complete exemption from punishment for the military offenders in both cases. In that way, the elite's right to kill the poor and repeal democracy whenever they deemed it necessary, was practically legitimised by the Venezuelan justice system. This is in line with how the army and judiciary have acted in similar instances throughout most of Latin America's history. From 1962 until the end of the Cold War, US allied military dictators in Latin America killed, tortured and imprisoned more non-violent dissidents than the communists regimes in Eastern Europe combined.[116] In that way, the army and judicial system ensured that the socio-economic apartheid system which Europe's middle class and working class began to reject almost a century ago, had survived in Latin America right up to the beginning of the twenty-first century.

The democratically elected governments of Latin America in the 1990s, of course appeared liberal in comparison to the dictators who ruled before them. Moreover they made no attempts to rein in the army or the judicial system. The perpetrators from the dictatorships continued to be exempt from punishment. By denying the poor and left-wing opposition due process, the justice system effectively cowed them into accepting the situation in silence. Additionally, the impunity of US supported right-wing coup-mongers has acted as an incentive to the privileged elite, greeting the left-wing wave of the 2000s in the usual manner: with violence and coups. When the Honduran supreme court gave its approval to the military coup leaders abduction of the country's elected president in 2009, it happened because Zelaya had allowed a judicial system established under the US allied military regime of the 1980s to remain intact. History repeated itself in Paraguay in 2012. The judicial system there, established during the forty years of the ultra-conservative Stroessner dictatorship, participated in removing the country's elected president, Lugo.

There is no doubt that both the judicial system and the army in Venezuela went to extreme lengths to protect the interests of the elite. Politicising an institution involves introducing political regulations to an institution that previously acted in a politically neutral manner. Since both the army and the judicial system of Venezuela already served the economic and political interests of the former elite, they cannot have been politicised by Chávez. What he did was to give both institutions a new political orientation, one which corresponded to his own political project. The Bolivarianisation of the army and parts of the judicial system was something Chávez received the most criticism for in the West. The image of a regime using military and judiciary force against the opposition in order to stay in power was not only exaggerated, but often based on outright lies. Still, the lack of a completely independent judiciary had grave consequences, as it severely limited the ability to limit corruption. And while Chávez refrained from using either the military or the judiciary against legal peaceful political activities, there was always a risk that future governments, be they from the left or the right, would take advantage of the opportunity for political interference in the two institutions for repressive purposes. However for the left wing of Venezuela and Latin America, this reorientation was one of Chávez' greatest achievements. Only in this way – with the military on their side – could the majority achieve social changes through peaceful and democratic means for the first time.

For the first time a left-wing Latin American president could survive a US supported military coup.

Protected by the loyalty of the military, he could also implement popular and modernising economic and social reforms which had a lasting effect on society.

If democracy means that the poor majority have the right to improve inhuman and reactionary social inequality – even if that went against the interests of the USA and the oligarchy – then democracy in Latin America is inconceivable without military protection

Chávez started by finding the physical common ground between the poor soldiers and the rest of the country's poor. By doing so, he created a split between the military and the upper class. This was achieved through an effective combination of political persuasion, personal leadership and pragmatism. While the mass media and the opposition were unwavering in their demands for the military to perform its traditional duty and remove him from power, in his speeches Chávez chose to point out the politically progressive function performed by the military in the independence wars led by Bolívar. He said that the role as 'the oligarchy's mercenary' was the lowest moral stage, the most unworthy task a soldier could do – and asked the question he had asked himself as a young soldier: 'Why should we soldiers from the poor families of Venezuela be used to suppress the people, ourselves, to protect the privileges of the oligarchy and their corrupt lackeys in politics?' There was nothing dictatorial about the way Chávez changed the military.

As president, he did not take away a single political freedom which existed in the era before him, back when Venezuela was called 'Latin America's most stable democracy.'

The designation 'military dictator' is also absurd when used to refer to a democratically elected leader. A leader who neither banned opposition parties, demonstrations or other political activities. A leader who implemented a constitution which gave the opposition the right to demand a referendum on the president's mandate to rule halfway through his term. A leader who subjected himself to the will of the people in a referendum in 2004, introduced a more secure voting system and was the first Latin American president to put constitutional changes up for referendum in 1999, 2007 and 2009. In Chávez' Venezuela, the opposition governed key states, had their own police forces and maintained close ties to the media. As the Uruguayan author Eduardo Galeano spoke ironically about in a New Left Review article: 'A strange dictator, this Hugo Chávez.' Galeano expressed the exact opposite of what most of the Western and Venezuelan media reported: 'This tyrant invented by the mass media, this fearsome demon, has just given a tremendous vitamin-injection to democracy.'[117]

Chávez' Final Battle

During the trip to Ecuador, Chávez sported a passion, the likes of which I had never seen before. He never showed any sign of wanting to rest, and only took a five-minute break during our twenty-hour work day. You could see from his body language that Chávez dove headfirst into the geopolitical power struggle with enormous delight. He did not appear to fear the attacks from the USA, but on the contrary enjoyed the furore around him, in the same way a soldier can end up enjoying the sound of explosions and gunshots. The stream of hateful characterisations and threats he was subjected to by the mass media, which would make most normal people fall apart, were outweighed by the jubilation, the adoration and the physically manifested love he received from his supporters.

The intensity of Chávez and of the battle he fought for, appeared to make him immune to advice from his doctors to get more rest. Chávez could not rest. Perhaps he did not want to either. The president said on several occasions that he often wished he could retire to the plains to work as a farmer, but that he was prepared to rule until 2021, something which became a genuine possibility after a referendum removed the limitation on how many terms a president could stand for election. In contrast to Bolivia, where Evo Morales came to power with the support of a strong, well-organised and trained mass movement, Chávez came to power in a country where the left wing was highly marginalised. The popular movement that shot up under his rule, was larger, better organised and more politically aware than the left wing had ever been in Venezuela. But the movement was still young and inexperienced. Chávez knew that his charisma, strategic abilities, nose for politics and unifying authority meant the difference between narrow victories and narrow defeats when the storm was at its worst. He knew that the Bolivarian revolution was vulnerable. Perhaps too vulnerable to defend a project which involved using the largest oil reserves in the world for the opposite of what the most powerful superpower in the world demanded.

The same applied to the international sphere. The movement Chávez started had undoubtedly made Latin America more independent than it had been since its colonisation five hundred years earlier. But intensive efforts by the USA to divide the region progressed at full speed, and the unification process was in no way consolidated. Even though practically the entire region was slowly dragged along, it was Chávez who had the economic resources and the political weight to take on the roles of spearhead and lightning conductor. His allies – like Argentina's Cristina Kirchner, Bolivia's Morales and Ecuador's Correa – were well aware of that. Chávez feared that despite the new regional organisations, the winds of independence and the climate of cooperation, he was still *the* driving force in the process. When I interviewed him in 2008, Chávez told me that his goal was to push the process of Latin American integration and independence from the USA to the point of no return. At that point, none of us knew how little time he had left.

On 30 June 2011 the answer arrived. In a televised speech from the Cuban capital, Chávez announced that he had cancer. Ten days earlier he had undergone an operation for what doctors believed was an abscess in the pelvic region. The laboratory investigations showed that they were dealing with a cancerous tumour. Chávez was pale and read with a quivering voice from a piece of paper. Since his first introduction to the Venezuelan people nearly twenty years earlier, Chávez had appeared in many different situations: in handcuffs in 1992, surrounded by hostile soldiers during the 2002 coup, with floodwaters above his knees during rescue operations for a flood, celebrating after election victories, moved, light-hearted, serious, furious and disappointed. But always with his characteristic strength. Never weak, like now. Perhaps it was the shock of hearing the diagnosis, perhaps it was the physical after-effects of the operation which changed his appearance almost beyond recognition. Omaira was one of many people who could not deal with seeing him like that. She told me that she had broken down in tears. It was quiet in Caracas that evening. Only on *Noticiero*

Digital, the right wing's most important internet news portal, were jubilant celebrations evident. There was a little over a year till the next election. Would cancer manage to break the Bolivarian revolution and remove Chávez from the world political stage?

However a few days later Chávez was back again. Surprisingly upbeat, he explained how he had a cancerous tumour 'the size of a baseball' removed by Cuban doctors. He said that Fidel Castro had practically forced him to get an examination and asked the people to forgive him for not taking his own health seriously enough. But according to Chávez the operation was successful and his body was now free of cancer cells. He immediately returned to his usual political combat mode and promised to take the revolution one step further by winning the presidential election in 2012. But the cancer had never been cured. In reality, his race towards death had entered its final phase.

Dying, but to all appearances unaffected, Chávez began the campaign with enormous energy. That year, in 2011, he launched one of the government's largest social drives. *Misión Vivienda*, Mission Housing. 'The housing crisis cannot be solved through capitalism. Here in Venezuela we will solve it through socialism and even more socialism,' he said, declaring that the goal was to build and apportion two million heavily subsidised homes over the next seven years.

Housing policy was one of very few social spheres where Chávez had not achieved better results than his predecessors. But after years with no visible progress on the housing front, step by step he had positioned himself to launch the big drive. He had nationalised the concrete and steel industries, launched window factories and quietly increased the necessary capacity. In 2010, when a catastrophic flood made 130 000 Venezuelans homeless, the national assembly, to heavy criticism, gave Chávez the authority to issue decrees. One of the first decrees was the new housing law. It gave the president wide-ranging powers to take control of economic sectors in order to accelerate homebuilding. Chávez expropriated hotels and unfinished shopping centres and opened government departments and other public buildings up to house tens of thousands of flood victims. At the same time, Chávez sent out an army of public officials, equipped with laptops and red tents, to register applicants. The 130 000 flood victims were first in the queue, but also those who lived in the slums and young couples who lived with their parents were told that they could claim free housing. Local grass roots organisations called *consejos comunales*, located, registered and suggested plots of land which could be used by the poor. With the enabling act, Chávez could expropriate where necessary.* Private and state-owned companies from Brazil, Cuba, Iran, China, Belarus, Russia, Portugal and Turkey were awarded contracts for homebuilding projects. The previous year Chávez had forced a ruthless and controversial showdown with the banking and finance industries, which included him nationalising several banks. It was not without risk: In Venezuela, the finance sector is also heavily involved in the ownership of the media. However, the financial showdown gave the president the upper hand he needed to compel private banks to set aside half of their credit for homebuilding. The state, assisted by a large loan from China, took care of the rest.

Chávez had recently appointed a new housing minister, Ricardo Molina. He looked like 'George Clooney in Ocean's Eleven,' a female friend of mine told me following his appointment.

---

* This was in stark contrast to neighbouring Colombia, which was also affected by the flood. While all the flood victims in Venezuela were supplied beds in public hostels as well as childcare, daily food handouts, regular doctors' visits and recreational offers, in Colombia, entire cities of improvised plastic tents appeared. In Venezuela, the victims organised demonstrations and complained to the media if the food handouts did not arrive or the living conditions in the hostels were poor, while they waited to have their free flat allocated. In Colombia, the flood victims disappeared from the news and returned to oblivion within a matter of days, with the government not deeming it necessary to do anything whatsoever. That was how it appeared in practice, the differences in a society where the poor had been given political power, and a society where they were sidelined as a matter of course, apparently without them realising that they had the right to more.

After a few months in the job, his hair had gone grey, his cheeks were hollow, his face was considerably narrower and his voice had changed. The president had decided that *the* symbol of the social and economic apartheid that existed in the country, the slums, would finally be overcome. With the cancer spreading quickly, and the upcoming presidential election in October 2012, achieving visible progress was urgent. Nothing would get in the way of that. Not even the health of government ministers.

In the summer of 2011, I found myself at an international press conference organised by the young state governor Henrique Capriles Radonsky from the right wing party, Primero Justicia (PJ).

For the first time, the opposition was going to elect its presidential candidate through internal elections. Some forces within the opposition were critical of supporting Capriles, a candidate from one of Venezuela's richest families – who had also been extremely prominent during the military coup in 2002. Particularly now as the opposition focussed on winning over Chavistas by appearing more moderate and imitating Chávez' use of symbols and rhetoric. For the Venezuelan opposition however, it was financial strength and access to the media, not party political activity that would decide whether you were selected as leader. Observing the way the TV channels spoke of Capriles was enough for me to realise that he was going to beat his competitors in the opposition. The amount of airtime dedicated to Capriles and the fact that his part in the military coup had been completely airbrushed from history by the private media, were clear indications, so I had decided to arrange an interview with him before he won the internal election and became even more sought after by international correspondents.

The press conference went as expected. Capriles introduced himself as a centre-left politician and insisted that Brazil's popular ex-president Lula da Silva was his role model. He said he would keep many of Chávez' social programmes, and that he wanted to 'reunite this divided nation.' Capriles offered some harsh but legitimate criticism of the corruption and crime that 'thrived under

Chávez.' He said Chávez had taken power because of popular discontent with the previous government, thus distancing himself from the policies of the pre-Chávez era, but that the time had come for change. 'The gap is closing now, and a tired runner must be replaced by one with the stamina to take Venezuela forward,' he said. However he avoided discussing ideology. The other correspondents at the press conference did not ask him any critical questions.

In the short interview after the press conference, I attempted to clarify what kind of political project Capriles actually believed in. PJ was founded by some of Venezuela's richest families. The money came from private donors and, to a lesser extent, from PDVSA. The company's PR director, Antonieta Mendoza, had arranged the donation to PJ in 1998, where her son, Leopoldo López Mendoza was forging his political career. Back then PJ was a radical neoliberal party which wanted to privatise the oil industry, and had close ties to US Republicans. When I asked him if the references to Lula meant that PJ had abandoned its former ideology, Capriles answered that 'Venezuela doesn't need ideology, we need good solutions and good government. And a leader with energy, who can offer Venezuela a fresh start and reunite the society which Chávez divided into ideological camps.' A few months later Capriles won the internal election by a wide margin.

Then he launched the most impressive election campaign I had ever seen from the opposition. This time the focus was on the *barrios*. For several months, Capriles travelled non-stop. He often visited several villages and neighbourhoods a day. He always came prepared with knowledge of the problems plaguing the local community and of the promises the Chávez government had not honoured. The crowds of people who greeted him were surprisingly large in some places. Some of the most remote villages had probably never been visited by a national opposition leader before.

In reality, Capriles was also reaping the fruits of a long-term and laborious plan that had been going on for several years beneath the surface, and which became public knowledge through WikiLeaks' publications in 2012 and 2013.

While the Venezuelan and international media portrayed Chávez' accusations of US interference as paranoid anti-Americanism, the US ambassador William Brownfield, in a top-secret document, described the goal for the USA in Venezuela. The strategy had four main points: 'penetrate Chávez' political base,' 'divide the Chavistas,' 'protect vital US business interests' and 'isolate Chávez internationally.' In a document from the embassy in Caracas dated 4 May 2006, it emerged how the US in particular worked purposefully to weaken support for Chávez in the *barrios* and foment discord in the Bolivarian movement. To achieve this, the US agency, USAID (United States Agency for International Development) had helped to support and establish '300 Venezuelan civil society organisations,' of which most operated with apolitical names and supposedly apolitical motives. The documents describes NGOs ranging from disability advocates to education programmes, but it appeared that many of them were in fact used as instruments by the US in their battle to topple Chávez. The apolitical cover made them effective – since the poor population would not allow themselves to be indoctrinated by organisations if they knew that they were carrying out the work of the right wing or the USA. Brownfield boasted of how a US financed organisation in Venezuela, called 'Democracy Among Us,' had reached over 600 000 Venezuelans in 'low income regions' without any of them knowing that the organisation formed part of a strategy to divide the Chavista movement and 'protect vital US business interests.'[118]

In 2010, the private US intelligence organisation, Stratfor reported the arrival of the Serbian-founded organisation CANVAS (Centre for Applied Nonviolent Action and Strategies) in Venezuela. In a secret communication published by WikiLeaks, Stratfor described the organisation as a: 'very impressive group of guys. They just go and set up shop in a country and try to bring the government down. When used properly, more powerful than an aircraft carrier battle group.' CANVAS, which had assisted in toppling several governments in the Middle East and Eastern Europe, seemed optimistic: 'Chávez is nothing compared to going against the old Soviet regimes,' they wrote in a document published by WikiLeaks.[119]

The presidential election was due to be held on 7 October 2012. Throughout 2012 Capriles toured Venezuela, *casa por casa*, 'house to house,' and as the election approached, Chávez grew more ill.

Capriles' argument that the president would be too weak to govern thrived on a rising torrent of rumours of the president's imminent death. Radiation therapy, chemotherapy and treating the side-effects meant that Chávez lost his hair and his face was swollen. Still he did not give in. In between his increasingly frequent and longer stays in Cuba, Chávez toured Venezuela and spoke to the people. At the same time, *Misión Vivienda* began to show results. Nearly ten million people out of a population of twenty-eight million registered – a clear indicator of a population who still trusted Chávez' promises after twelve years in power. Lorries with reinforced steel bars, concrete and building materials filled the motorways. Then the new buildings began to rise up in great clusters in cities and urban areas across all of Venezuela at an impressive rate.

The president insisted that he would beat the cancer, and that his treatment in Cuba was yielding good results. But certain events made me think that Chávez sensed that death was approaching.

The first was a church service in April 2012. Chávez talked about his childhood on the plains with tears streaming down his face. Then he addressed Jesus directly: 'Give me your crown of thorns, Christ. Give it to me and let me bleed. Give me your cross, a hundred crosses, I can bear them,' he said. 'But give me life. Don't take me yet. A life in pain, that's fine, but give me life. I have much left to do.'

Then there was a speech Chávez gave at a campaign event three months before the election.

'Chávez is no longer me. Chávez is a people, we are millions of Chávezes. Women, young people, children, soldiers, fishers, farmers, students, workers, tradesmen, you too are Chávez. Because I am no longer Chávez, Chávez has become an entire people,' he shouted to his enthusiastic supporters.

Seen from the outside, the words the president was using in more and more speeches, could seem like megalomaniacal nonsense. To me though, there was a clear message: The president is going to die, and he wants each and every one of his supporters to have a sense of ownership, of responsibility and a duty to continue his life's work, the Bolivarian Revolution.

But Chávez was clinging to his life. From the end of September 2012, he prepared for his final election duel: the closing demonstration in Caracas on 4 October, three days before the election.

Capriles had just held the opposition's largest ever campaign demonstration, giving a huge boost to his campaign, so Chávez had to respond with a mobilisation at least as big in order to maintain morale in his camp. That meant he needed to fill all eight lanes of Avenida Bolívar with his supporters and make a passionate appeal to show that he still had political and physical strength. Anything else would be a huge loss of prestige, which could influence the election result. So when the day of Chávez' mass assembly began with a powerful rainstorm, the opposition sensed victory. Firstly, they assumed the rain would reduce the turnout. Secondly, an ill Chávez with a weakened immune system – according to the rumours he now had a chest infection – would certainly be ordered by his doctors to stay out of the rain and instead make a televised speech from his office. And even if he did make an appearance outdoors in Avenida Bolivar, he would come across as weak in front of a reduced group of supporters. For a movement where the charismatic Chávez played the role of motivator, that could be incredibly demoralising. So on the opposition website Noticiero Digital, many expected the event to be cancelled. According to the rules set by the electoral commission, that was the final day of campaigning, meaning that the president might not be able to hold any closing campaign event whatsoever.

But again Chavistan Venezuela surprised and was surprised. Venezuela. In spite of the rain, hundreds of thousands of red-clad supporters filled Avenida Bolivar and even spilled over into the side streets and parallel avenues. Inspired by the enormous turnout, Chávez ignored the tropical downpour and raced out of the covered area where he was meant to give his speech. 'God bless the rain,' he shouted, soaked through in a matter of seconds. He spoke for ninety minutes. 'This battle of ours is long. This battle has lasted five hundred years. We are children of the indigenous people's resistance fight, of the slaves' resistance fight. We are the children of Simón Bolívar. We have battled a long way. We come from *el Caracazo*, we come from the fourth of February [Chávez' military rebellion in 1992], damn it. We have paid dearly to get to where we are now, to a free and independent Venezuela. A Venezuela where the people and the children, thanks to the revolution, have food on the table, where the poor have doctors. We have founded twenty-two new universities,' Chávez said. 'I have made mistakes, like everyone else. But has Chávez ever sold out to the bourgeoisie? Has Chávez ever given in to imperialism? You know that several times I have been close to death because I stayed true to the Venezuelan people.'

The jubilation intermingled with the noise of the heavy raindrops falling on the ground, on the buildings and on the hundreds of thousands of red-clad people.

The presidential election turned out to be not so much a competition with the opposition candidate Capriles, whose great efforts and skilful campaign had likely maximised his potential. Instead, for Chávez it was a final battle with the undermining influence of the USA; with the power and international mudslinging by the Venezuelan media; with the economic warfare that again cropped up as food disappeared from the shelves in the months leading up to the election; with the deadly cancer, and not least with a merciless political law of nature – the inescapable decline in popularity that comes with being in government for long periods. A political law that in Venezuela was strengthened by what Chávez called 'imperialism' and the oligarchy's political and economic war of attrition.'

On the night of 8 October 2012, it was clear that he had defeated them all.

Chávez won his fourth presidential election with fifty-five per cent of the votes. It was one per cent lower than in 1998, but with a vote tally that had increased from 3.6 million to 8.2 million, and a turnout that had risen from sixty-three per cent to eighty-one.

Two months later, Chávez' socialist party PSUV had its best regional elections and won in twenty of twenty-three states.

The last few months before the election, Chávez' health appeared to have improved. During the closing event of his final campaign, standing between skyscrapers and hillsides under heavy rainclouds, with water pouring down his face from his soaking hair, his aura of invincibility had returned. The visible side effects of the cancer treatment were gone: His face was no longer swollen; his eyebrows and curly hair were back. Omaira and many others believed, or intensely wanted to believe, that his show of strength meant that Chávez had miraculously recovered. The truth may have been that the president knew death was only months away and chose to end the exhausting radiation treatment and chemotherapy that could have extended his life, but which sapped him of the strength he needed to win his final presidential election.

It would be his last victory.

On 5 March, at 16:25, Hugo Chávez died at a military hospital in Caracas.

By that time, he had managed to break his way through some of the world's most backward social structures that had been lodged in Latin America since colonial times.

It was expressed both at street level and in the statistics. Media like the *New York Times*, *The Economist* and the Norwegian newspaper, *Aftenposten*, often wrote sensational articles about Chávez' 'catastrophic rule' without providing any statistics. While the media presented reports of impending economic collapse, Venezuela's GDP had an accumulated real term growth of twenty-four per cent per inhabitant under Chávez.[120] In comparison, growth in the twenty years preceding him was negative – that is GDP decreased. The media often used the high inflation as evidence that Chávez had destroyed the economy with his irresponsible populism. And inflation was high under Chávez – on average about twenty-five per cent annually. However, it was half of the average inflation in the decade preceding his time in power – which according to the IMF was fifty-two per cent.[121] Unemployment was reduced from 14.9 per cent in 1999 to 6.5 per cent in 2011, according to Venezuela's central bureau of statistics.

Presumably Venezuela is the only country in the world where turning a falling GDP into growth, and reducing inflation and unemployment by half, is considered an economic catastrophe by the media and experts.

In a way, Chávez got his revenge for the constant attacks directed at the Venezuelan economy, which could have become a self-fulfilling prophecy with investors being scared out of the country. It came when the American financial company Lehman Brothers – which had long been predicting Venezuelan bankruptcy – went bankrupt in 2008, a year when all economic indicators in Venezuela were pointing upwards. Chávez did not miss the chance to gloat over their bankruptcy.

During Chávez' rule, infant mortality was reduced from nineteen to thirteen deaths per thousand live births, according to UNICEF.[122] Caloric intake increased by nearly fifty per cent, and protein intake, which is always too low among the poor, increased by sixty per cent. After the state began selling subsidised foodstuffs in 2004, malnourishment was reduced by more than seventy per cent, from eighteen to below five per cent, according to UNECLAC.[123]

Many older *Caraqueños* still tell the story of the ritual where hungry pensioners protested in front of public buildings due to missing welfare payments, and were removed by the police with water cannons. During Chávez rule, the number of people who received a pension increased from half a million to two million, partly by including housewives, domestic workers and other occupations that previously had not qualified. The number of recipients increased by four hundred per cent, and the size of the payments increased drastically, a result of Chávez linking the minimum pension to the minimum wage, which had also increased to the second highest in Latin America. In all, poverty was reduced by forty-two per cent and extreme poverty by fifty per cent, according to UNECLAC. [124] Calculating from 2003, when the Chávez government gained control of the state oil company, PDVSA, enabling it to launch its social reforms, the figures from the same source show that poverty was halved and extreme poverty reduced by seventy per cent.[125]

This happened not just as a result of increased oil prices, but also because of clear prioritisation, resulting in a number of serious conflicts for Chávez. For example, the percentage of the national budget that went to social spending was doubled. In the 1990s, Venezuela had one of the greatest disparities between rich and poor in Latin America. After fourteen years of Chávez in power, Venezuela, along with Uruguay, had the lowest level. The so-called Gini coefficient, a measure of income inequality, fell from 0.498 in 1999 to 0.397 in 2011. Where before the richest twenty per cent of the population in 1999 earned fifteen times more than the poorest twenty per cent, they now earned eight times more – nearly halving the divide.[126]

In Venezuela, much like the rest of a patriarchal Latin America, women were traditionally in a weak position relative to men. In general, they would be the ones to benefit most from Chávez' social programmes, not just the ones with a specific female profile. In addition, the government founded a 'Women's Development Bank,' which among other things, offered credit to cooperatives run by women.

The head of the UN commission UNECLAC, Alicia Bárcena, shocked CNN when she corroborated Chávez' figures for poverty reduction and declared that Venezuela had 'extremely positive indicators on the social level,' and made 'impressive progress' and that UNECLAC would look closer at the social programmes that were the cause of these advances. After the president's death, the UNECLAC leader wrote that 'America's face changed for the better' when Chávez entered the stage with his 'uncompromising loyalty to the poor.'[127]

While the international media praised Obama and told off Chávez, the *New York Times* reported that for the first time, the USA had higher social inequality than 'the banana republic' of Venezuela.[128] And whilst the Spanish government evicted nearly half a million families from their homes, at the behest of the banks, Venezuela's government provided homes for 249 368 poor families through *Misión Vivienda* – in part by forcing the banks to participate in financing the project.[129]

Over the course of the Chávez era, the number of Venezuelans in higher education rose from fewer than half a million to nearly two million, according to the government (although the quality of the education varies and in some instances is very poor) In 1998 Venezuela had twenty doctors per one hundred thousand inhabitants. Ten years later, this had increased to sixty, according to the government. Many of these were Cubans and Venezuelan doctors who had recently graduated from a Cuban university, all working for *Misión Barrio Adentro*.

On the competitive level, before Chávez, Venezuela was known for winning beauty pageants and losing football matches. When Chávez died, the country had climbed ninety-three places on the FIFA rankings from number 129 in 1998 to number 36 in the world in 2013. They continue to win beauty pageants, however. The

2012 Miss Venezuela was even a Chavista. When Chávez recommended Noam Chomsky's book *Hegemony or Survival: America's Quest for Global Dominance* to the UN general assembly, during the same speech he called Bush the devil, the book climbed from number 26, 000 on Amazon's bestseller list to number one.[130] At a summit in Trinidad and Tobago, Chávez presented Obama with a copy of Eduardo Galeano's classic, *Open Veins of Latin America*, with the message: 'To Obama, with affection.' The book rose from 54 000 on Amazon's sales list to number two overnight. Another example of Chávez' impact was during the climate summit in Copenhagen. There he stated that 'if the climate were a bank, it would already have been saved' – probably the only quote from the unproductive summit that is still remembered by many people. Chávez set a record with eighteen election and referendum victories in fourteen years. He was nearly unbeatable on Twitter as well. Of all the national leaders on Twitter, only Obama had more followers.

A lot of things changed over the course of Chávez' fourteen years that cannot be measured in numbers.

After the opposition abandoned its ambitions of a military coup, and the USA began to place stronger emphasis on using so-called *soft power* – undermining from within instead of open confrontation – a different mood could be felt in the streets. The opposition's rhetoric softened. With that, the relationship between Chavistas and anti-Chavistas on the streets also softened. There were fewer confrontations, fewer arguments between my friends as well. I noticed that with Antonio. He was far from your typical ultra-conservative, racist oligarch. But he actively participated in the battle against Chávez both politically and economically, for example when he closed his company during the lockout in December 2002. Antonio remained an anti-Chavista for as long as Chávez lived but over the final years, his position softened considerably. The first sign was when he told me about a meeting with the Cohen family, Venezuela's largest shopping centre magnate, who he had done a lot of work for. It was in 2008 and Antonio had asked them if they believed it was possible to run a business under Chávez' socialism. They answered that 'making money in Venezuela is no problem as long as you don't try to use your business to attack Chávez.' At first Antonio had seemed a little disappointed when he told me. But two years later he too had signed his first contracts with Caracas' socialist mayor, to restore and upgrade local parks, pedestrian areas and outdoor areas. Had Antonio changed under Chávez? 'This has been a chaotic period of misrule, but I don't believe Venezuela can be the same as before Chávez either. I believe we must take better care of the poor. Maybe that has taught us something,' he admitted reluctantly.

Omaira for her part, only grew happier with Chávez over time, calling him 'the love of my life.'

In 2010 she signed up to the Bolivarian militia to 'defend the fatherland' as she put it. Her son trained as a firefighter, and both of her daughters were trained as laboratory assistants. For her, all these things were completely unthinkable before Chávez. However when he died, she despaired. She did not doubt that there were good candidates who wanted to achieve the same things as Chávez politically, but she was not confident that any of them had the same strength to stay in power. Neither did Omaira have any trust that the opposition's new rhetoric would mean that people like her would be treated more humanely if there was a change of government. The class hatred and racism of the Venezuelan upper class was gone from the opposition representatives and the major media outlets, but beneath the surface, it still flourished. I discovered a typical example of this on the opposition's website, Noticiero Digital. Someone had started a discussion about what you should do with domestic servants who supported Chávez. Cleaning ladies and maids were referred to as 'apes, stupid slaves, slum sluts and jealous subhumans' by their own employers – highly educated Venezuelans with good finances from the same social elite as the opposition's leading politicians.

I asked Omaira whether she was angry that the truth about Chávez' cancer had been kept secret during the election campaign.

She did not understand what I meant. It was probably like asking an Argentinian is he was angry with Maradona for scoring 'the hand of God' goal in the World Cup quarterfinals against England in 1986. That was exactly why she loved Chávez, because facing an oligarchy that always played dirty, he was just as tough in return. There was only one thing she could not forgive *el comandante* for: dying.

Simón Bolívar died lonely and in exile, hated by the majority in the areas he had liberated. A lot indicates that the mudslinging against Chávez was even more intense than what Bolívar was subjected to. According to the journalist John Pilger, no president has been lied about as much as Chávez. Mark Weisbrot, from the independent Washington-based think-tank CEPR and a regular columnist for The *Guardian*, says Chávez received worse press coverage in the USA than Saddam Hussein. In Norway, *Aftenposten* gave considerably friendlier coverage to the Islamic dictatorship of Saudi Arabia than of Chávez' Venezuela. The same goes for serious media outlets like the BBC. Of more than three hundred BBC articles about Venezuela between 1998 and 2008, only three mentioned positive aspects of Chávez' policies.[131] 'They lied about you, like they lied about Bolívar. But they never managed to defeat you, *comandante*,' a tearful Nicolas Maduro said at his funeral. And it was true. Chávez did not die in exile and hated – he went down in history with a popularity of seventy per cent after having won a record number of elections. He was carried through Caracas by millions of weeping supporters before he was laid to rest with thirty-three state leaders present, while sixteen countries declared a state of national mourning for his passing.

So how will Chávez' legacy contribute to world history? While his failure to diversify an economy heavily dependent on oil and to combat rising crime and corruption are the norm rather than the exception in modern Venezuelan history, Chávez did break new ground in certain respects to earn himself a place among the most important historical figures of the twentieth and twenty-first

centuries. Chávez shaped the national and international scenes in three truly historically unique ways:
1. During Chávez' government, the formerly excluded majority reached its highest degree of political protagonism since colonisation in 1492.
2. The process of increased Latin American cooperation, the diversification of economic and political relations with the rest of the world (such as BRICS) and the weakening of US hegemony over the region, as a whole constitute the most important geopolitical shift pushed forward by democratic elections since the fall of communism in the Soviet Union.
3. The aforementioned process ensured the highest level of autonomy from external powers enjoyed by Latin America since colonisation.

While none of these changes would have materialised without bold and astute initiatives and leadership by Chávez and other Latin American presidents, as well as a massive increase in grassroots activism, they were also aided by high commodity prices. And none of the three achievements are truly irreversible.

Nadie te quita lo bailado, they say in Venezuela. 'Nobody can take away the dances you have already had.' For fourteen years Omaira and Venezuela danced to the beat of a president who for the first time in the country's history put the poor majority of the population in the driver's seat, forcefully pushing the oligarchy to the side. Even if the absence of Chávez tips the balance of power in favour of the former elite, things will never be the same as before. As long as the echo of 'Hurricane Hugo' continues to resound through the hillsides of Caracas and the villages and *barrios* in the rest of Venezuela, never again will the majority quietly accept being forced into degradation.

Endnotes

[1] *Aftenposten*, 13.04.2002.
[2] *Quinto Día*, 30.08.2002.
[3] *El Universal*, 21.04.2003.
[4] *El Universal*, 16.03.2003.
[5] *El Universal*, 24.01.2003.
[6] *El Nacional*, 14.10.2002.
[7] The estimates are found on the human rights blog *Derechos Humanos*, 'El Caracazo, 1989.' Accessible on the website: http://derechoshumanosunefamonasterio.blogspot.no/
[8] Jones, Bart (2007): *Hugo: The Hugo Chávez Story. From Mud Hut to Perpetual Revolution*. London: The Bodley Head.
[9] *New York Times*, 25.04.1999.
[10] Bartley, Kim and O'Briain, Donnacha (2003): *The Revolution Will Not Be Televised* (documentary).
[11] *El Nacional*, 29.10.2001.
[12] *El Nacional*, 21.10.2001.
[13] *Newsweek*, 11.11.2001.
[14] Elizalde, Rosa Miriam and Baez, Luis (2004): *Chávez Nuestro*. Casa Ediotra Abril. The book contains interviews with several ministers and family members who were inside the presidential palace on 11 April.
[15] Elizalde, Rosa Miriam and Baez, Luis (2004): *Chávez Nuestro*. Casa Editora Abril, pp. 143-162.
[16] Villegas, Ernesto (2010): *Abril Golpe Adrentro*, Editorial Galac, p.67 and p.289; Palacio, Ángel (2004): *Puente Llaguno Claves de una masacre* (documentary); Ultimas Noticias, 14.04.2002; Nelson, A. Brian (2009) *The Silence and the Scorpion: The Coup Against Chávez and the Making of Modern Venezuela*, Nation Books.
[17] Palacio, Ángel (2004): *Puente Llaguno: Claves de una masacre* (documentary).

[18] Nelson, A. Brian (2009): *The Silence and the Scorpion: The Coup Against Chávez and the Making of Modern Venezuela*. Nation Books. This book goes a long ways to defend the military coup leaders version and avoids mentioning the most central, obvious and irrefutable evidence to the opposite. But the author still acknowledges that the coup leaders threatened to attack the presidential palace with bombers.
[19] Elizalde, Rosa Miriam and Baez, Luis (2004): *Chávez Nuestro*. Casa Editora Abril, p. 152.
[20] The scenes from the presidential palace, including Chávez being bundled off and the aforementioned man's parting words, are in the documentary, *The Revolution Will Not Be Televised*. Bartley, Kim and O'Briain, Donnacha (2003).
[21] Bartley, Kim and O'Briain, Donnacha (2003): *The Revolution Will Not Be Televised* (documentary).
[22] Bartley, Kim and O'Briain, Donnacha (2003): *The Revolution Will Not Be Televised* (documentary).
[23] Palacio, Ángel (2002): *Asedio a una Embajada* (documentary).
[24] Video recording of the events is found on the *Manifest Analyses* webpage: http://manifestanalyse.no/-/page/show/5155_oslo-freedom-forum-2010. (read: 06.05.2013).
[25] Bartley, Kim and O'Briain, Donnacha (2003): *The Revolution Will Not Be Televised* (documentary).
[26] Elizalde, Rosa Miriam and Baez, Luis (2004): Chávez Neustro. Casa Editora Abril, pp.303-304.
[27] Elizalde, Rosa Miriam and Baez, Luis (2004): *Chávez Neustro*. Casa Editora Abril, pp.298-304.
[28] Elizalde, Rosa Miriam and Baez, Luis (2004): *Chávez neustro*. Casa Editora Abril, p.179
[29] Elizalde, Rosa Miriam and Baez, Luis (2004): *Chávez neustro*. Casa Editora Abril, pp.270–276.
[30] *El Nacional*, 29.07.2002.
[31] *El Universal*, 24.11.2002.
[32] *El Universal*, 24.11.2002.

33 *El Nacional*, 30.09.2002.
34 The recording is accessible on the website: http://www.youtube.com/watch?v=FpJz3zPAkQ8. (Read: 05.05.2013).
35 Britto, Luis García (2008): *Dictadura Mediatica en Venezuela: Investigación de unos medios por encima de toda sospecha.* Coleccion Analisis, p. 145.
36 *2001* (newspaper), 14.12.2002.
37 Britto, Luis García (2008): *Dictadura Mediatica en Venezuela: Investigación de unos medios por encima de toda sospecha.* Coleccion Analisis, p. 152.
38 *El Nacional*, 04.01.2003.
39 *El Nacional*, 05.01.2003.
40 *Reuters*, 23.01.2003 and *Los Angeles Times*, 24.01.2003. Accessible on the website: http://articles.latimes.com/2003/jan/24/world/fg-venez24.
41 Kozloff, Nikolas (2007): *Hugo Chávez, Oil, Politics and the Challenge to the United States.* New York: Palgrave Macmillan, p. 32.
42 *Bergens Tidende*, 19.12.2002.
43 The recording is available on the website: http://www.youtube.com/watch?v=px04jhigE-0. (Read: 05.05.2013)
44 Interview with Dr Alcántara, President of the Chamber of Venezuelan Oil Companies, Cámara Petrolera de Venezuela.
45 Consejo nacional electoral, www.cne.gov.ve.
46 Instituto Nacional de Estadistica (INE).
47 Instituto Nacional de Estadistica (INE).
48 *El Universal*, 20.02.2004.
49 *El Mundo*, 04.03.2004.
50 *Ultimas Noticias*, 04.03.2004.
51 *The Economist*, 11.09.2003. Accessible on the website: http://www.economist.com/node/2054474?story_id=E1_NDVQQSQ

52 *WSWS*, 09.03.2004. Accessible on the website: http://www.wsws.org/en/articles/2004/03/ven-m09.html. (Read: 06.05.2013)
53 *El Nacional*, 17.03.2004.
54 http://www.terra.com.ve/actualidad/articulo/html/act172006.htm
55 *The Independent*, 08.10.1994. Accessible on the website: http://www.independent.co.uk/news/world/cia-helped-to-set-up-terror-group-in-haiti-1441438.html
56 *Washington Post*, 21.09.1991.
57 Britto, Luis García (2008): *Dictadura Mediatica en Venezuela: Investigación de unos medios por encima de toda sospecha*. Coleccion Analisis, p. 160.
58 Britto, Luis García (2008): *Dictadura Mediatica en Venezuela: Investigación de unos medios por encima de toda sospecha*. Coleccion Analisis, p. 165.
59 *2001* (newspaper), 04.03.2004.
60 Britto, Luis García (2008): *Dictadura Mediatica en Venezuela: Investigación de unos medios por encima de toda sospecha*. Coleccion Analisis, p. 164.
61 Britto, Luis García (2008): *Dictadura Mediatica en Venezuela: Investigación de unos medios por encima de toda sospecha*. Coleccion Analisis, p. 173.
62 *El Nacional*, 25.07.2004.
63 *IPS Noticias*, 09.03.2005. Accessible on the website: http://ipsnoticias.net/print.asp?idnews=33139
64 *Ultimas Noticias*, 10.02.2008.
65 Instituto Nacional de Estadística (INE).
66 *Financial Times*, 21–22.12.2002, referred to in *Le Monde Diplomatique*, April 2013.
67 http://vtv.gob.ve/videos-emisiones-anteriores/41990 video 2 and 3.

[68] *The Carter Center* (2005): 'The Venezuela Presidential Recall Referendum: Final Reports'. Accessible on the website: www.cartercenter.org
[69] *National Catholic Reporter*, 03.09.2004.
[70] *Klassekampen*, 14.09.2004.
[71] Galeano, Eduardo (1992): *Open Veins of Latin America*. Oslo: Pax Forlag, p. 126.
[72] *BBC*, 02.11.2005. Accessible on the website: news.bbc.co.uk/2/hi/business/4399084.stm
[73] Munevar, Santiago (2010): 'Un balance de la "larga noche neoliberal"', *Observatorio Político de América Latina y del Caribe*. Available on the website: http://www.opalc.org/web/index.php?option=com_content&view=article&id=478:un-balance-de-la-qlargan-noche-neoliberalq&catid=47:les-politiques-publiques-en-amerique-latine&Itemid=78. (Read: 06.05.2013)
[74] Stiglitz Joseph (2003): 'El rumbo de las reformas. Hacia una nueva agenda para América Latina,' *Revista de la CEPAL*, n. 80, pp. 7–40.
[75] *Washington Post*, 03.11.2005 and *New York Times*, 02.11.2005.
[76] From the conservative Argentinian newspaper *Clarin*. Mentioned on the website: www.minci.gob.ve/opinion/7/6442/el_cachorro_del.html. (Read: 06.05.2013).
[77] Smith, Adam (1937): *An Inquiry into the Nature and Causes of the Wealth of Nations*. New York: The Modern Library, p. 591.
[78] The term was introduced by the Argentinian author, Manuel Dugart, who wrote a book entitled *La Patria Grande* in 1922.
[79] Chávez Frías, Hugo (2005): *Construyendo el ALBA*, Caracas, p. 115.
[80] *BusinessWeek*, 14.05.2006.
[81] Vold, Eirik (2007): 'Enhancement and capture of value. The case of the Venezuelan petroleum industry,' Department of Sociology and Human Geography, University of Oslo. p.55.
[82] Bernard Mommer quoted in Lander, Luis (2003): *Poder y petroleo en Venezuela*, Caracas, Faces-usv, PDVSA, p. 28.

[83] *Reuters*, 10.02.2008. Accessible on the website: http://www.reuters.com/article/2008/02/10/us-exxon-venezuela-chavez-idUSN0846080120080210
[84] See for example, *The Economist* 14.02.2008. Accessible on the website: http://www.economist.com/node/10696005
[85] Ryggvik, Helge (2010): *Til siste dråpe. Om oljens politiske økonomi.* Oslo: Aschehoug.
[86] Shah, Sonia (2004): *Crude: The story of oil.* New York: Seven Stories Press, p. 14.
[87] The Americans' account of Operation Ajax, which ended with the fall of the popular Iranian prime minister, is accessible on the website: web.payk.net/politics/cia-docs/published/one-main/main.html. (Read: 05.06.2013).
[88] Shah, Sonia (2004): *Crude: The story of oil.* New York: Seven Stories Press.
[89] Shah, Sonia (2004): *Crude: The story of oil.* New York: Seven Stories Press, p. 31.
[90] *Taipei Times*, 23.09.2006. Accessible on the website: www.taipeitimes.com/News/world/archives/2006/09/23/2003328878.
[91] Some examples using 'delusions of grandeur' and 'megalomania' concerning Chávez' international politics: Globovisión (04.07.2008): www.Globovision.com/articulo/e-ntorno-nacional-una-politica-absurda; Globovisión (31.07.2010): www.globovision.com/articulo/cara-de-culpable; the major Spanish paper ABC (04.05.2009): http://archivo.abc.com.py/2009-05-04/articulos/518334/vil-entrega-a-pdvsa-de-la-soberania-nacional-en-combustibles
[92] *Times World*, 02.12.2011. Accessible on the website: http://world.time.com/2011/12/02/
[93] Castañeda, Jorge (2004): 'Latin America's two lefts', *Project Syndicate*. Accessible on the website: http://www.project-syndicate.org/commentary/latin-america-s-two-lefts

⁹⁴ *USA Today*, 13.03.2008. Accessible on the website: http://usatoday30.usatoday.com/news/washington/2008-03-13-2265536436_x.htm.
⁹⁵ *Apublica.org*, 18.08.2011. Accessible on the website: www.apublica.org/2011/08/amorim-a-pedra-no-meio-do-caminho/.
⁹⁶ *ABC News*, 08.02.2008. Accessible on the website: abcnews.go.com/print?id=4262036
⁹⁷ https://wikileaks.org/plusd/cables/07ASUNCION396_a.html
⁹⁸ Revealed by WikiLeaks' leaked embassy cables.
⁹⁹ *USA Today*, 22.08.2005. The recording and quote are also available on YouTube: www.youtube.com/watch?v=DykgMyTjWU-I.
¹⁰⁰ Gaffney, Frank J. (2004): *War Footing: 10 Steps America Must Take to Prevail in the War for the Free World, Annapolis*, Naval Institute Press, p. xi.
¹⁰¹ The figure is from Jack Anderson, referred to in the book: Escobar, Roberto (2009): *Escobar: The Inside Story of Pablo Escobar the World's Most Powerful Criminal*, Hodder General Publishing Division, p. 58.
¹⁰² *Página* 12, 26.11.2007.
¹⁰³ *BBC Mundo*, 02.03.2008. Accessible on the website: http://news.bbc.co.uk/hi/spanish/latin_america/newsid_7274000/7274169.stm.
¹⁰⁴ *VG*, 03.03.2008. Accessible on the website: http://www.vg.no/nyheter/utenriks/artikkel.php?artid=504235 and TV2, 03.03.2008. Accessible on the website: http://www.tv2.no/nyheter/utenriks/chavez-truer-med-krig-1648202.html
¹⁰⁵ *Bloomberg*, 11.03.2008. Accessible on the website: http://www.bloomberg.com/apps/news?pid=newsarchive&sid=azsjP6yNwkXM&refer=latin_america.
¹⁰⁶ *New York Times*, 12.07.1998 'A Bombers tale.'
¹⁰⁷ *NRK*, 17.03.2011. Accessible on the website: http://www.nrk.no/nyheter/verden/1.2062012

108 *New York Times*, 25.11.1986. Accessible on the website: http://www.nytimes.com/learning/general/onthisday/big/1125.html.
109 https://wikileaks.org/plusd/cables/09QUITO225_a.html
110 *The Guardian*, 22.05.2008. Accessible on the website: http://www.guardian.co.uk/commentisfree/2008/may/22/seeingthroughtransparencyinternational.
111 Chris, Carlson (30.11.2012): 'What the statistics tell us about Venezuela in the Chávez' era', *Venezuelaanalysis.com*. Accessible on the website: http://venezuelanalysis.com/analysis/7513. (Read: 06.05.2013).
112 *The Guardian*, 02.12.2010. Accessible on the website: http://www.guardian.co.uk/world/2010/dec/02/chavez-uribe-summit-wikileaks.
113 *El Nacional*, 18.03.2002.
114 Galeano, Eduardo (1992): *Open Veins of Latin America*. Oslo, Pax Forlag, pp.126-127.
115 The chapter 'Plan Colombia' in Chomsky, Noam (2000): *Rogue States. The Rule of Force in World Affairs*. South End Press. Accessible on the website: http://www.chomsky.info/books/roguestates08.htm.
116 Fløgstad, Kjartan (02.06.2012): 'Marxist Hunter', *Klassekampen*.
117 Galeano, Eduardo (2004): 'Nothingland – or Venezuela', *New Left Review 29*. Accessible on the website: http://newleftreview.org/II/29/eduardo-galeano-nothingland-or-venezuela
118 Referenced by the independent US organisation, *Fairness and Accuracy in Reporting* (FAIR). Accessible on the website: http://www.fair.org/blog/2013/04/08/wikileaks-was-chavez-right-about-u-s-meddling/. (Read: 06.05.2013).
119 Referenced in *Venezuelanalysis.com*. Accessible on the website: http://venezuelanalysis.com/news/7907. (Read: 06.05.2013).

[120] Weisbrot, Mark (30.01.2013): 'Media Hate Fest for Venezuela Keeps on Keepin' On', *Al Jazeera*. The figures are taken from IMF statistics, starting from 2004.
[121] The figures are found on IMF's website: http://www.imf.org/external/pubs/ft/weo/2009/01/weodata/weo rept.
[122] UNICEF's figure accessible on the website: http://www.childinfo.org/mortality_imrcountrydata.php. (Read: 06.05.2013).
[123] *Agencia Latinoamericana de Información*, 06.04.2013. Accessible on the website: http://alainet.org/active/63055. (Read: 06.05.2013). Figure from UN organisation UNECLAC. Accessible on the website: http://www.eclac.cl/publicaciones/xml/3/28063/LCG2332B_1.pdf and http://www.eclac.org/publicaciones/xml/2/48862/AnuarioEstadistico2012.pdf. (Read: 06.05.2013)
[124] Figure from the UN organisation UNCECLAC. Accessible on the website: http://www.eclac.org/publicaciones/xml/2/48862/AnuarioEstadistico2012.pdf. (Read: 06.05.2013)
[125] UNECLAC'S figure referred to in *Que Pasa*, 13.02.2012. Accessible on the website: http://www.quepasa.com.ve/index.php?option=com_content&view=article&id=201:cepal-confirma-disminucion-de-pobreza-en-venezuela&catid=92:seccion2&Itemid=55. (Read: 06.05.2013)
[126] UNECLAC'S figure referenced in *La Nacion*, 05.03.2013. http://www.eclac.org/publicaciones/xml/2/48862/AnuarioEstadistico2012.pdf. (Read: 06.05.2013)
[127] Bárcena's statement is accessible on UNECLAC's website: http://www.eclac.org/cgi-bin/getProd.asp?xml=/prensa/noticias/comunicados/1/49301/P49301.xml&xsl=/prensa/tpl/p6f.xsl&base=/tpl/top-bottom.xsl. (Read: 06.05.2013)

[128] *New York Times* 06.11.2010. Accessible on the website: http://www.nytimes.com/2010/11/07/opinion/07kristof.html?_r=0.

[129] The Venezuelan opposition disputes this figure, like most other figures: http://www.vtv.gob.ve/articulos/2012/09/06/gran-mision-vivienda-venezuela-ha-concluido-249.368-viviendas-hasta-la-fecha-3327.html. (Read: 06.05.2013).

[130] Chomsky, Noam (2004): *Hegemony or Survival: America's Quest for Global Dominance*. New York: Henry Holt and Company.

[131] The finds come from researchers Lee Salter and Dave Weltman, from the UWE (University of the West of England), who have studied ten years of Venezuelan coverage by the *BBC*. According to the researchers the extreme bias in the BBC's coverages is systematic. Accessible on the website: http://venezuelanalysis.com/analysis/5003. (Read: 10.04.2013)

www.ingramcontent.com/pod-product-compliance
Lightning Source LLC
Chambersburg PA
CBHW070716160426
43192CB00009B/1211